IMAGES
of America

WOONSOCKET

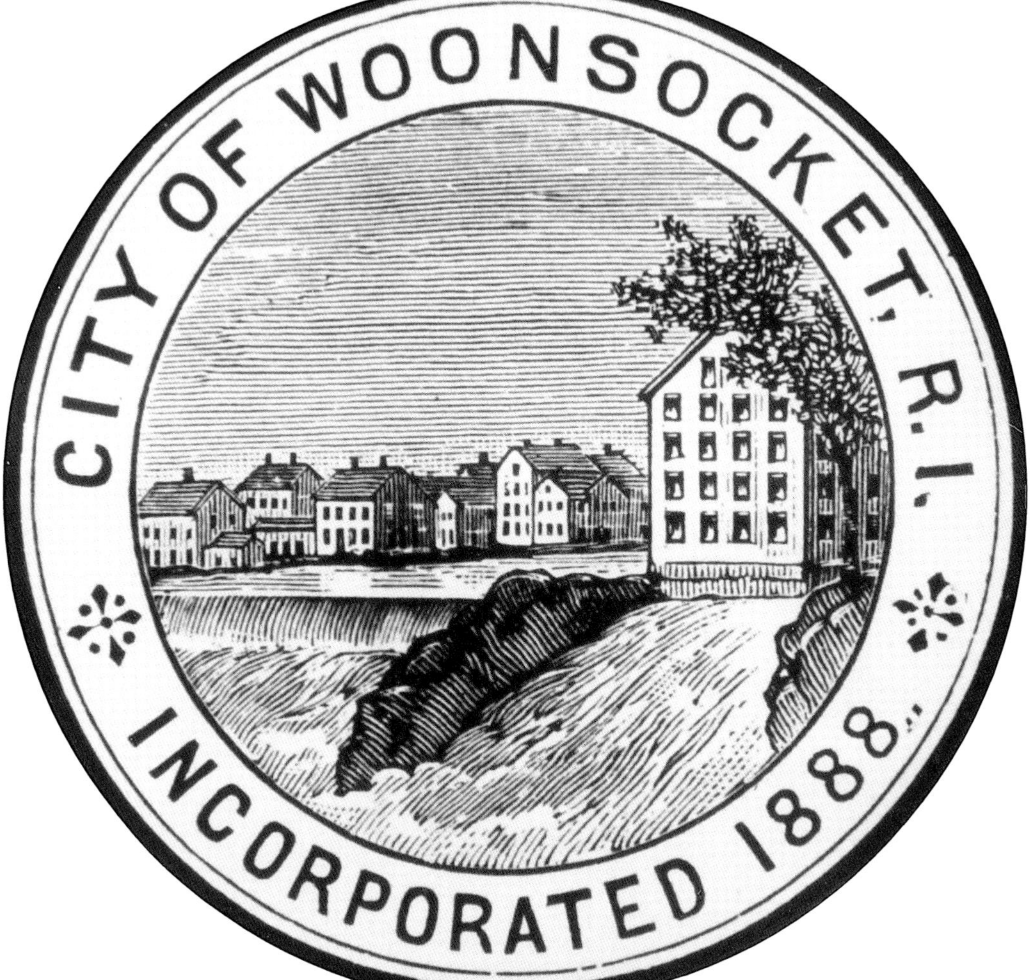

The seal of the City of Woonsocket depicts several mill buildings at Woonsocket Falls. The seal prominently features the Cotton Mill owned by George Ballou which was demolished in the 1960s.

IMAGES
of America

WOONSOCKET

Robert R. Bellerose

ARCADIA
PUBLISHING

ISBN 978-0-7385-1296-9

Published by Arcadia Publishing
Charleston, South Carolina

Printed in the United States of America

Library of Congress Catalog Card Number: Data applied for

For all general information contact Arcadia Publishing at:
Telephone 843-853-2070
Fax 843-853-0044
E-mail sales@arcadiapublishing.com
For customer service and orders:
Toll-Free 1-888-313-2665

Visit us on the Internet at www.arcadiapublishing.com

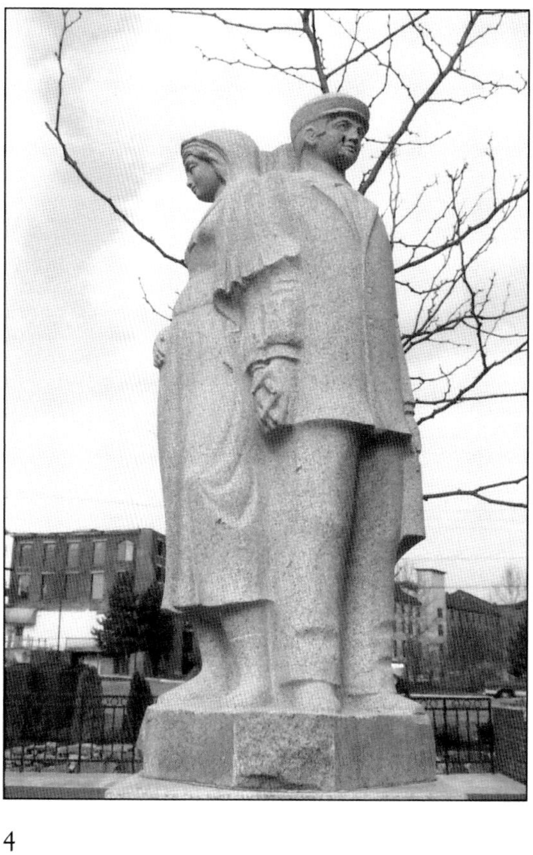

This book is dedicated to the working people and their families who fought our nation's wars, built this great city, and created a standard of living unsurpassed in the world. Pictured is the "Working People's Monument" designed by Robert B. Lamb of Lincoln, Rhode Island, in 1977. The monument depicts a young man and young woman standing holding hands before a panorama of the city. The sculpture originally stood in the Social District in the city. In 1996 the monument became the centerpiece of a plaza next to the new museum of "work and culture" at Woonsocket Falls.

Contents

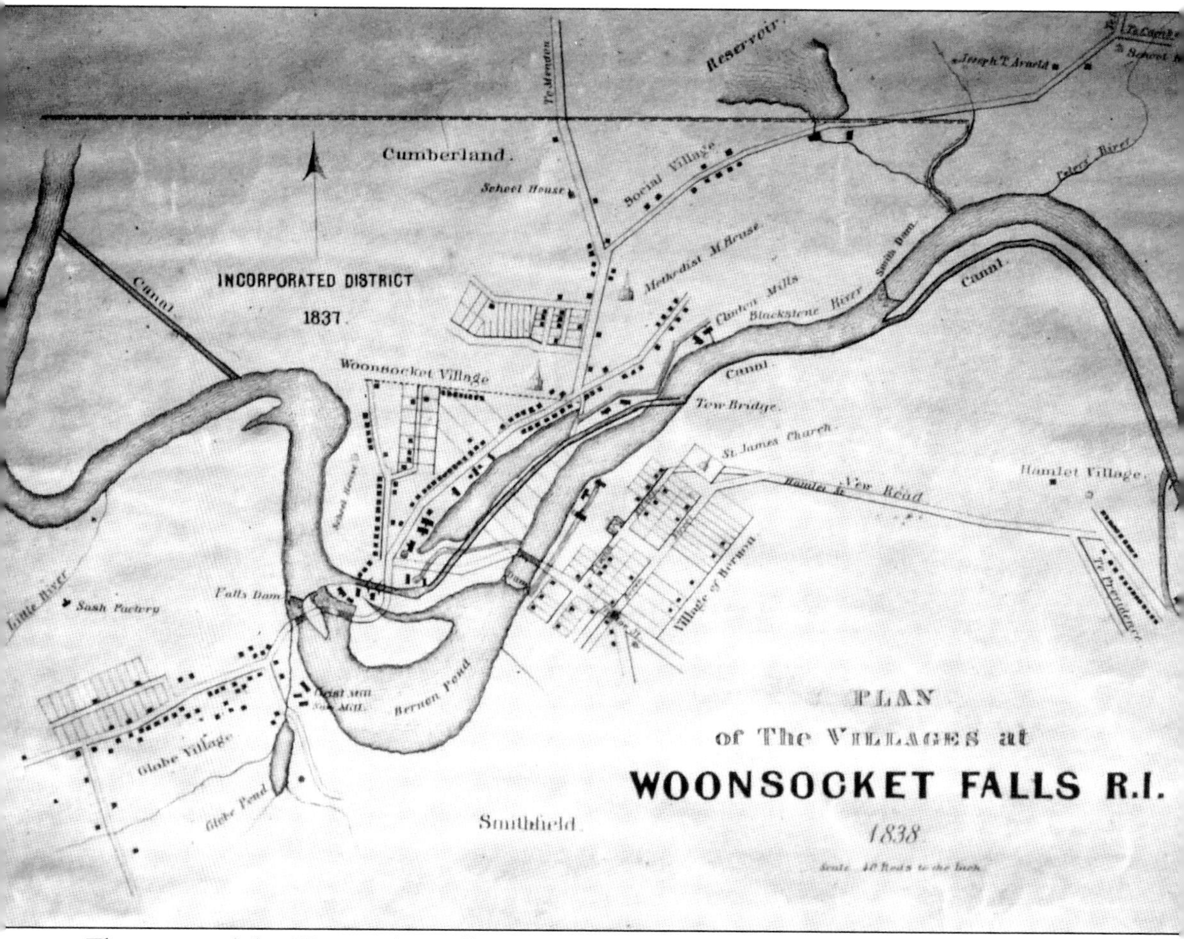

This insert of the Woonsocket Falls region is from an 1838 map of Cumberland. It depicts five of the six distinct mill villages which would be the keys to the development of the city of Woonsocket. The mill villages of Bernon, Globe, and Hamlet were along the Smithfield side of the Blackstone River. Along the Cumberland side of the river were the three mill villages of Woonsocket Falls, Social, and just off the map, Jenckesville. (Woonsocket Harris Public Library.)

Introduction

Nestled along "the hardest working river in America," the Blackstone River, is the city of Woonsocket. This story of an industrial mammoth reflects the dreams and aspirations of its many immigrants and is a history of our great country in miniature. Entrepreneurs and workers alike saw the river as their opportunity to improve life for themselves and their families.

Though countless books and scholarly articles have recounted the history of this city, it has been the photographer who has brought these words to life. With the "click of a shutter" a moment in time becomes a window to the past for historians and future generations to study. A photograph can show what takes a historian hundreds of words to describe.

Since the inception of photography, librarians and archivists have seen the benefit of preservation efforts of this medium. Even families are gathering their treasures, identifying persons and locales, and preserving them for future generations. The use of private and public photographic collections is helping to tell the story of communities such as Woonsocket. These collections are in effect helping to give each generation a sense of place and an idea of where they fit in the total historical perspective.

Many photographs in this book are from the collection of the Woonsocket Harris Public Library. Another source for fine images was the collection of the Blackstone River Valley National Heritage Corridor Commission.

I was exceedingly fortunate and grateful to have had access to many private photographic collections. I would like to thank Mr. and Mrs. Aram Archambault, Mr. and Mrs. George E. Brin, Mr. and Mrs. Robert C. Brin, and Saint Antoine's Residence. Pictures from each of these collections are designated accordingly. Where no credit line accompanies a picture, the source is from the author's personal collection.

This undertaking was possible with the grateful assistance of Kathy Ellen Bullard, Director, and Michael V. Silvia, Reference and Adult Service Librarian, of the Woonsocket Harris Public Library. Romeo G. Berthiaume, Chair of the Social Studies Department at the Woonsocket Senior High School, provided access to the photographic collection. Mary Ann Altrui, Administrator, and Rachel Brin, Supervisory Nurse, at Saint Antoine's Residence graciously provided access to their archives.

I would like to extend a special thank you to Raymond Boswell, a dear friend, who saw in me the potential for such a project. His initial reassurance and support persuaded me that this undertaking was possible.

A special word of thanks to my wife, Therese, who continually encouraged and supported me throughout this project. Finally, I would like to thank my parents, Mr. and Mrs. Emile E. Bellerose. They instilled in me an appreciation of my ancestral heritage, respect for working-class people, and especially for life itself.

This effort, as created, would not have been possible without the assistance of everyone mentioned. I extend a special thank you to all.

Prologue

This city that our forebears knew
Had days of glory; hard times, too,
Learned lessons that it hoped would last,
And took advantage of the past.
The past is never really dead
When it can help one look ahead.

WOONSOCKET

The vast mosaic of the days
Falls slowly, neatly into place—
A river traced its winding course
Through glacial rocks deep-rimmed with moss.
And from the woods the Indians came
To give the spot its proper name;
This hollow that the rainbow kissed
They called "Woone" (thunder) "Suckete" (mist).

About three hundred years ago
Came colonists; to them we owe
Ideas of freedom that they brought,
(The precepts Roger Williams taught).
They hacked out homesteads on the ridges,
The Arnolds, Inmans and Aldriches,
To face, stout hearted, unafraid,
The threat of a King Philip raid.

A grist mill was their primary need
And they turned wishing into deed—
It rose upon the river's edge,
Deep planted in the granite ledge,
Bedecked with brilliant rainbow shower,
And harnessing the water power.
Then to the mill the grain was brought,
Where, in the stones, the meal was caught.

Thus through the Blackstone's natural force,
Was born Woonsocket's destined course;
Nor would it hesitate or dwindle
The while there was a whirring spindle,
For Samuel Slater's priceless gift
Gave the new town a needed lift,
When cotton turned the shining page
That ushered in a Golden Age.

Though many years have passed, we find
Woonsocket's skills have not declined.
Our heritage of knowing how
To get things done awaits us now.
So in the eras still to come,
The wheels of industry will hum
And knowledge passed on, like a light,
Will help to make the future bright.

—Louis P. Genereux

[Louis P. Genereux was a post office worker who was also a gifted artist, musician, and poet. At the time of his death in 1975 he was president of the Woonsocket Fine Arts Society. It is with the kind permission of his widow, Rhea Genereux, that I have included this poem.]

One

A Working River Is Harnessed

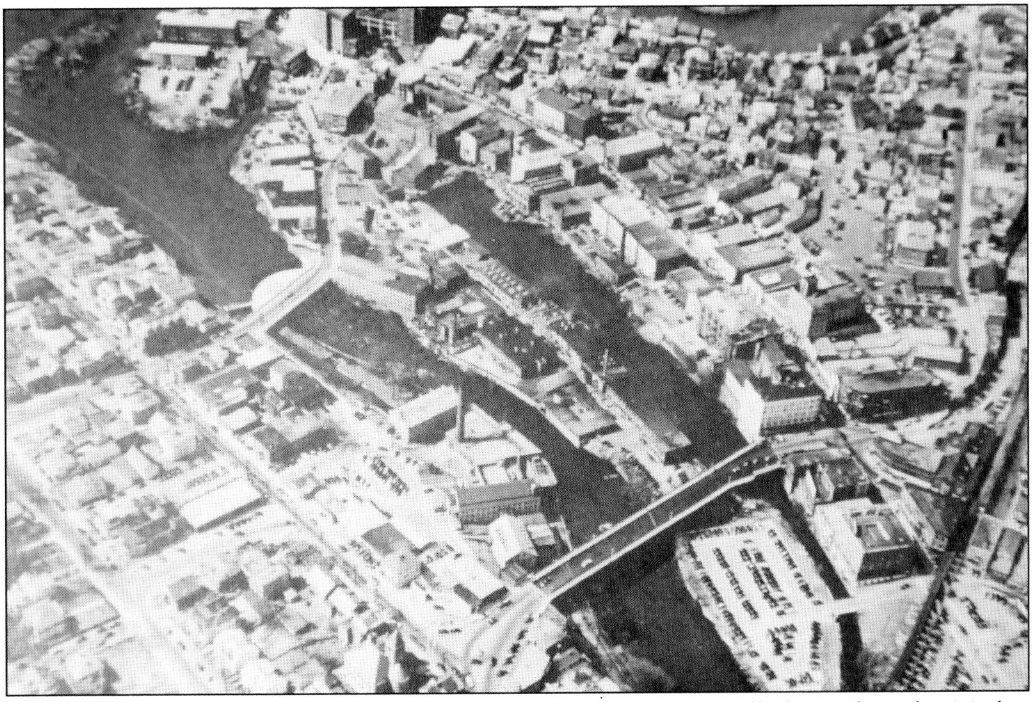

A c. 1950 aerial view of downtown Woonsocket showing the mills located in the Market Square area, the buildings along Main Street, Bernon Dam, Clinton Pond, and the Court Street Bridge. (Woonsocket Harris Public Library.)

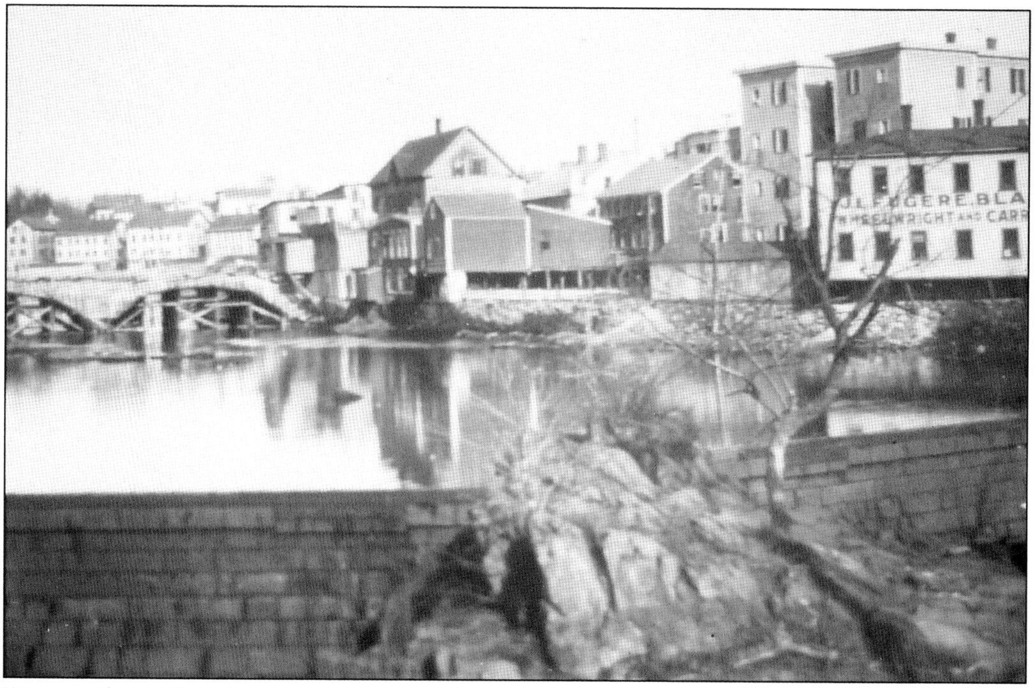

Woonsocket Falls at low water, photographed by Charles S. Lawton, *c.* 1890. The natural falls in this area were the largest along the Blackstone River at 32 feet and provided more than 2,000 horsepower. The area was a maze of power trenches and mills springing to life from the waters of the river.

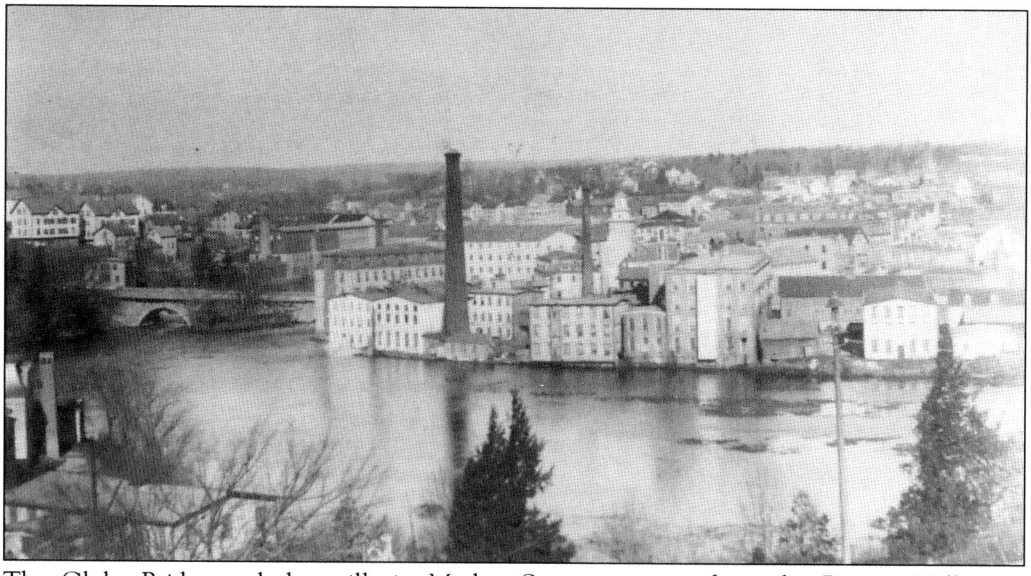

The Globe Bridge and the mills in Market Square as seen from the Bernon Hill area. Photographer Charles S. Lawton captured this scene *c.* 1890. Many of these mills are no longer standing. Today (1997) this area is a revitalized gateway to Main Street. The former Lincoln Textile Mill will become a new museum. Themes for this museum will include the rise of the French-Canadian community in Woonsocket and the evolution of the city's labor unions. (Woonsocket Harris Public Library.)

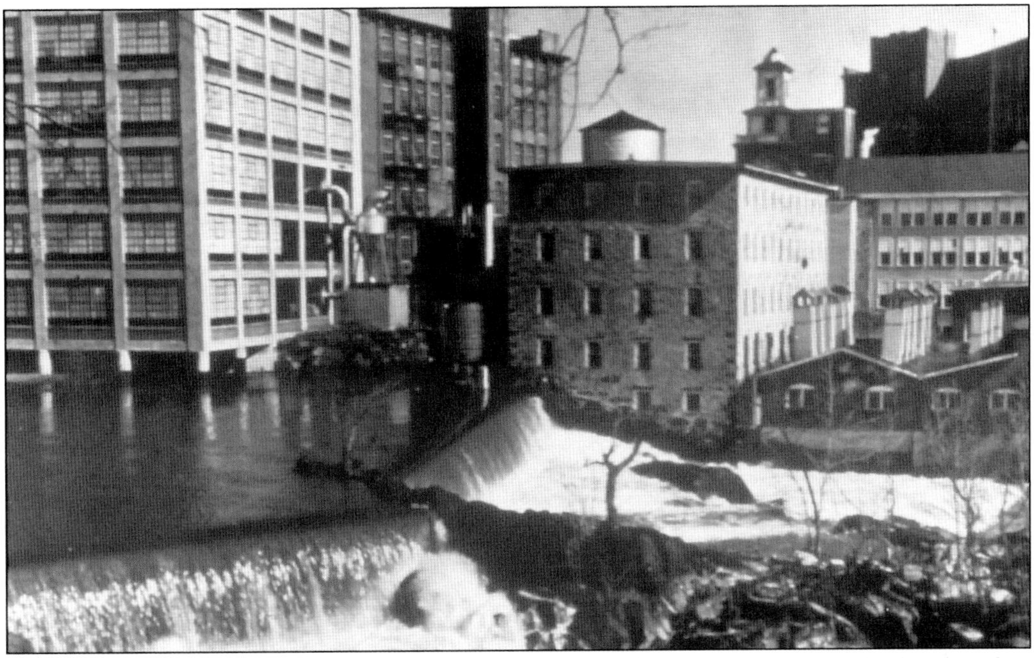

A *c*. 1940 view of Woonsocket Falls and the area around Market Square at the height of its industrialization. In the center is the stone mill owned by George Ballou and featured on the seal of the City of Woonsocket. The demolition of these mills, seen in the background, occurred in 1961.

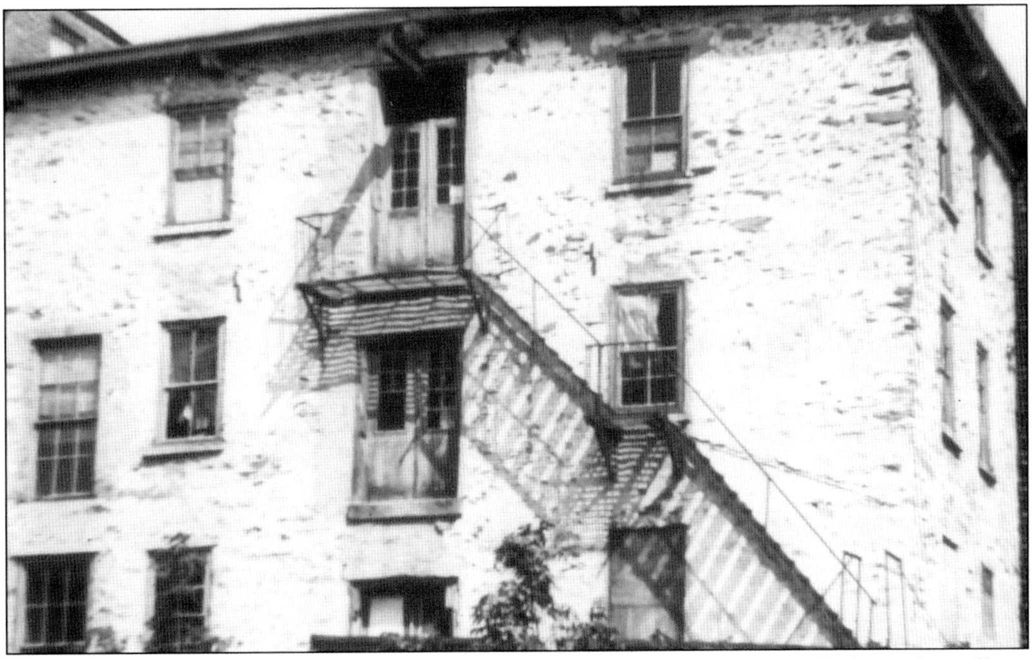

The Bartlett Mill. Dan A. Daniels built this four-story stone-rubble-walled textile mill on Bernon Street in 1827, and he spun cotton yarn here on 6,000 spindles. John Bartlett purchased the structure in 1840. Fire destroyed the mill in 1976. This photograph of the mill is from 1940. (Woonsocket Harris Public Library.)

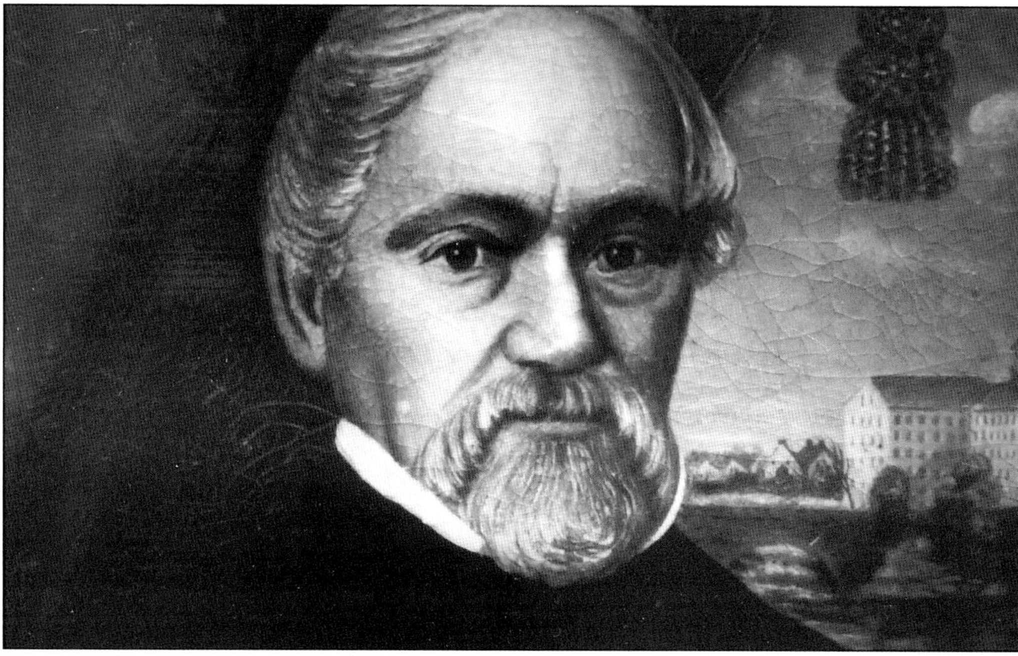

George Ballou. One of Woonsocket's first industrialists is depicted here in an 1860 painting. Of particular note is the inclusion of his Cotton Mill at Woonsocket Falls and the Globe Bridge. (Woonsocket Harris Public Library.)

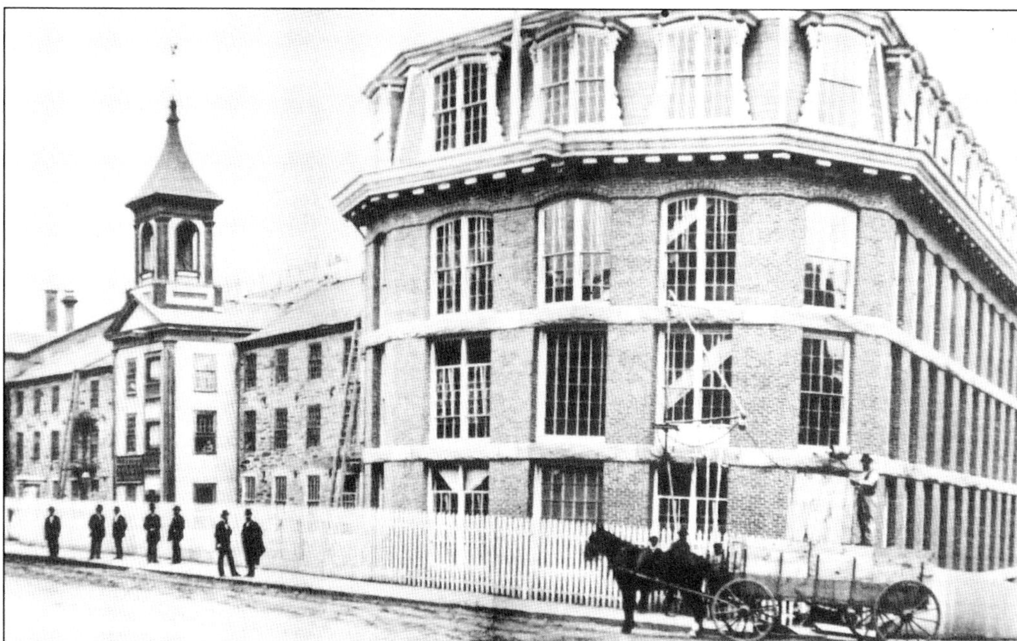

The Lippitt Woolen Company built this mill in 1865. Shown here ten years later, it was a three-and-one-half-story, granite-trimmed, mansard-roofed building at the vital intersection of Main Street and Market Square. The Lippitt Woolen Company produced woolen goods here through World War II. Before construction this was the site of Dan Daniels' store where Woonsocket's first post office could be found. (Woonsocket Harris Public Library.)

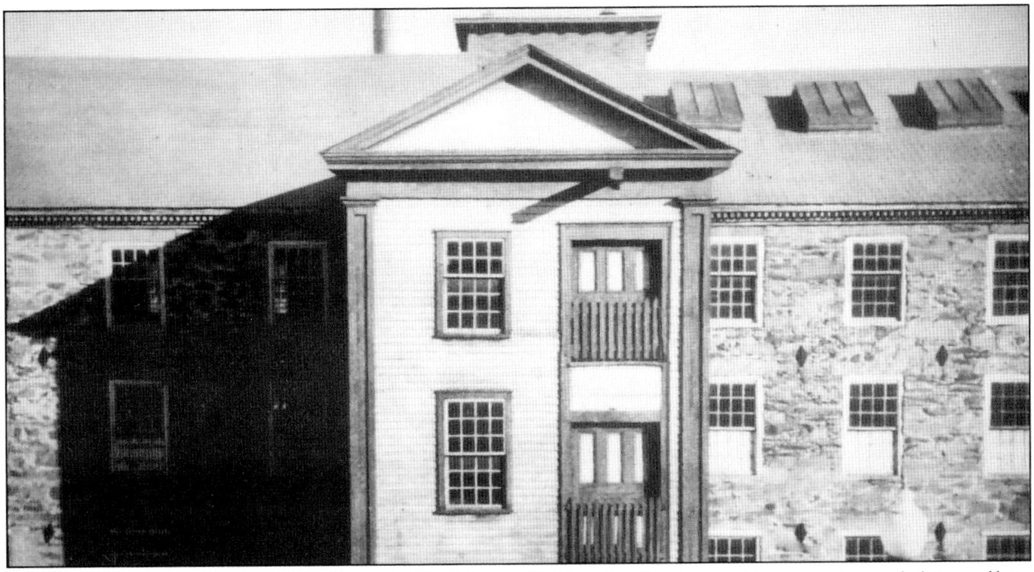

The former Dexter Ballou mill in 1940. Hosea Ballou built the earliest section of this mill in 1827. Constructed of brick, it is now largely hidden. Dexter Ballou, in 1832, built the main part of the complex in stone rubble with a brick cornice. The Greek Revival wooden stairtower added later was his inspiration. The Lippitt Company bought the property in 1865 from the Harrison Cotton Mills and made it a part of their woolen mill complex. This renovated complex opened as housing for the elderly on August 17, 1982. (Woonsocket Harris Public Library.)

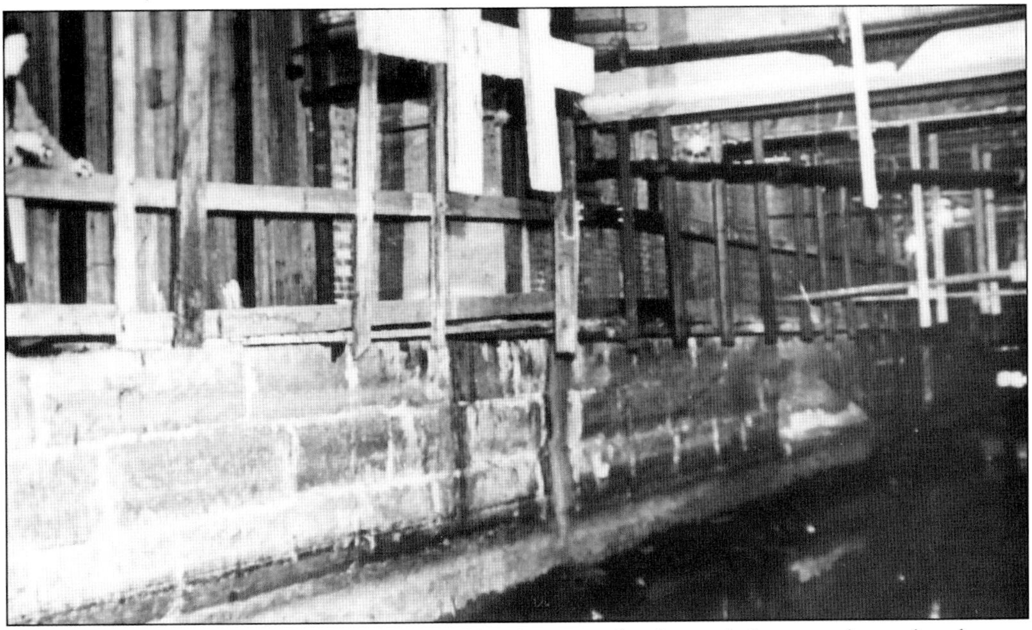

The Lyman-Arnold Trench. Built *c.* 1827, this trench channeled water from the dam at Woonsocket Falls and powered the mills along Main Street. The Ballou-Harris-Lippitt mill complex drew water from this power trench to operate the machines in the mill. This photograph, taken in February 1974, shows the trench under the Buell Building. Dr. Alton P. Thomas, noted local historian, is at left. (Woonsocket Harris Public Library.)

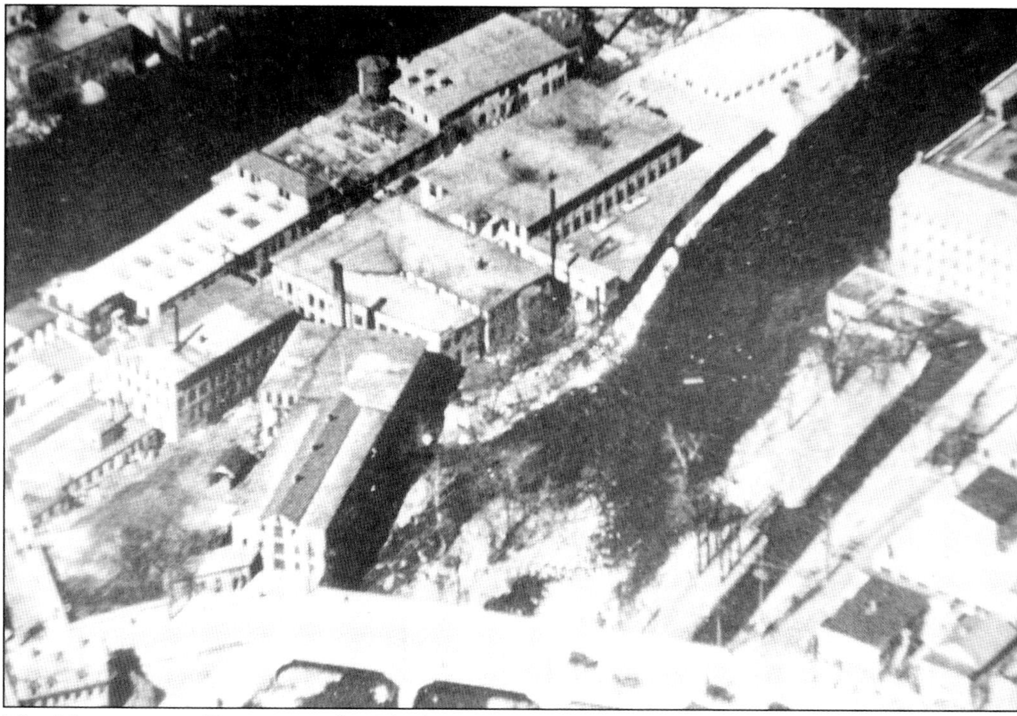

The Narragansett Knitting Mills, Blackstone River, and the Bernon Mills power trench in a c. 1950 aerial view. The Narragansett Knitting Mills, which began as the Leicester Knitting Mill, is located in the center-left of this photograph. The reinforced concrete span shown is the Bernon Street Bridge, constructed in 1912. (Woonsocket Harris Public Library.)

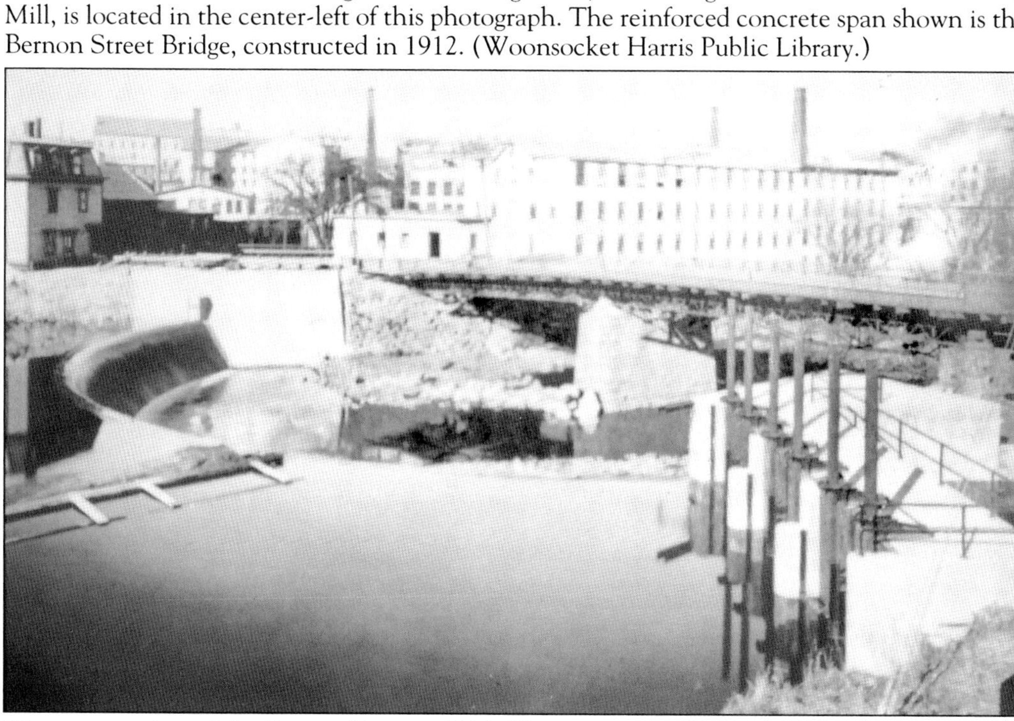

The construction of the Bernon Dam in 1911. The power trench gate to the right controls the flow of water to the Woonsocket Company Mills. (Woonsocket Harris Public Library.)

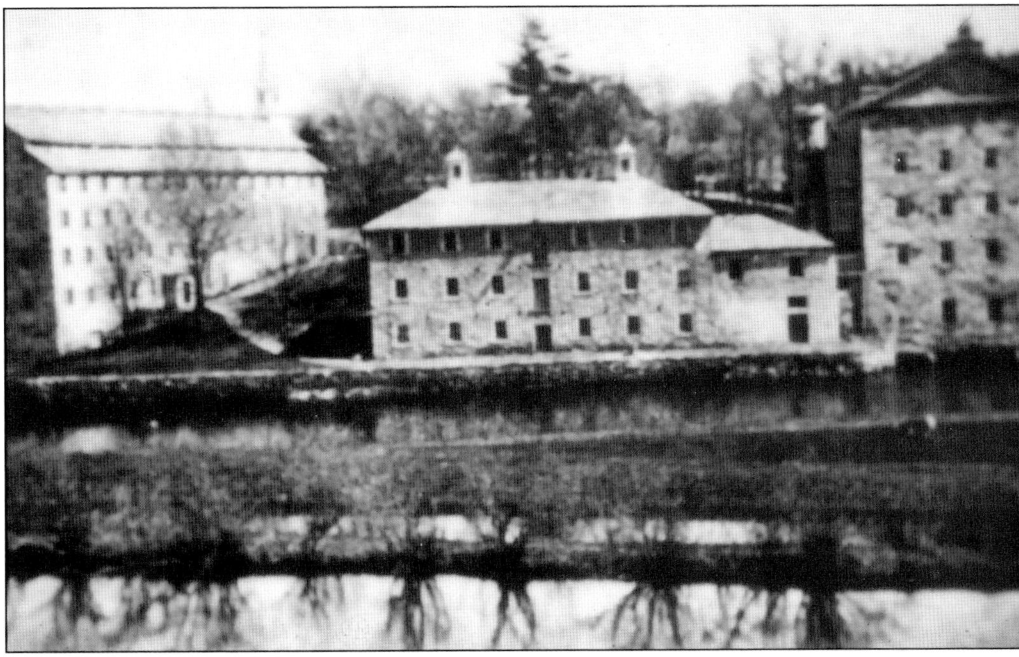

A *c.* 1860 view of the Woonsocket Company Mills and the Blackstone Canal and River. Mill Number One, erected in 1827–28, is at left. It is the earliest known mill constructed in this country according to "slow-burning" architectural specifications. Mill Number Three, built in 1835, is in the center. Mill Number Two, seen at right, is a Greek Revival structure built in 1833. (Woonsocket Harris Public Library.)

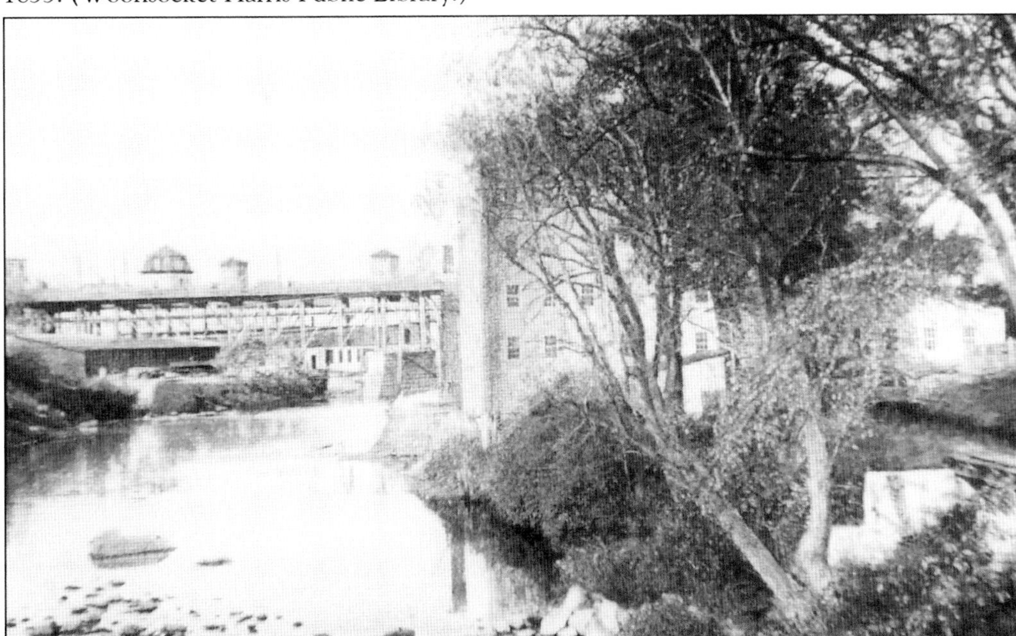

The Blackstone River in a view looking toward the Court Street Bridge from the Bernon Street Bridge in 1915. Woonsocket Company Mill Number Two, built in 1833 in the Greek Revival style, can be seen on the right bank of the river. (Woonsocket Harris Public Library.)

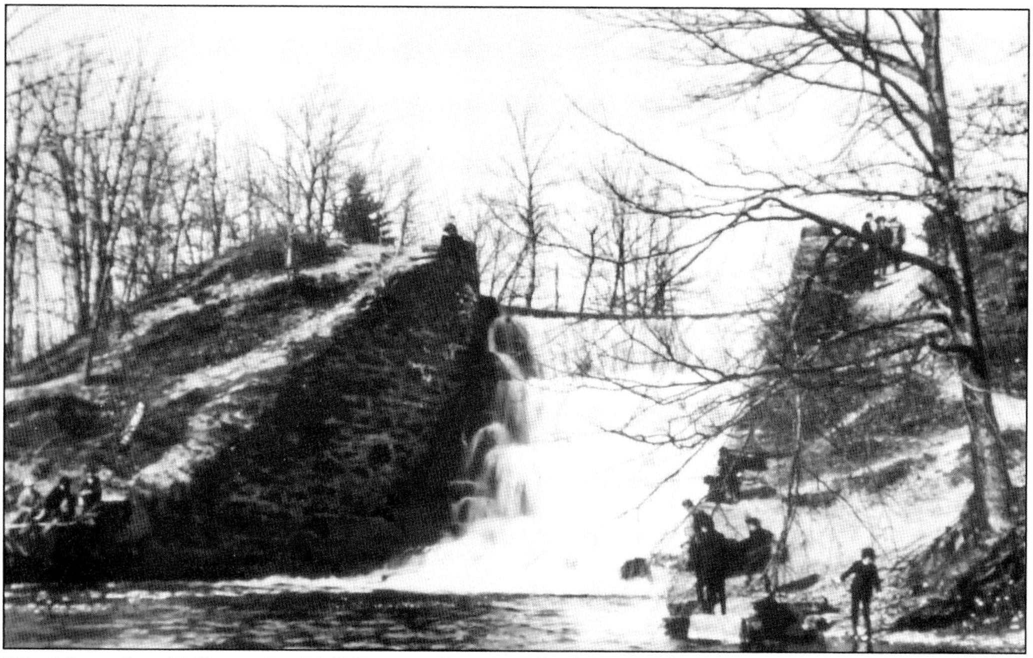

The Horseshoe Falls on the Mill River, photographed *c.* 1900 by Charles S. Lawton. This dam, built by Edward Harris in 1864–65, created a mill pond for his new Privilege Mill complex. In 1955 the earthen embankments on both sides of the falls were breached, sending a wall of water nearly 20 feet high roaring toward the heart of the Social District. (Woonsocket Harris Public Library.)

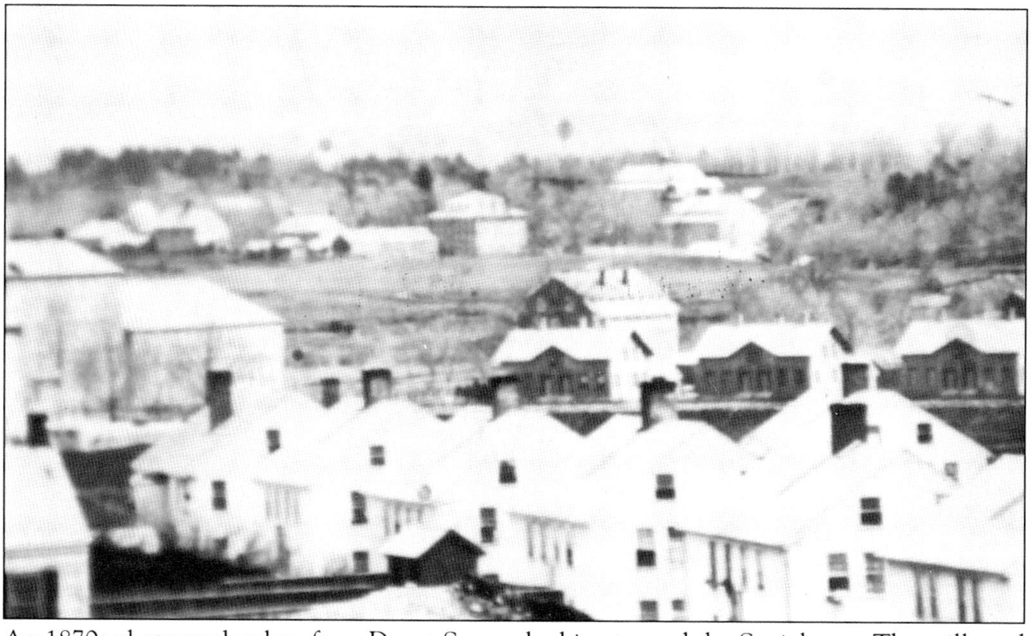

An 1870s photograph taken from Depot Square looking toward the Social area. The mills and mill housing in the distance are in Jenckesville. The Jenckes established a mill along Peter's River in 1822. Their #1 Mill was the first stone factory building in the vicinity. Later, in 1828, they constructed their #2 Mill farther down stream. (Woonsocket Harris Public Library.)

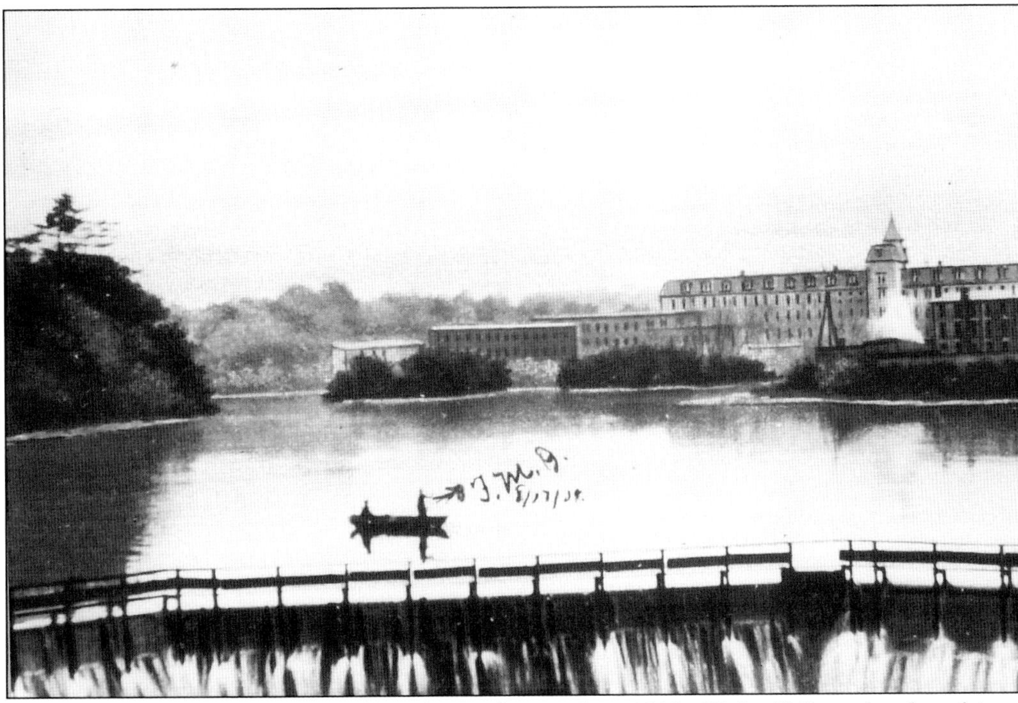

Bernon Dam with the Globe Mill in the background, *c.* 1928. Globe Village developed in an area southeast of Woonsocket Falls and was named for the Globe Mills that stood between Front Street and the river. (Woonsocket Harris Public Library.)

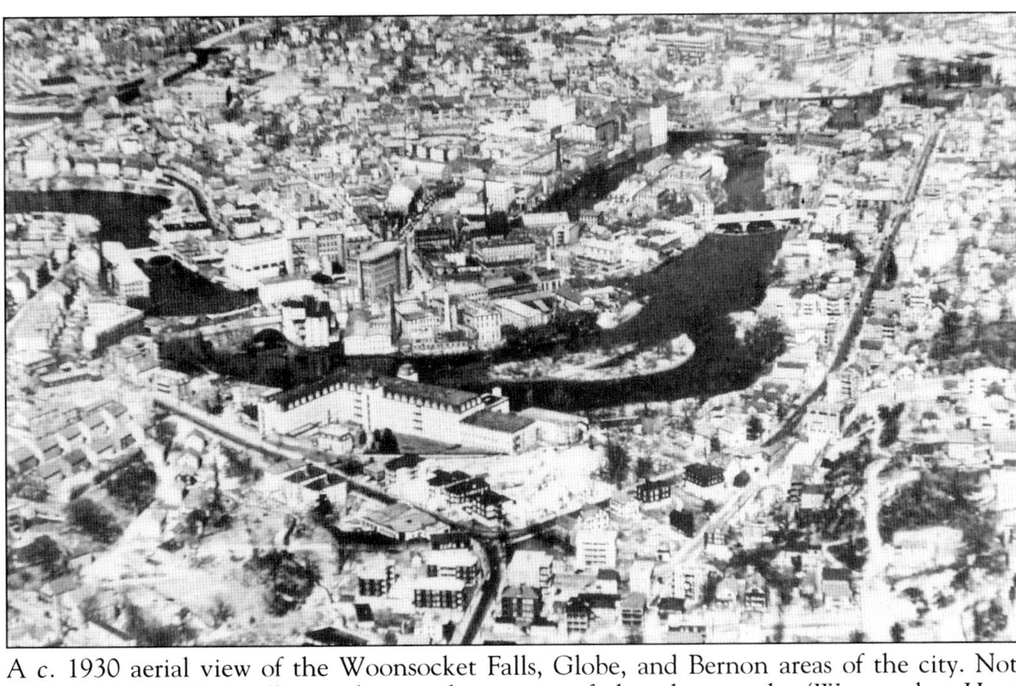

A *c.* 1930 aerial view of the Woonsocket Falls, Globe, and Bernon areas of the city. Note the massive Globe Mill complex in the center of the photograph. (Woonsocket Harris Public Library.)

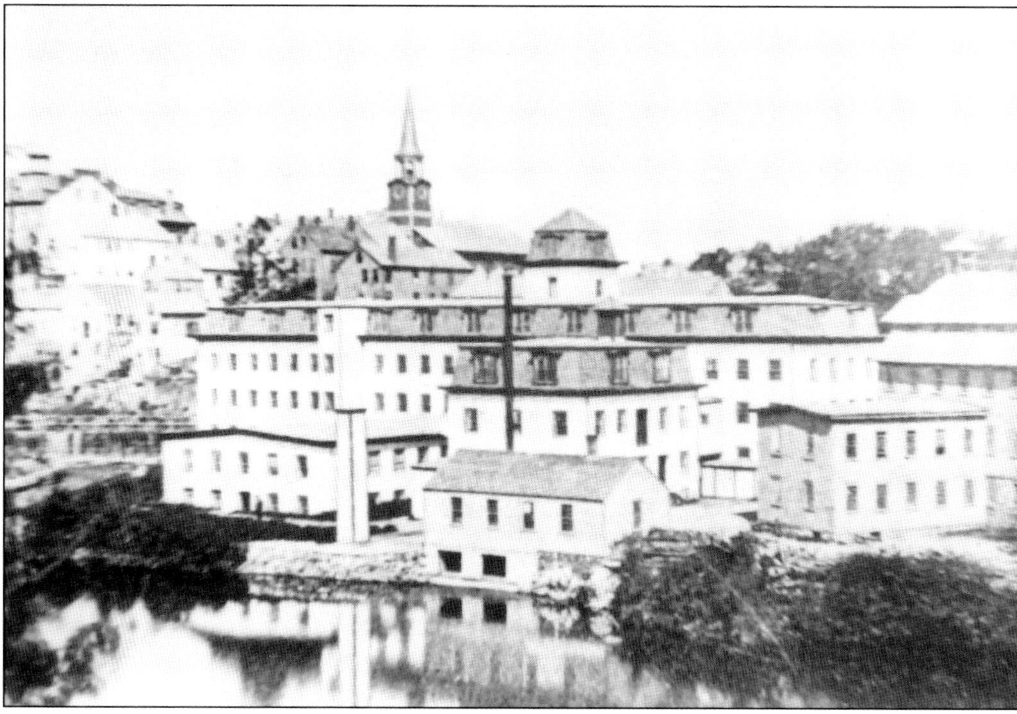

A *c.* 1880s photograph of the Eagle Mill. The original factory dates back to 1831, with additions built between 1867 and 1888. (Woonsocket Harris Public Library.)

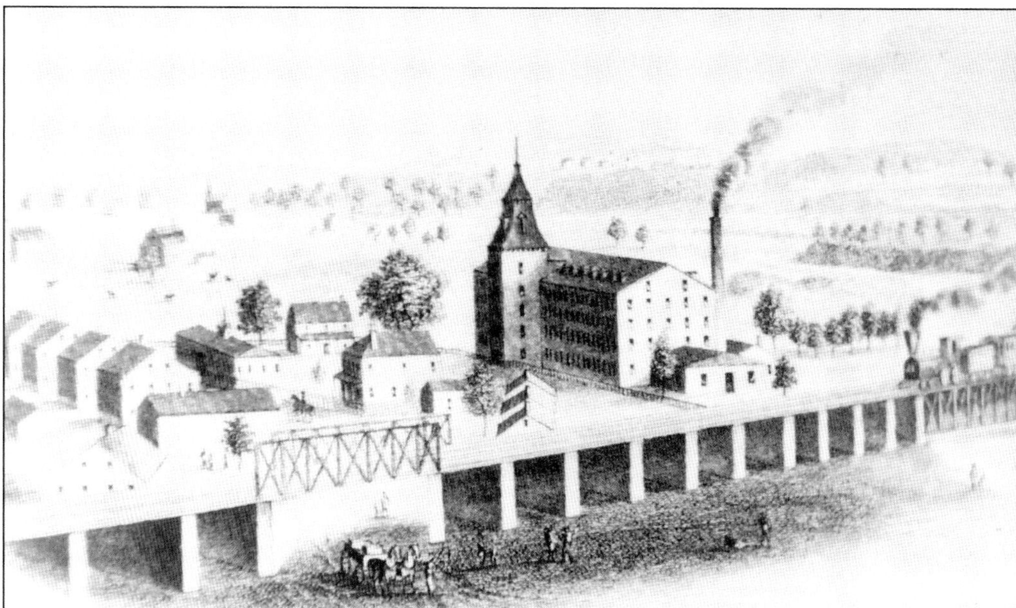

Clinton Mill Village, *c.* 1850s. Associated with the large mill are the mill houses that provided shelter for the many immigrants who came to work at the Clinton Mill. This landscape played out repeatedly throughout the Blackstone River Valley as each mill and village developed along similar lines. The tracks of the Providence and Worcester Railroad are in the foreground. (Woonsocket Harris Public Library.)

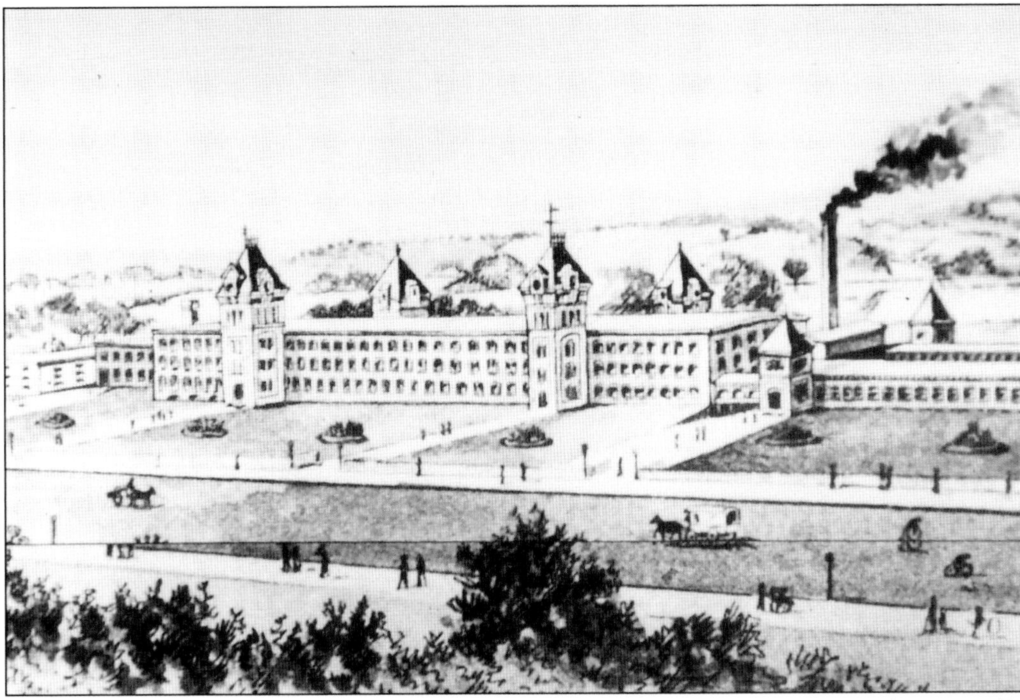

An 1890 view of the Nourse Mill on Clinton Street, built in 1883. In 1929 the Manville-Jenckes Company purchased the complex and operated their rayon manufacturing subsidiary, the Woonsocket Rayon Company, here. During demolition, the mill became engulfed in a spectacular general alarm fire that occurred on October 6, 1956. (Woonsocket Harris Public Library.)

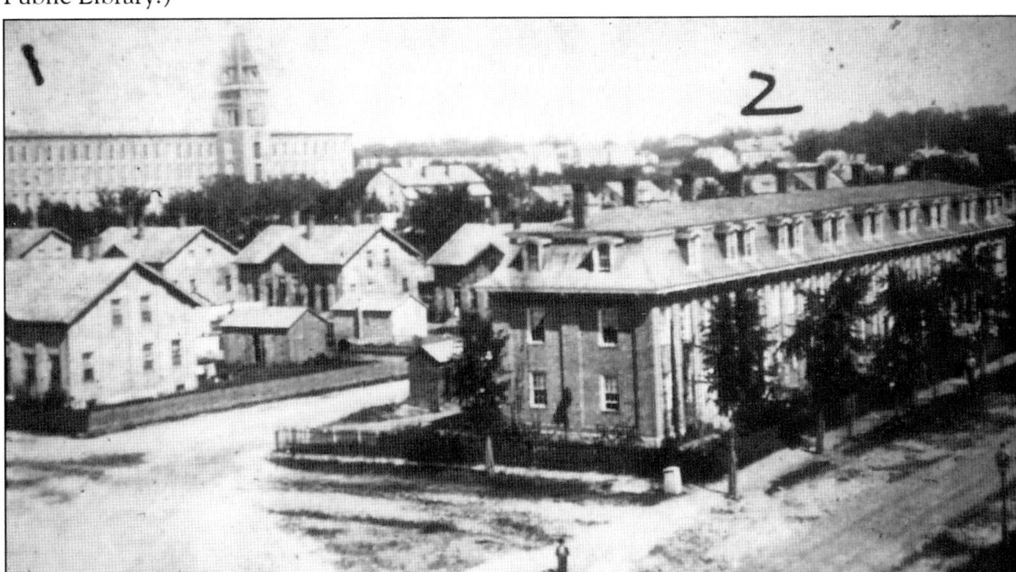

The Social Mill and Nourse Mill Village in a *c*. 1900 photograph. The Nourse village consisted of several well built and historical buildings. In the name of progress, demolition of the village took place in the early 1970s. It also wiped out such streets as Page, Collier, Gobeille, Sampson, and Nourse. (Woonsocket Harris Public Library.)

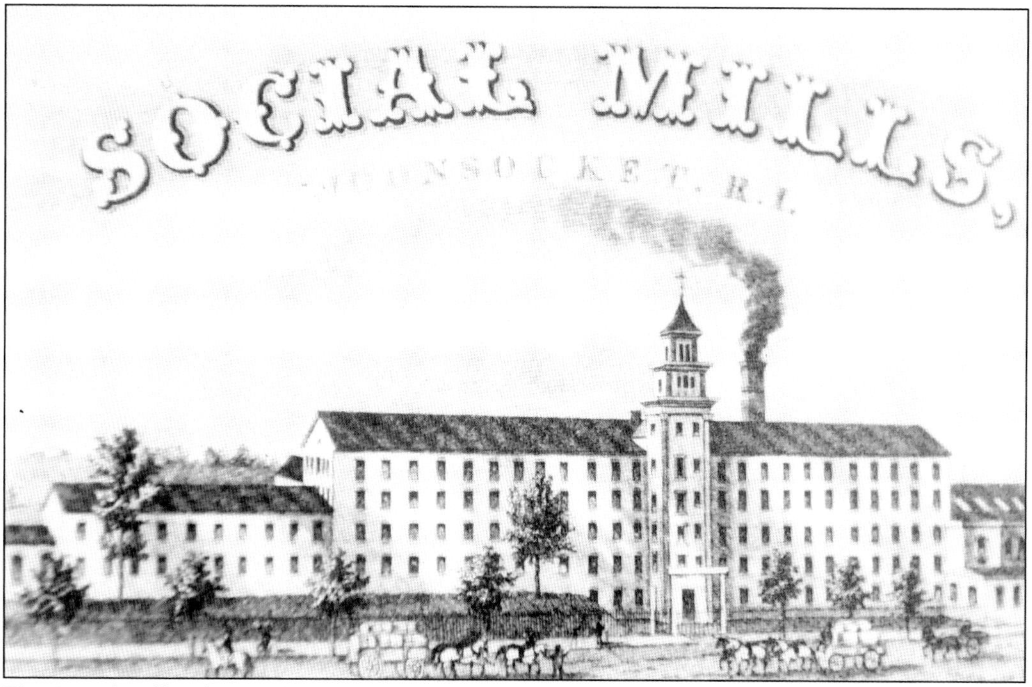

The Social Mill as depicted on a cloth label from the 1860s. The Social Manufacturing Company, formed in 1810, purchased a site on the Mill River. The Social Mill was Woonsocket's first textile concern. This huge plant closed permanently in 1927. (Woonsocket Harris Public Library.)

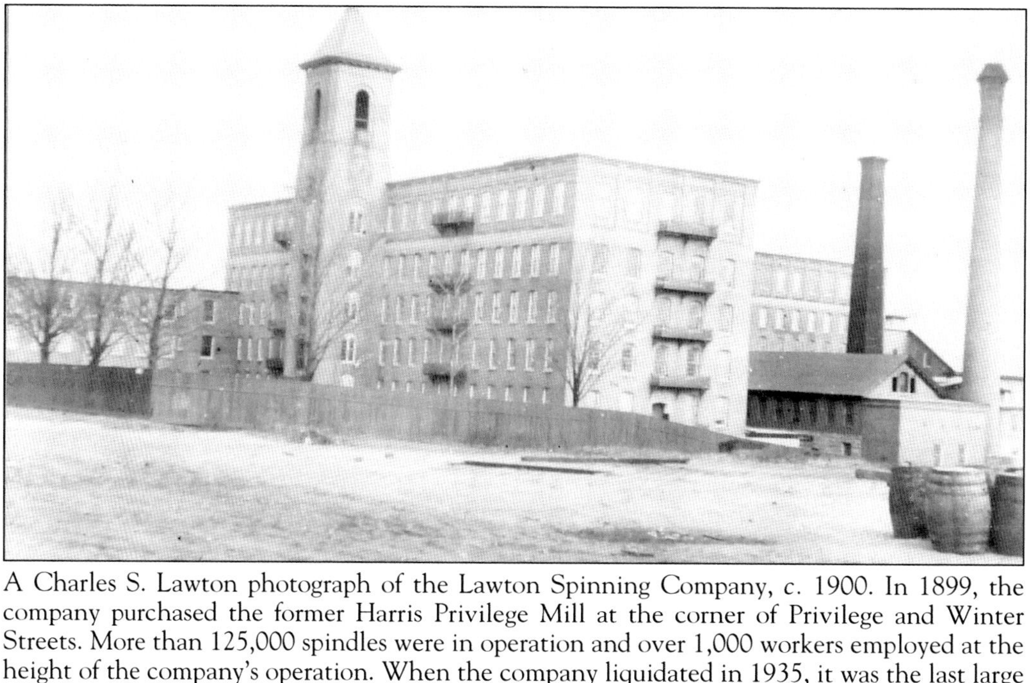

A Charles S. Lawton photograph of the Lawton Spinning Company, *c.* 1900. In 1899, the company purchased the former Harris Privilege Mill at the corner of Privilege and Winter Streets. More than 125,000 spindles were in operation and over 1,000 workers employed at the height of the company's operation. When the company liquidated in 1935, it was the last large cotton mill in Woonsocket. (Woonsocket Harris Public Library.)

Edward Carrington as depicted in the *History of Providence Plantations*, published in 1886. He was an investor in the original Hamlet Mill and Village, which was established in 1825. Carrington was also a major influence in the creation of the Blackstone Canal that linked the port of Providence to Worcester. (Woonsocket Harris Public Library.)

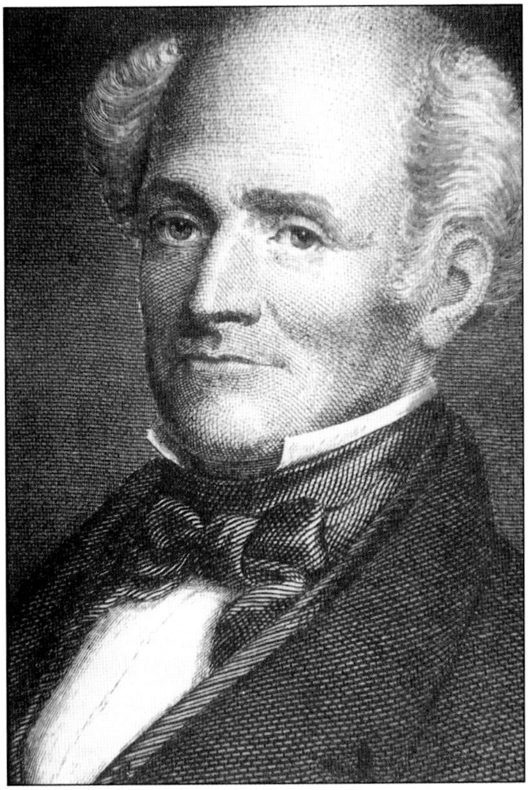

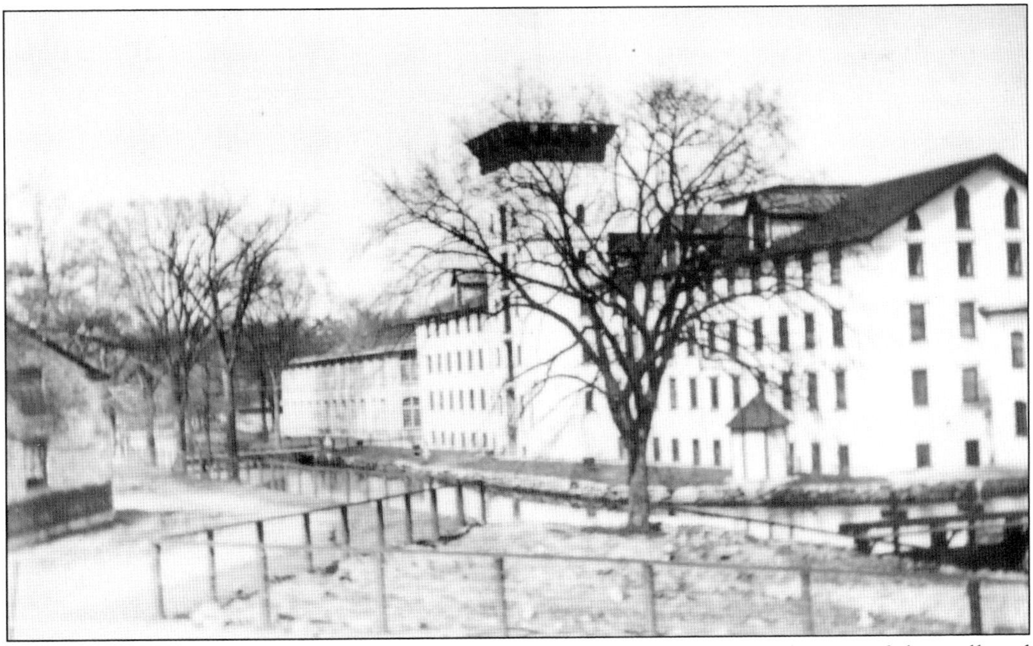

The Hamlet Mill with an excellent view of the mill trench, *c.* 1900. The site of the mill and village would be near today's Davison Street and Hamlet Avenue. The development of this area dates from 1825, when Edward Carrington established a textile mill here. (Woonsocket Harris Public Library.)

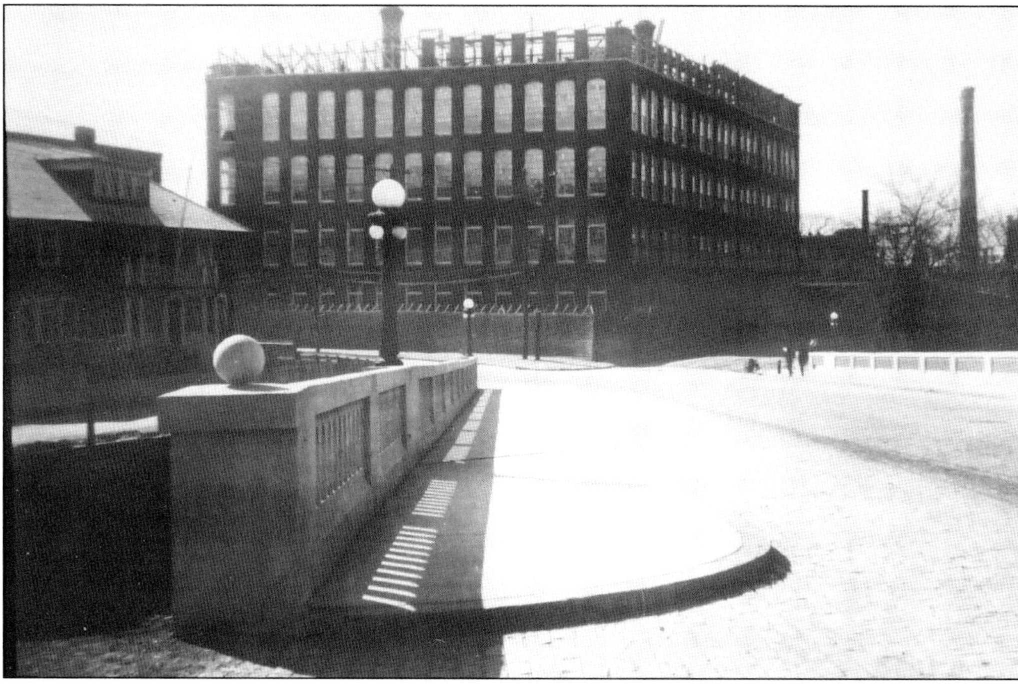

A 1920 view from the Hamlet Avenue Bridge of the Lafayette Worsted Mill with the fourth-floor addition. M. Simonis and M. Mali, two Belgians, and Charles Devine, a Frenchman, established the Lafayette Company in 1889. They came to Woonsocket at the invitation of Aram Pothier. The firm produced worsted by the French method. (Woonsocket Harris Public Library.)

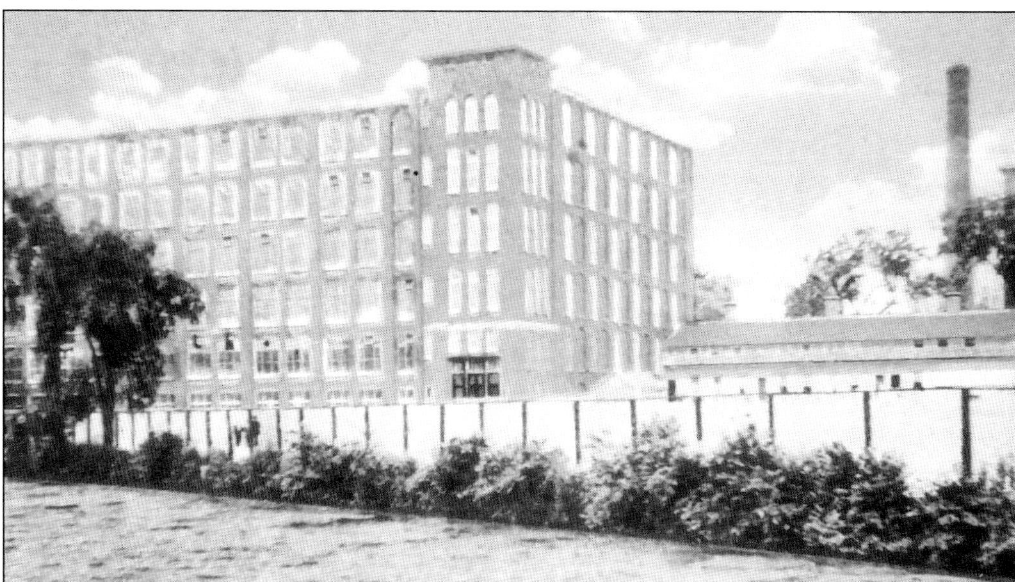

The French Worsted Mill, located on Hamlet Avenue, as seen *c.* 1915. The firm of Charles Tiberghien and Sons of Tourcoing, France, established the French Worsted Company in 1906. At the invitation of Aram Pothier they established a five-story building across the street from the Lafayette Worsted Company. (Woonsocket Harris Public Library.)

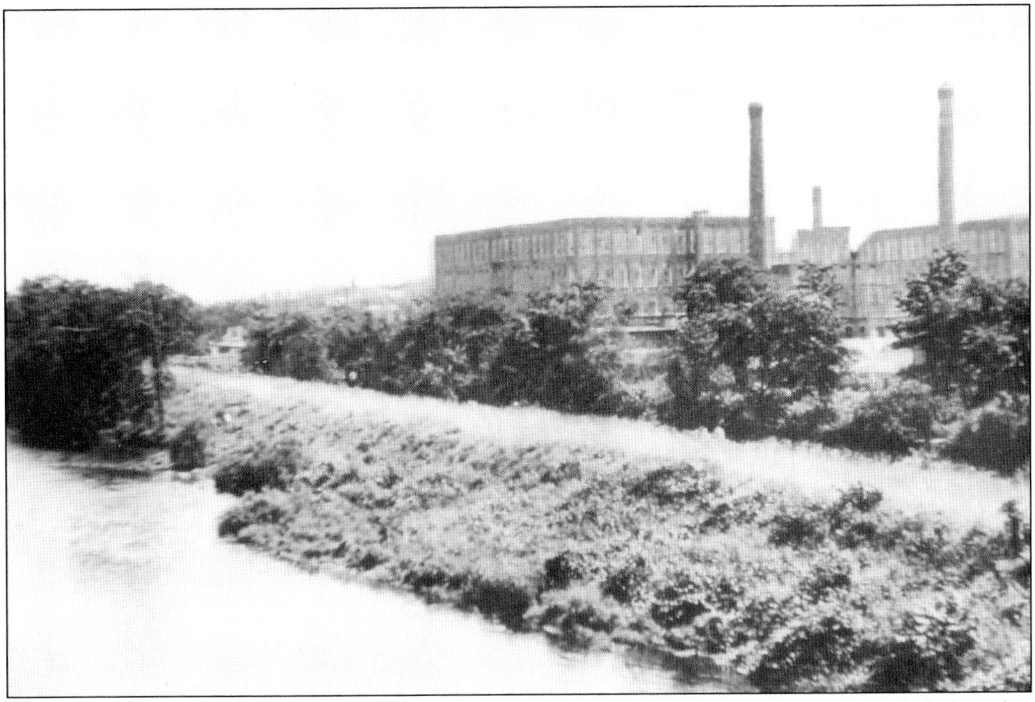

A view of the mills, including the Nyanza Mill, along Singleton Street *c*. 1915. Included in this photograph are the former Samoset Worsted Mills, built *c*. 1911, and the former Nyanza Mills, constructed *c*. 1910. These mills were the last textile mills built in Woonsocket. (Woonsocket Harris Public Library.)

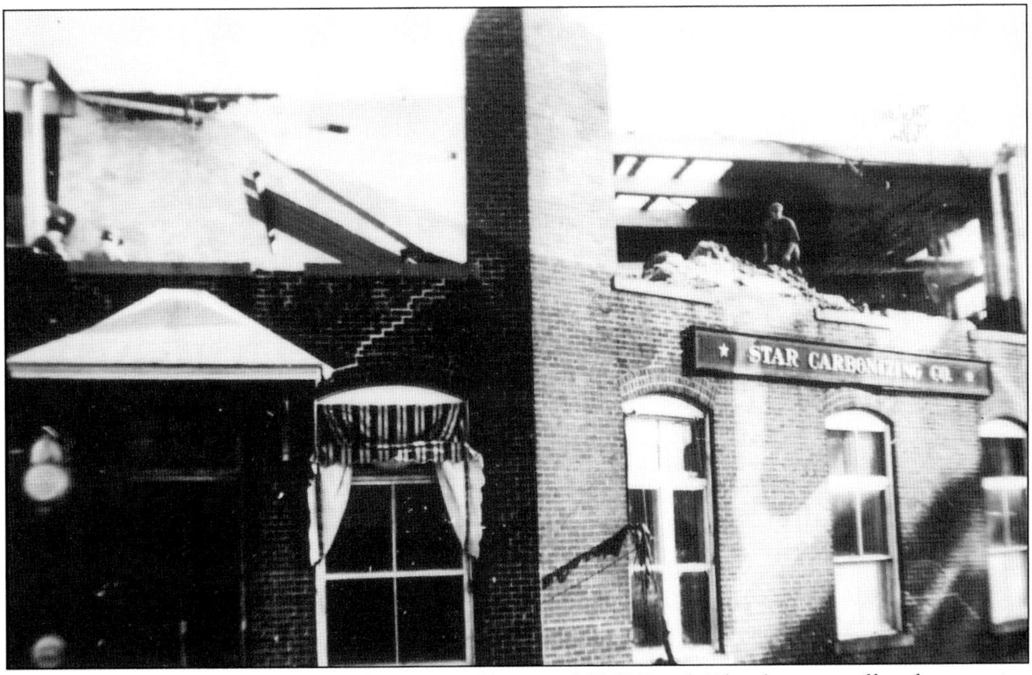

The Star Carbonizing Company factory on Diamond Hill Road. The factory suffered extensive damage to its roof in the 1938 hurricane. (Woonsocket Harris Public Library.)

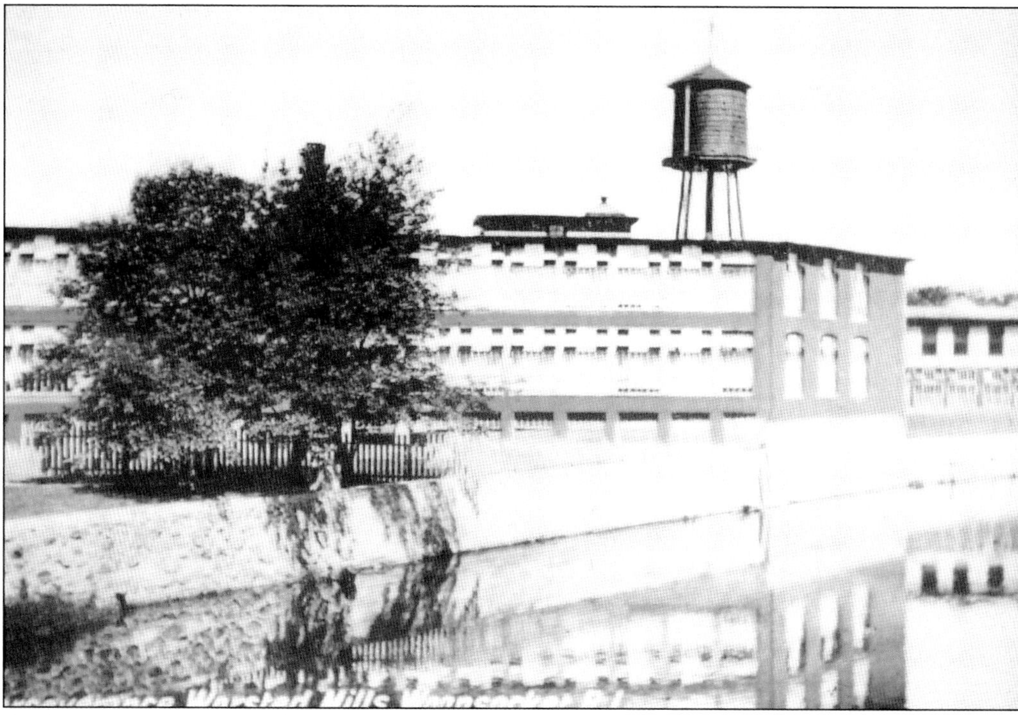

A 1915 postcard of the Perseverance Worsted Company on River Street. This mill, started in 1880 by the Singletons, had 233 employees by the year 1900. (Woonsocket Harris Public Library.)

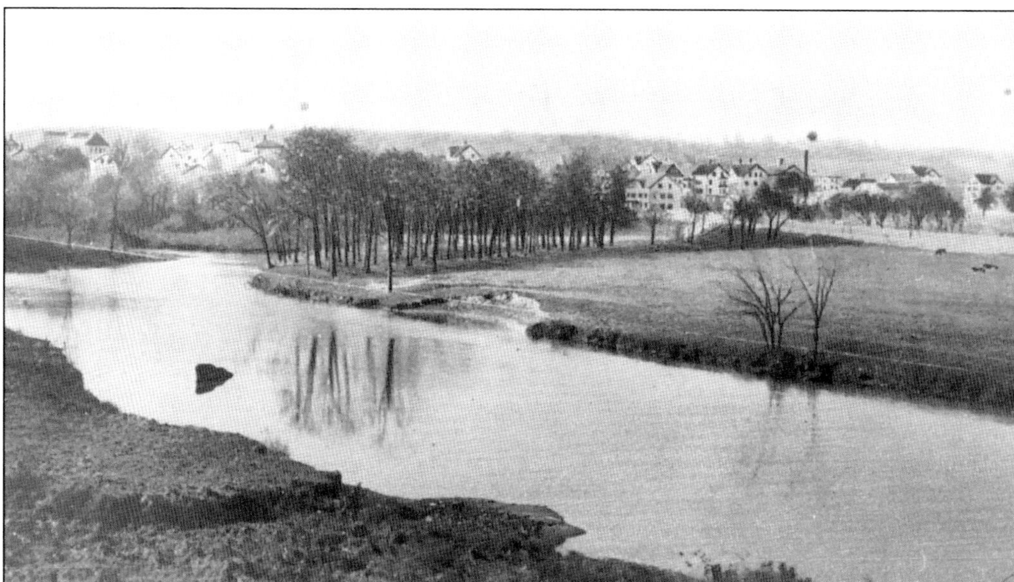

The Blackstone River and the Fairmount neighborhood, *c.* 1910. Fairmount is the largest nineteenth-century working-class residential subdivision in Woonsocket. It is in the northwestern part of the city, near the North Smithfield border. Designed in a grid pattern, it has Fairmount Street as its main thoroughfare. (Blackstone River Valley National Heritage Corridor.)

Two

The Backbone of the Industry: The Worker

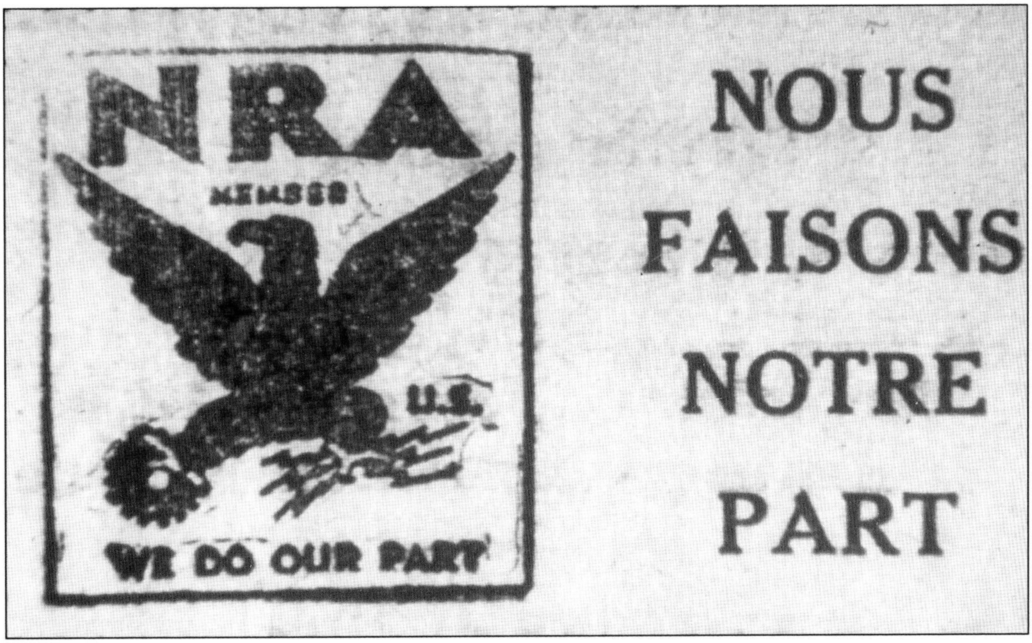

Over 70% of Woonsocket's population was of French-Canadian origin, according to the 1930 census. This made Woonsocket the third largest city with a French-speaking population in North America and "la ville la plus francaise aux Etats-Unis." You can see the French flavor of the community in this National Recovery Act emblem from the 1930s.

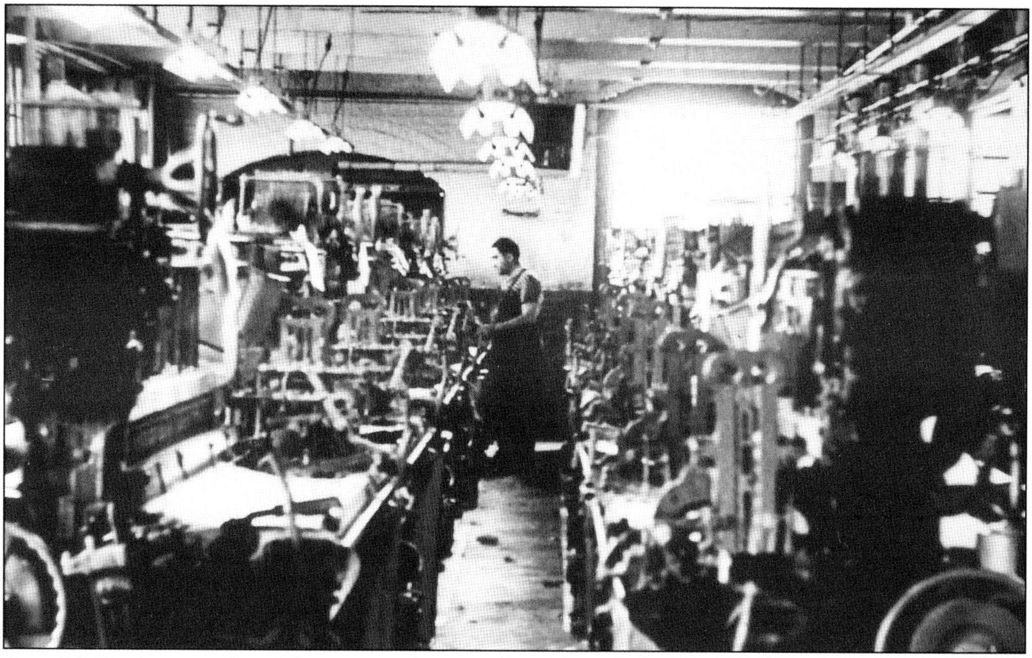

A *c.* 1945 photograph of the weave shop in the Glenark Worsted Mill. The former Glenark Mill is on the edge of the Blackstone River immediately above the Falls. The original stone section dates back to 1865, when it was built by the Ballou family. (Woonsocket Harris Public Library.)

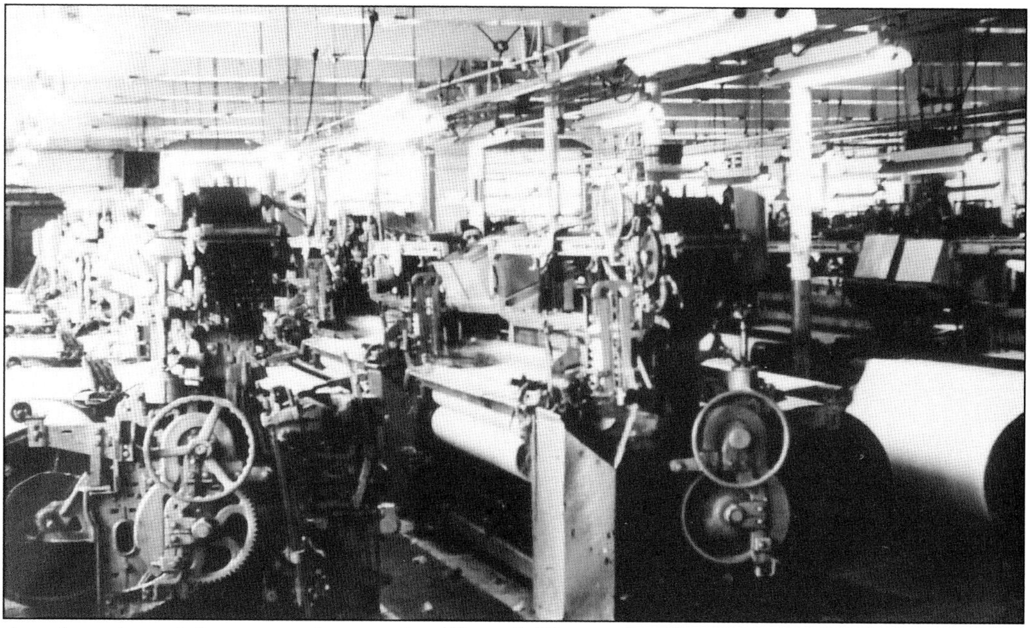

Another view of the weave shop in the Glenark Worsted Mill in 1940. This textile complex, constructed in 1865 with an addition in 1885, has seen many uses. Originally a cotton mill, it later became a knitting mill, and then a worsted mill. Fire seriously damaged the Glenark Mill in April 1987. Today the structure serves as subsidized housing. (Woonsocket Harris Public Library.)

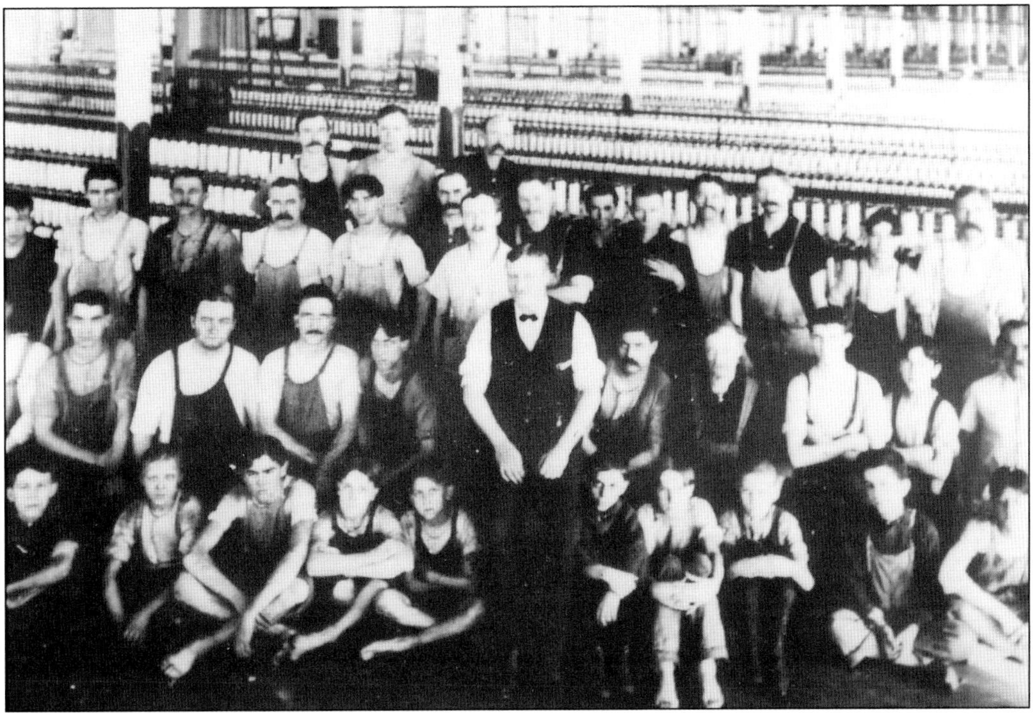

Nourse Mill operatives *c.* 1900. The Nourse Mill, built in 1883 and located on Clinton Street, was by the beginning of the twentieth century one of Woonsocket's largest cotton-manufacturing companies. (Woonsocket Harris Public Library.)

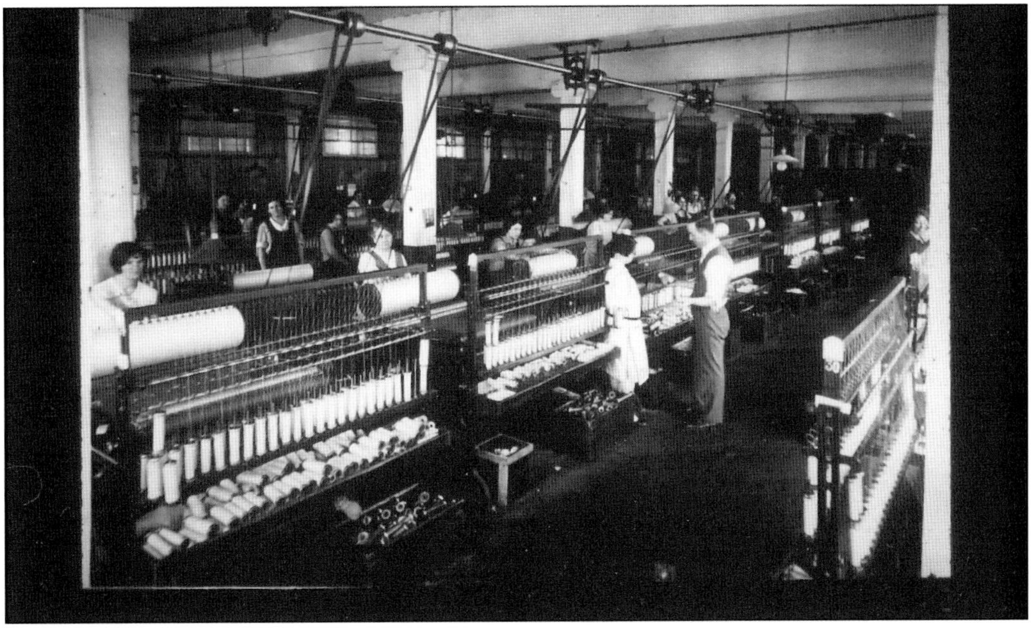

The Spool Room in the Jarret Mill in 1929. Shortly after this photograph was taken, the Great Depression of the 1930s collapsed Woonsocket's economy. Only 50% of the city's textile workers would remain employed during the height of the Depression. (Woonsocket Harris Public Library.)

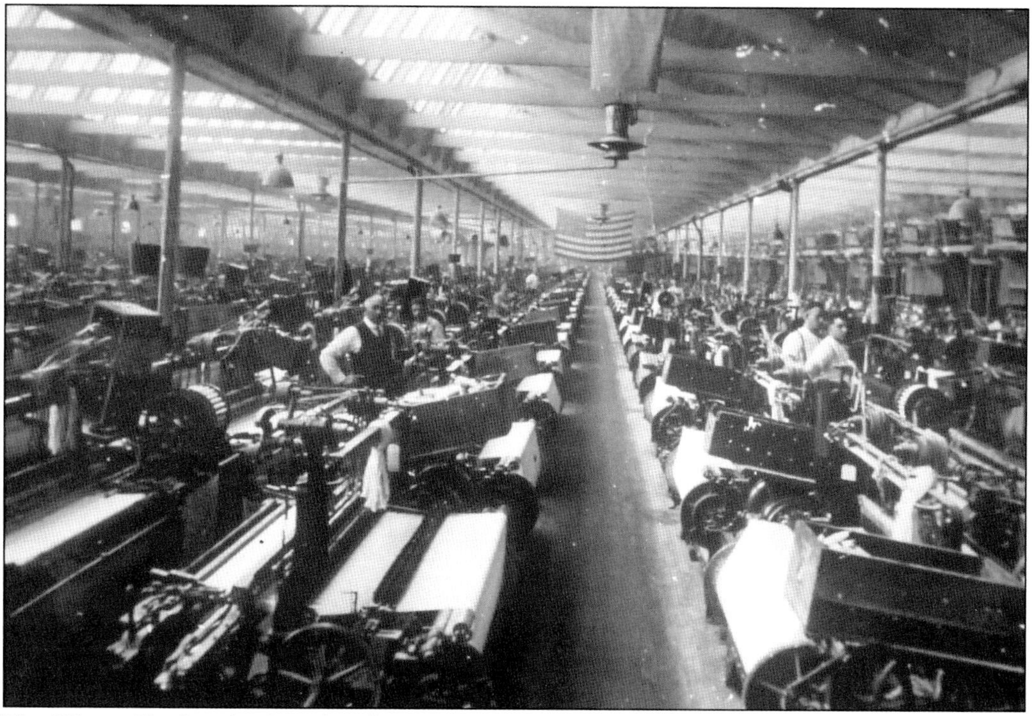

The Weave Shed in the Social Mill *c.* 1920. The formation of this mill and village along Social Street occurred in 1810. This huge mill, eventually owned by the Manville-Jenckes Company, closed permanently in 1927. Razing of the Social Mill occurred in 1932. (Woonsocket Harris Public Library.)

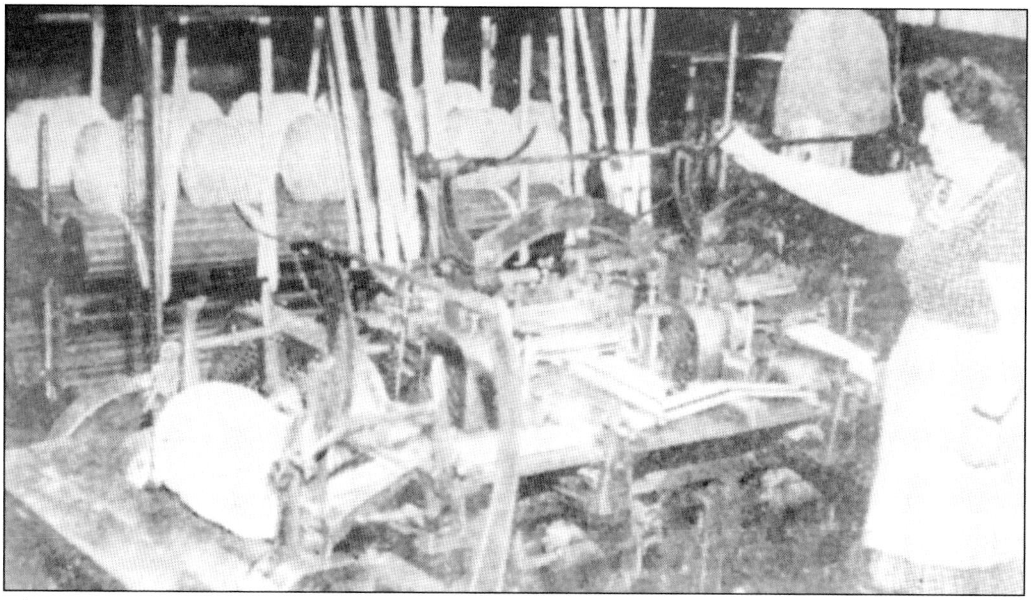

The interior of the French Worsted Mills *c.* 1950. Located along Hamlet Avenue, the French Worsted Company was built in 1906 by the French firm of Charles Tiberghien and Sons. Aram Pothier helped the company in building a mill in Woonsocket. (Woonsocket Harris Public Library.)

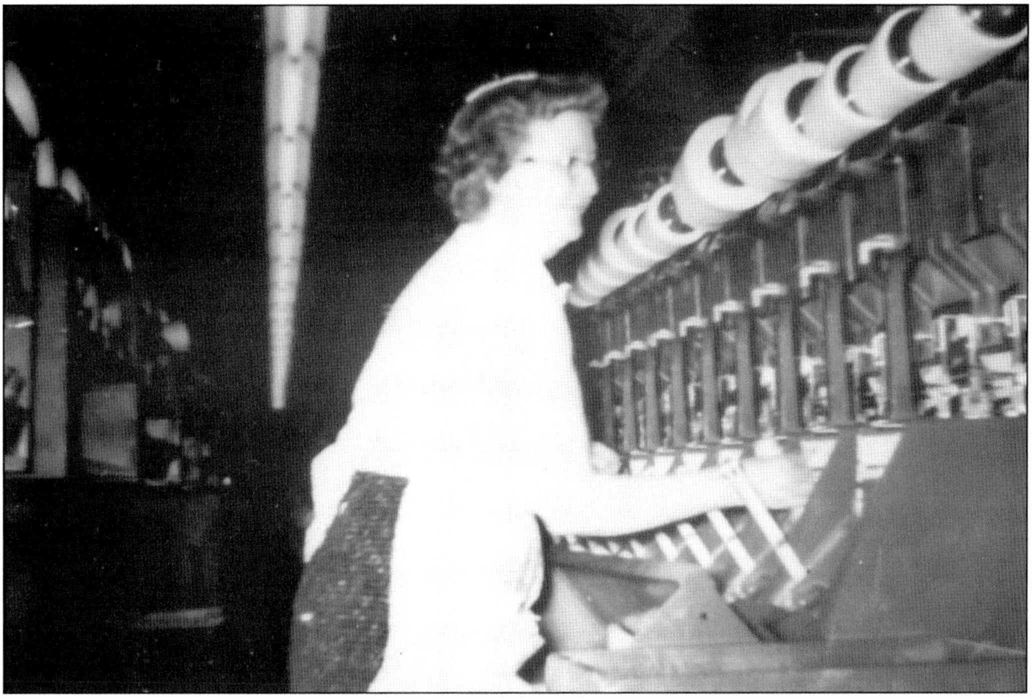

An employee "doubling" in the French Worsted mills in the 1950s. During this period the French Worsted mills had over 900 employees in their Hamlet Avenue operation.

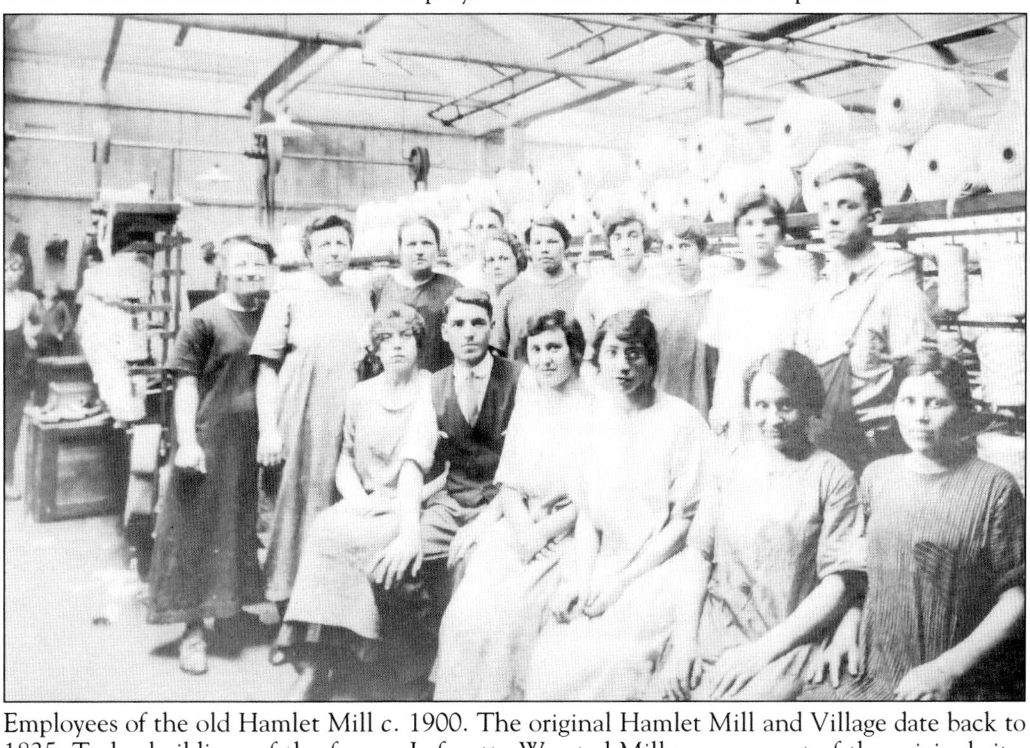

Employees of the old Hamlet Mill c. 1900. The original Hamlet Mill and Village date back to 1825. Today buildings of the former Lafayette Worsted Mills occupy part of the original site. (Woonsocket Harris Public Library.)

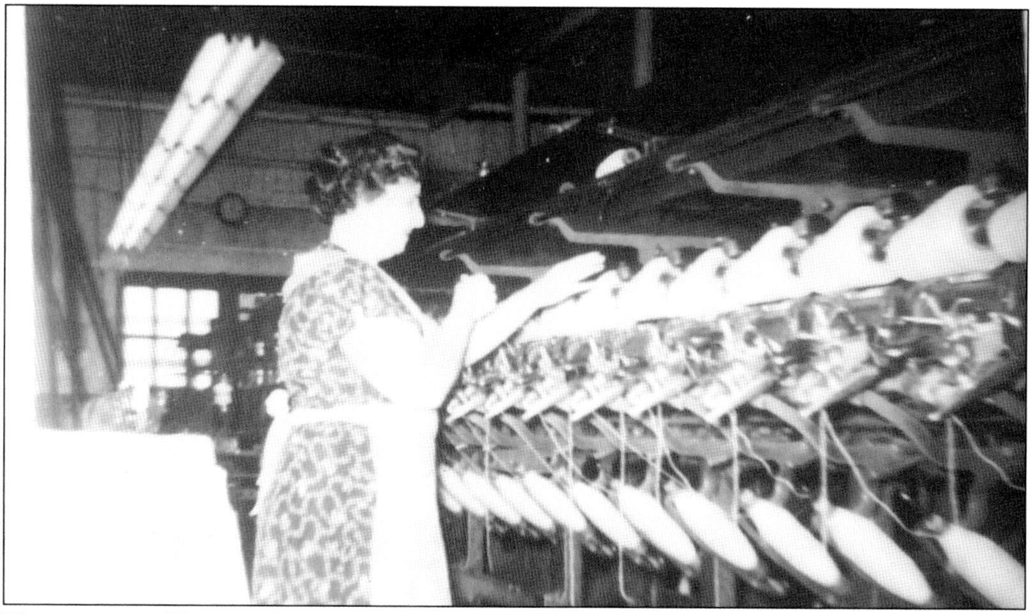

The interior of Bonin Spinning as photographed in 1954. Incorporated in 1923, the Bonin Spinning Company established a new plant on Mendon Road. The company's founders were Aime E. Bonin and Wilford E. Lamarine. (Woonsocket Harris Public Library.)

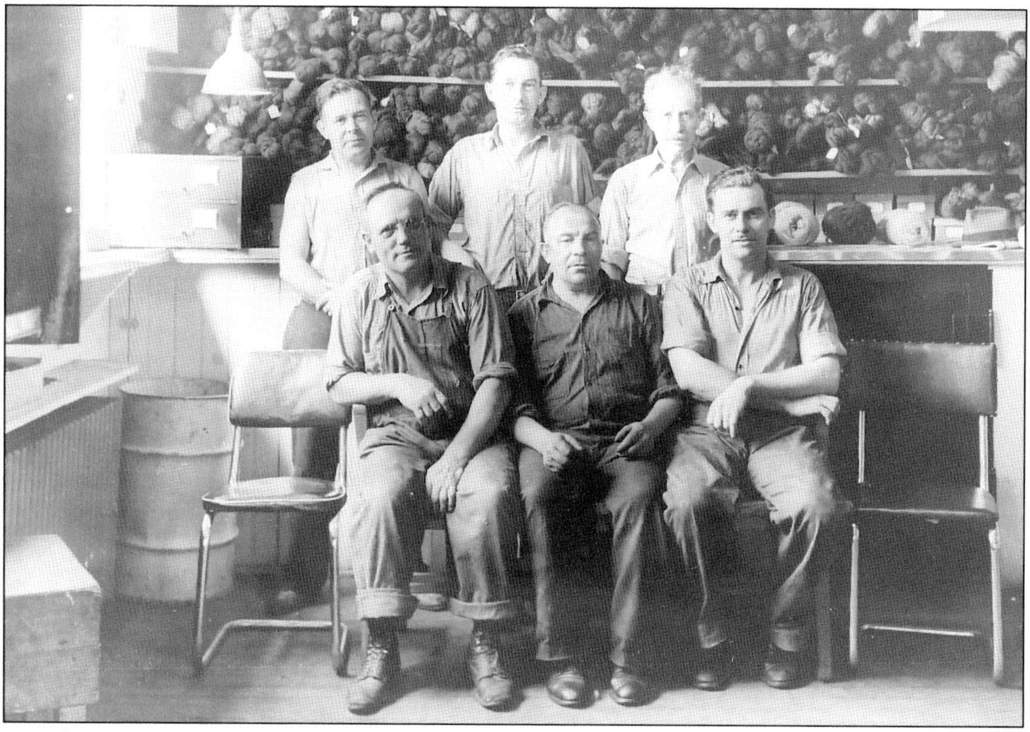

Six of the many hardworking employees of the Fairmount Dye House c. 1930. The gentleman, seated on the right, is Romeo Brousseau. Located at the corner of First Avenue and Fairmount Street, Fairmount Dye Works was incorporated in 1924 by Joseph E. Kelly and Jules Lejeune. (Mr. & Mrs. George E. Brin.)

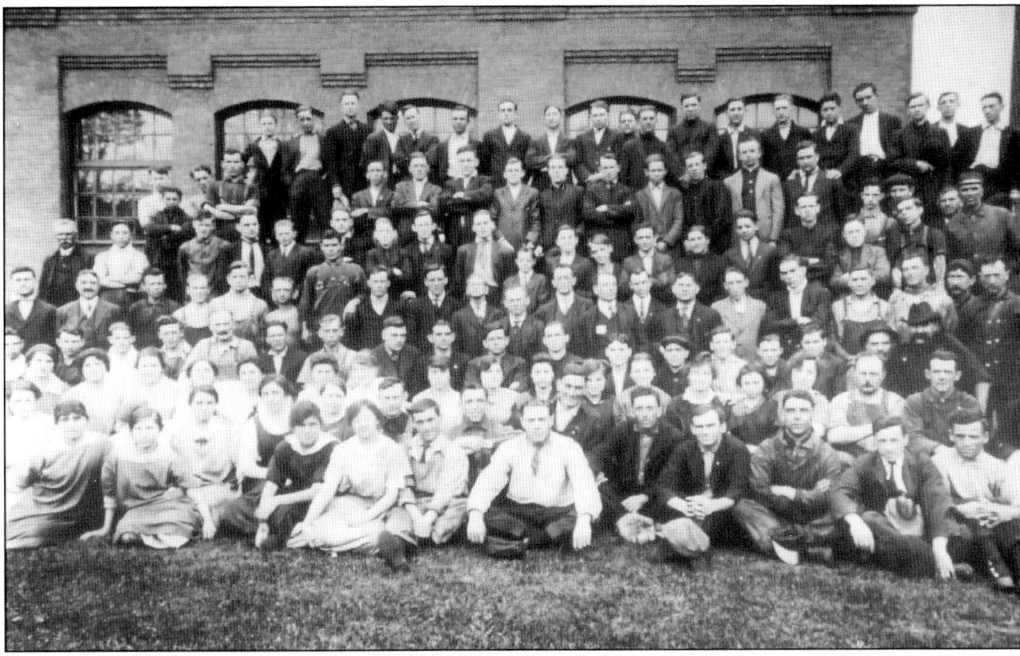

Employees of the Bonin Spinning Company outside the plant in the early 1920s. The Bonin Spinning Company, located on Mendon Road, was a manufacturer of fine woolen and merino yarns.

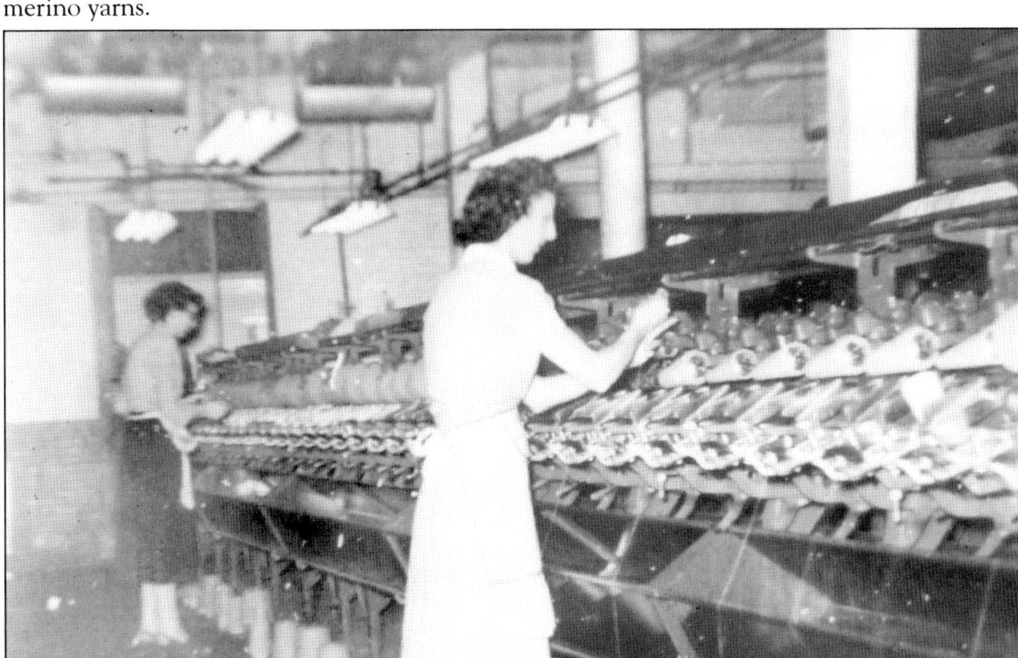

Workers and winding machines in the Woonsocket Falls Mill, *c.* mid-1950. Incorporated in 1913 and located in the "Old White Mill" at Market Square, the Woonsocket Falls Mill was a manufacturer of pile and other fabrics. By the end of the 1950s, the company succumbed to a battered textile industry and disappeared from Woonsocket. (Woonsocket Harris Public Library.)

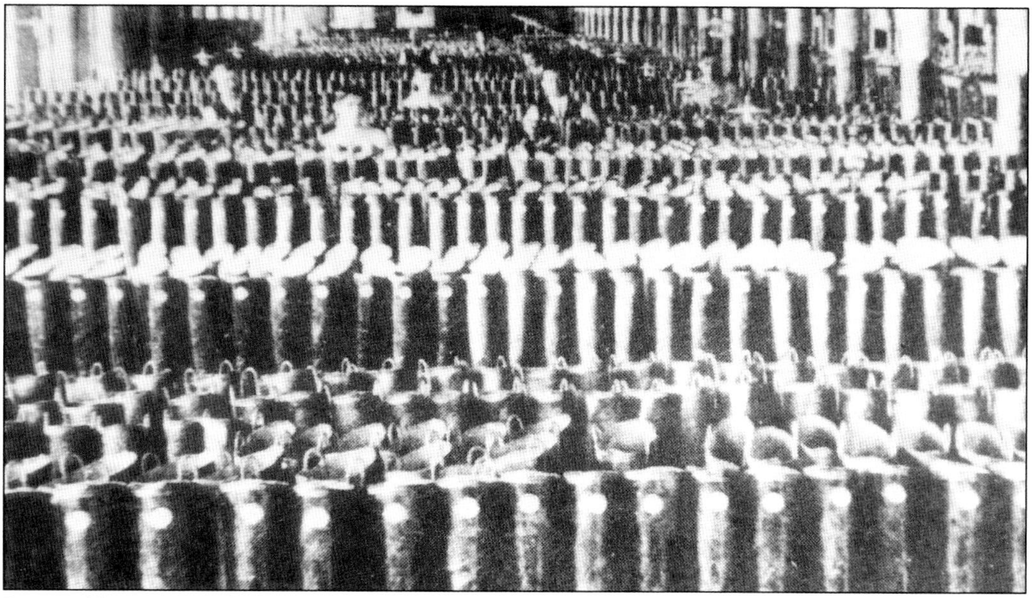

Rows of boots manufactured in the Woonsocket Rubber Company's Alice Mill on Fairmount Street *c.* 1900. Headed by Joseph Banigan, the Woonsocket Rubber Company was the leading importer of raw rubber into the United States. At the height of its operation, 2,000 hands were working here and it was the largest rubber goods factory in the world. (Woonsocket Harris Public Library.)

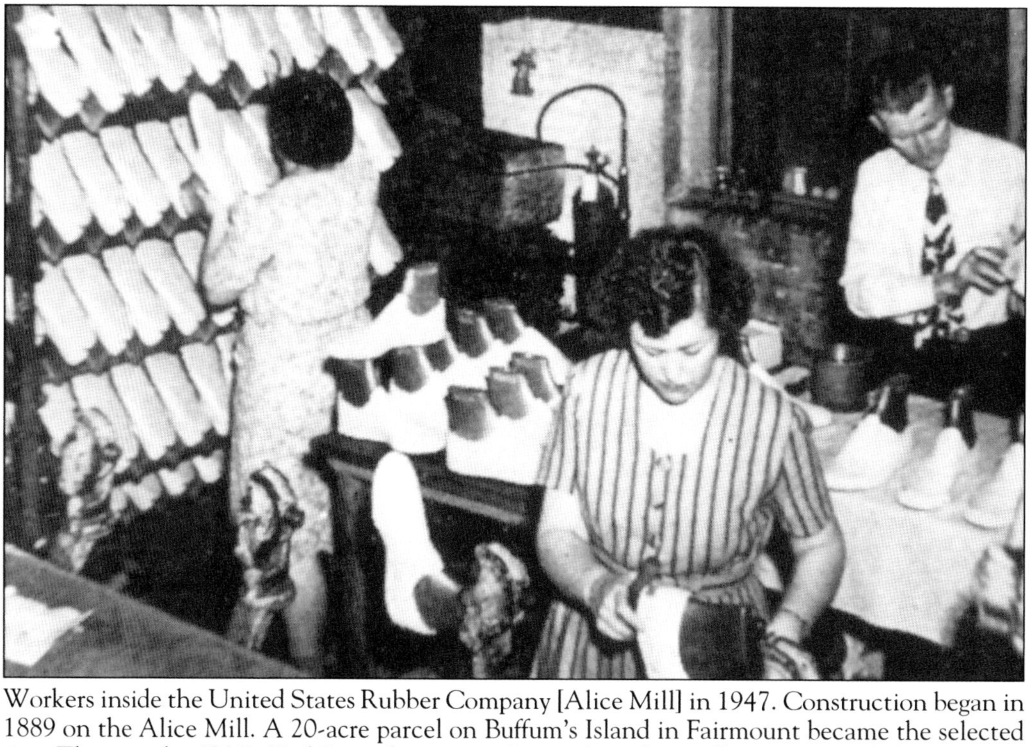

Workers inside the United States Rubber Company [Alice Mill] in 1947. Construction began in 1889 on the Alice Mill. A 20-acre parcel on Buffum's Island in Fairmount became the selected site. The popular "U.S. Keds" sneakers manufactured in this mill were part of the footwear division of the United States Rubber Company. (Woonsocket Harris Public Library.)

Three

A Working City Grows

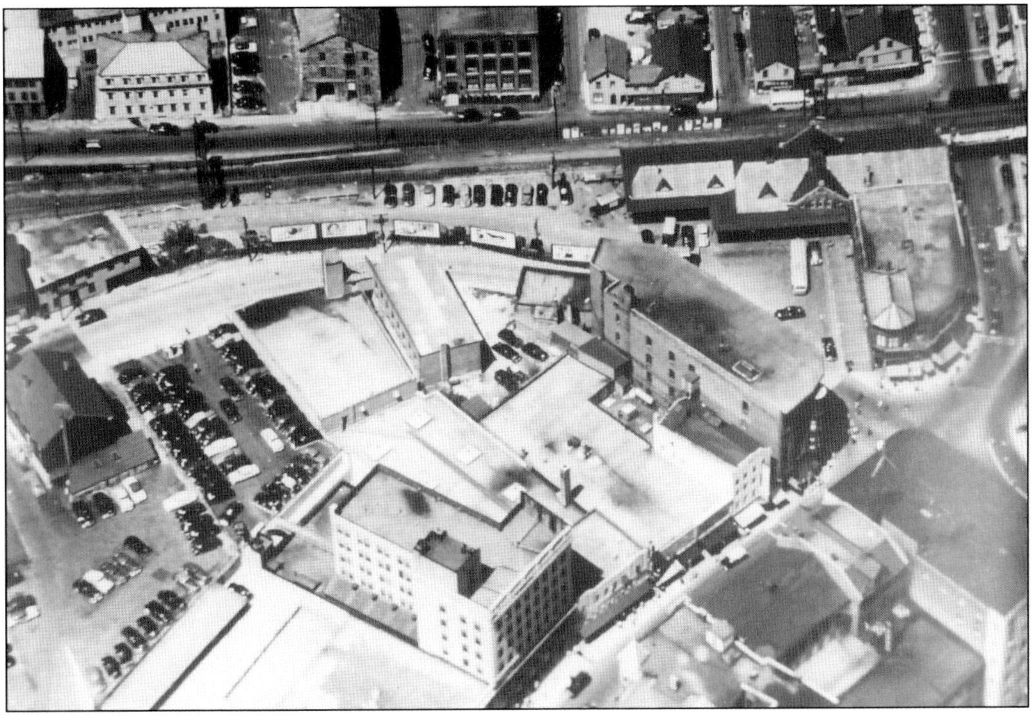

A *c.* 1951 aerial photograph of the Depot Square area. Included in this view are: the Rhode Island Hospital Trust Building (1929) in the lower center; city hall (1856–1891) across the street; the Longley Building (1890) is just right of the center; McCarthy's Building is across the street; and the Railroad Depot (1882) with Edwards Block is at the intersection of Main and High Streets. (Woonsocket Harris Public Library.)

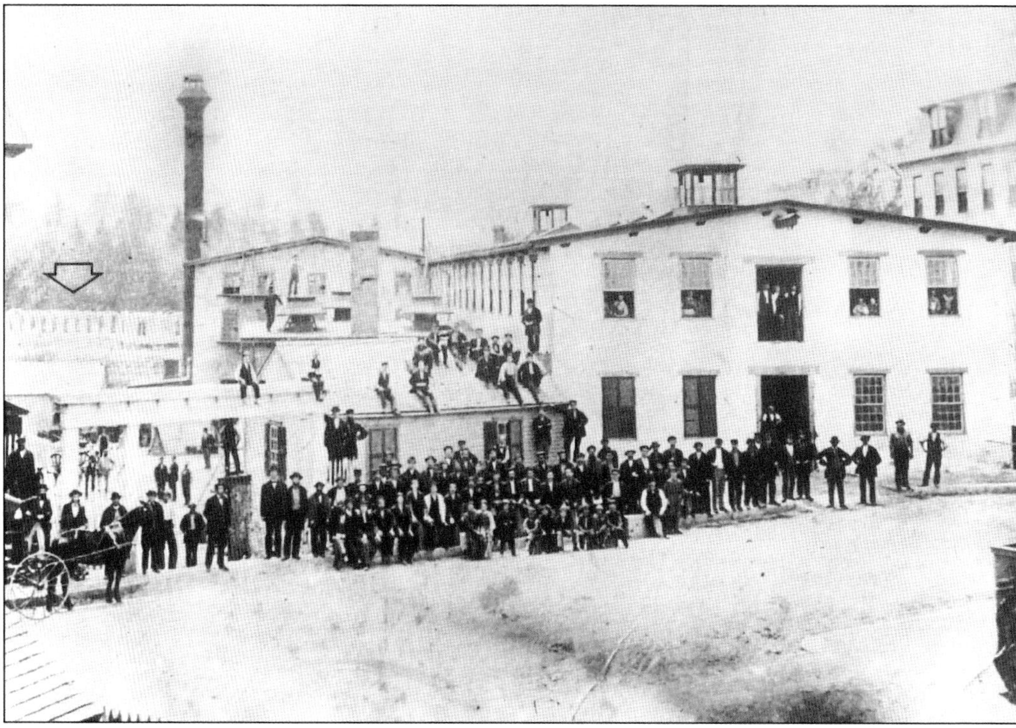

The Woonsocket Rubber Company at Market Square, c. 1870. Members of the Cook family and Joseph Banigan of Providence founded the firm in the late 1860s. Banigan would eventually dominate the firm. (Woonsocket Harris Public Library.)

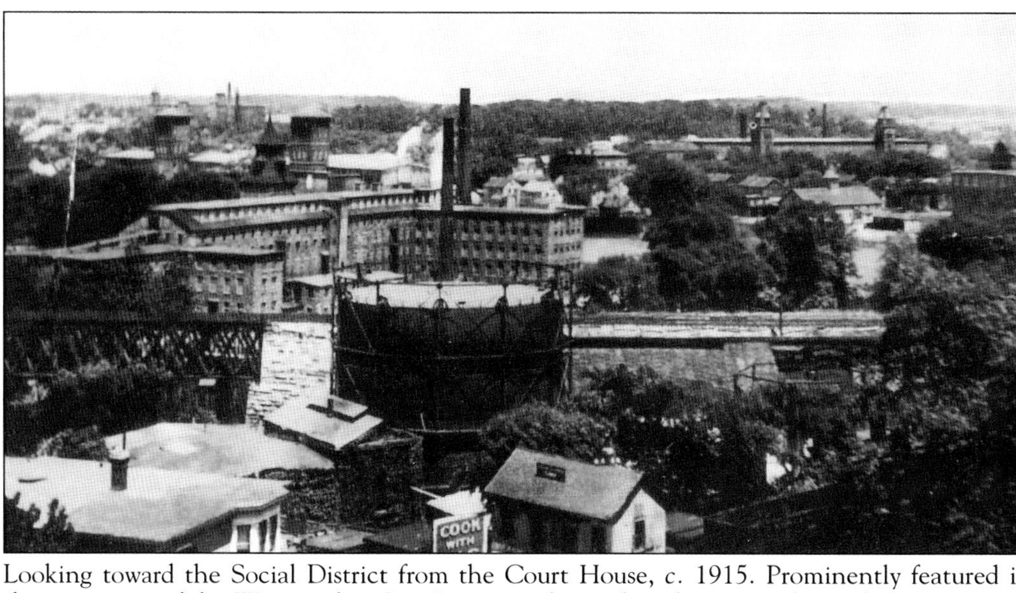

Looking toward the Social District from the Court House, c. 1915. Prominently featured is the gasometer of the Woonsocket Gas Company, located in the gas works yard on East Front Street. The Clinton Mill is just left of the center and in the distance is the Social District. (Woonsocket Harris Public Library.)

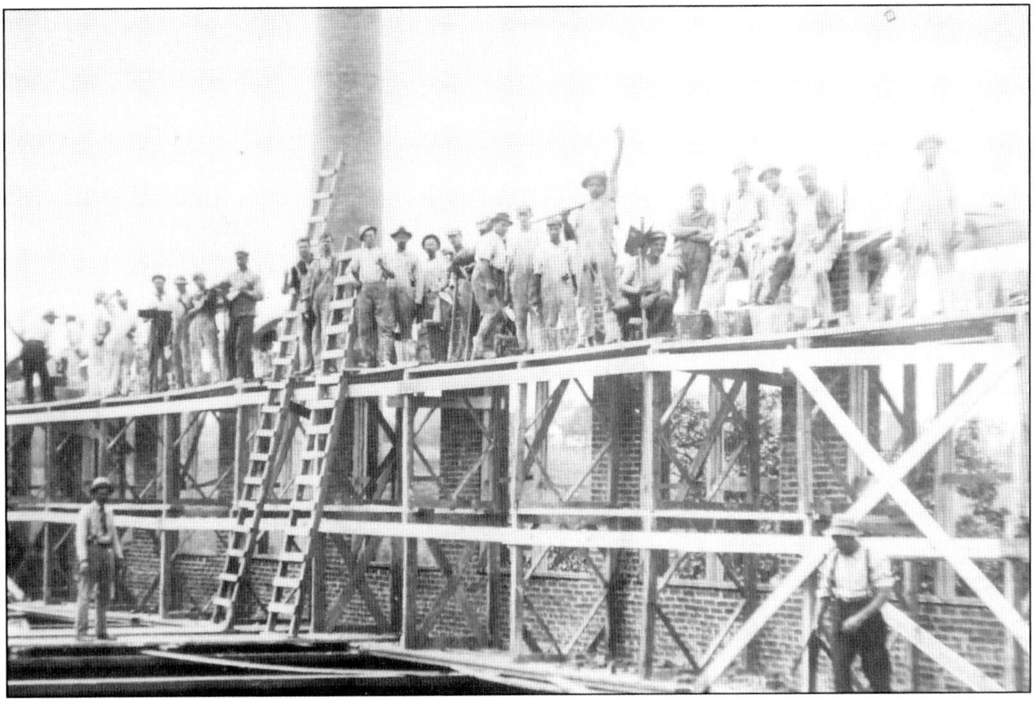

The construction of an addition to the Woonsocket Machine and Press Company, *c.* 1890. This mill provided the first substantial growth of the Fairmount Neighborhood by prompting many workers to settle in the area. (Woonsocket Harris Public Library.)

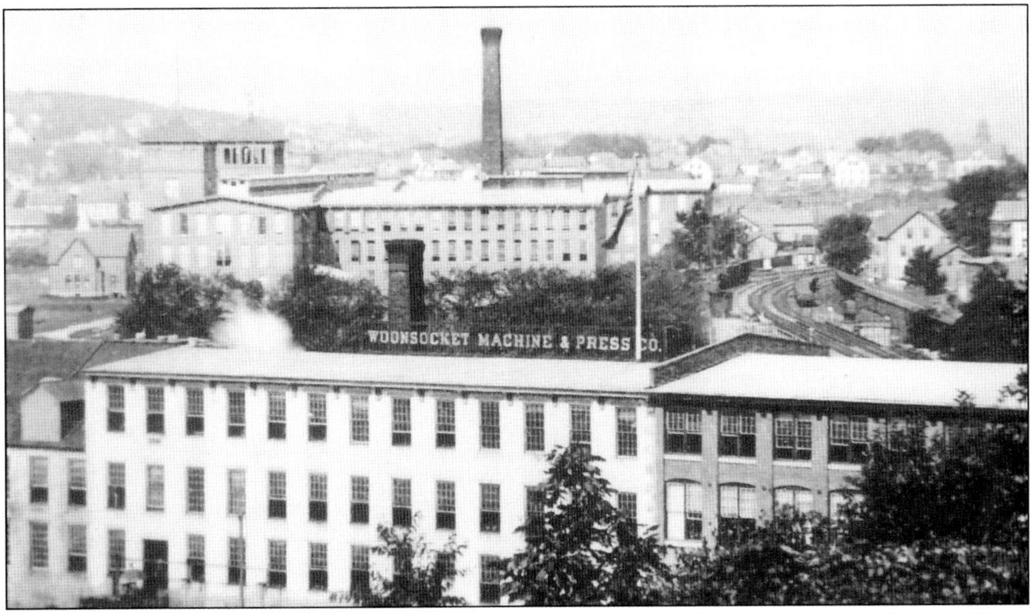

The Woonsocket Machine and Press Company, *c.* 1900. The company built a mill on Second Avenue in the Fairmount Neighborhood in 1879. This firm was the world's leading manufacturer of fly frames. In April 1984, this converted complex became the Fairmount Manor, providing 139 apartment units for the city's elderly. (Woonsocket Harris Public Library.)

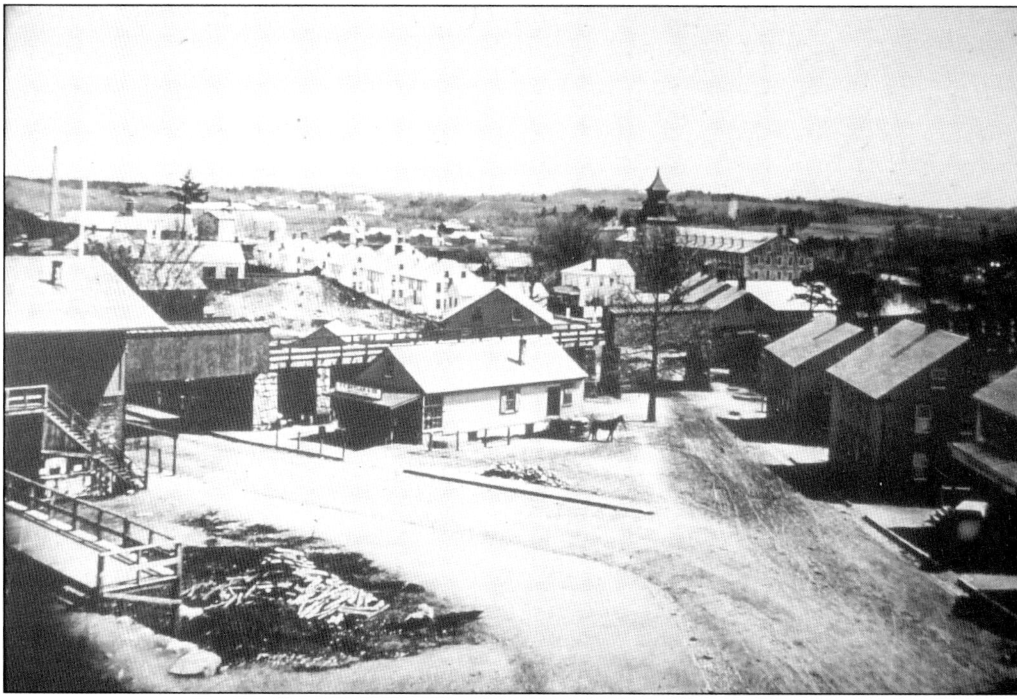

Depot Square as captured by a photographer *c.* 1870. The view is of the Clinton Mill and Village looking down Clinton Street. The railroad tracks are those of the Providence and Worcester Railroad, and the original depot (1847) is at left.

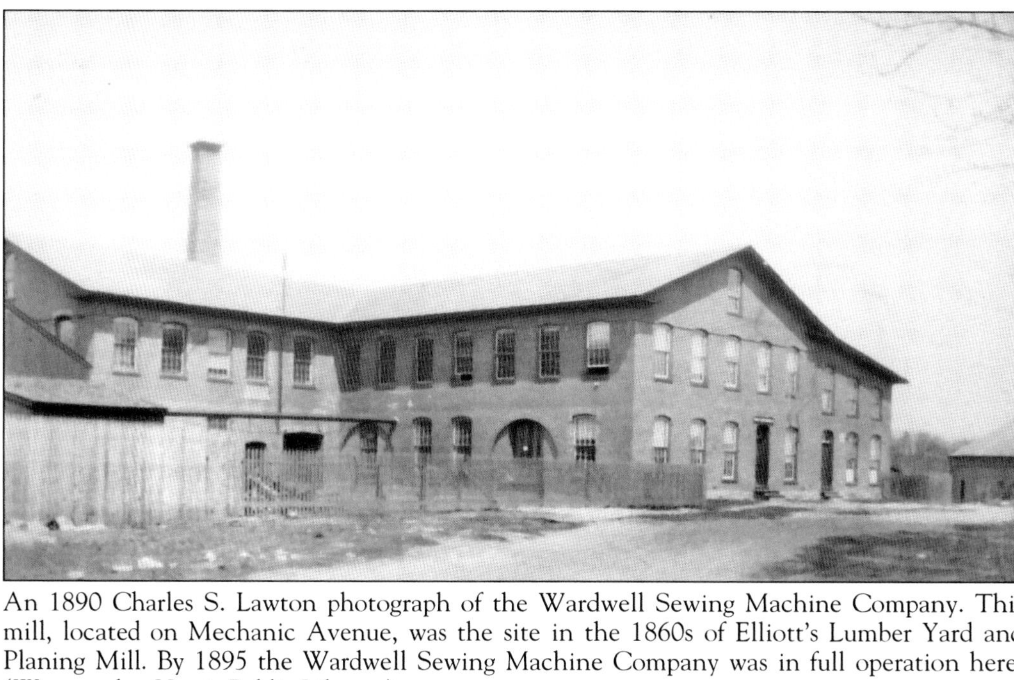

An 1890 Charles S. Lawton photograph of the Wardwell Sewing Machine Company. This mill, located on Mechanic Avenue, was the site in the 1860s of Elliott's Lumber Yard and Planing Mill. By 1895 the Wardwell Sewing Machine Company was in full operation here. (Woonsocket Harris Public Library.)

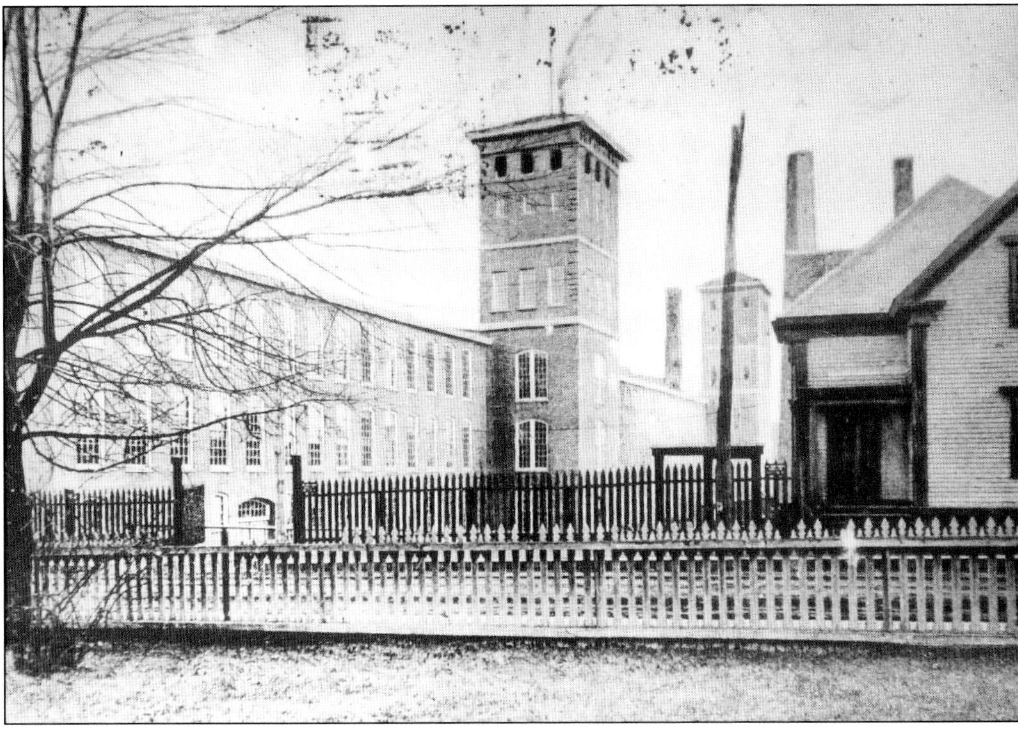

The American Wringer Mill in 1911. This mill, located in the block between Clinton and Social Streets, is today the site of the Woonsocket Police Station and the post office. The company began as the Bailey Wringer Company in the 1860s, but later changed its name to the American Wringer Company. Clothes wringers manufactured here were in use throughout the world. (Woonsocket Harris Public Library.)

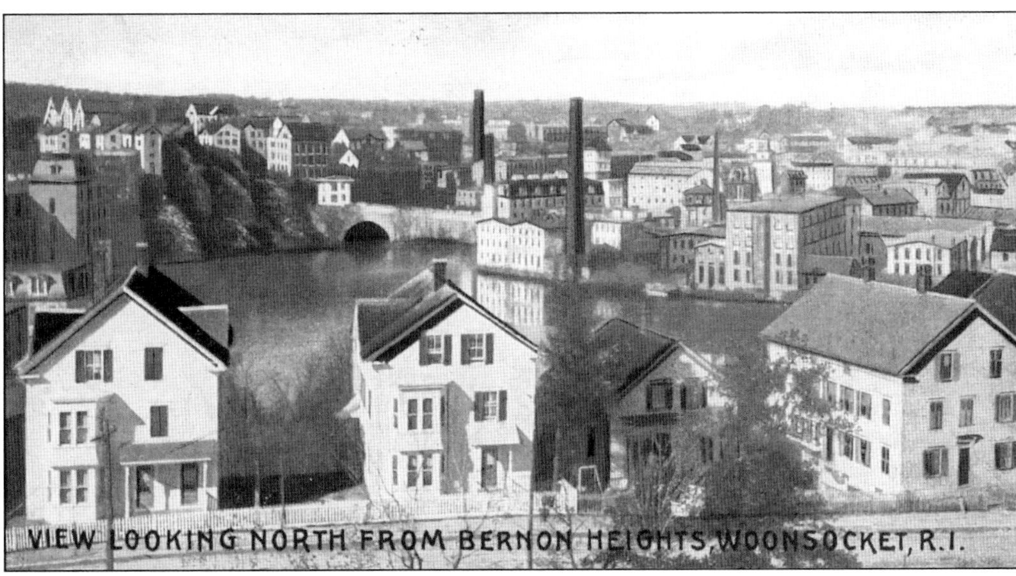

A view looking north from Bernon Heights, *c.* 1900. The Globe (South Main Street) Bridge and the mills located in the Market Square area can be seen here, as well as the Globe Mill (at left). The houses in the foreground are on Front Street. (Mr. & Mrs. Robert C. Brin.)

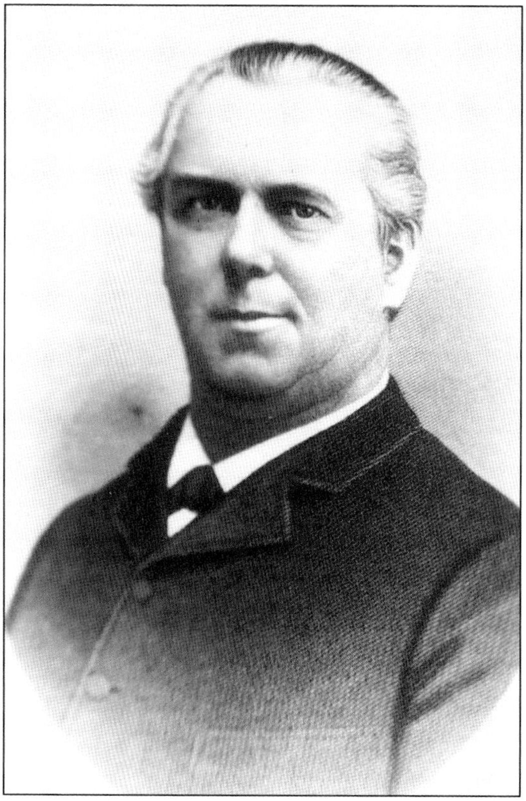

Joseph Banigan, an Irish immigrant who became a self-made millionaire. He headed the Woonsocket Rubber Company, which was the leading importer of raw rubber into the United States. Banigan later helped create the United States Rubber Company. He was a most munificent philanthropist to Rhode Island institutions, especially to Catholic charities. (Woonsocket Harris Public Library.)

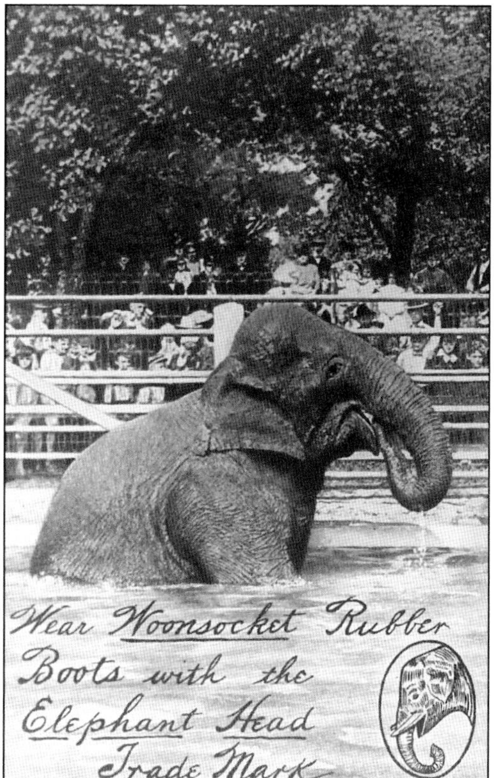

A Woonsocket Rubber Company Trade Card, *c.* 1890. Sales associates distributed these cards throughout the nation to mercantile store operators. (Blackstone River Valley National Heritage Corridor Commission.)

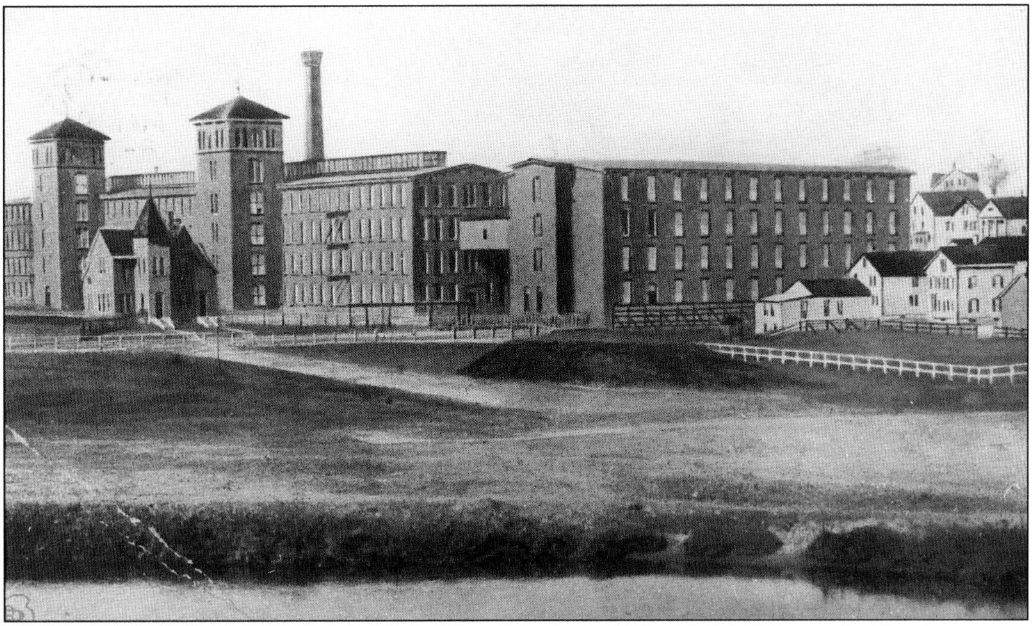

The Alice Rubber Works, the largest rubber shoe factory in the world, *c.* 1900. This enormous four-story brick mill was constructed in 1889. Joseph Banigan, who was the head of the Woonsocket Rubber Company, named the mill in honor of his mother. (Blackstone River Valley National Heritage Corridor.)

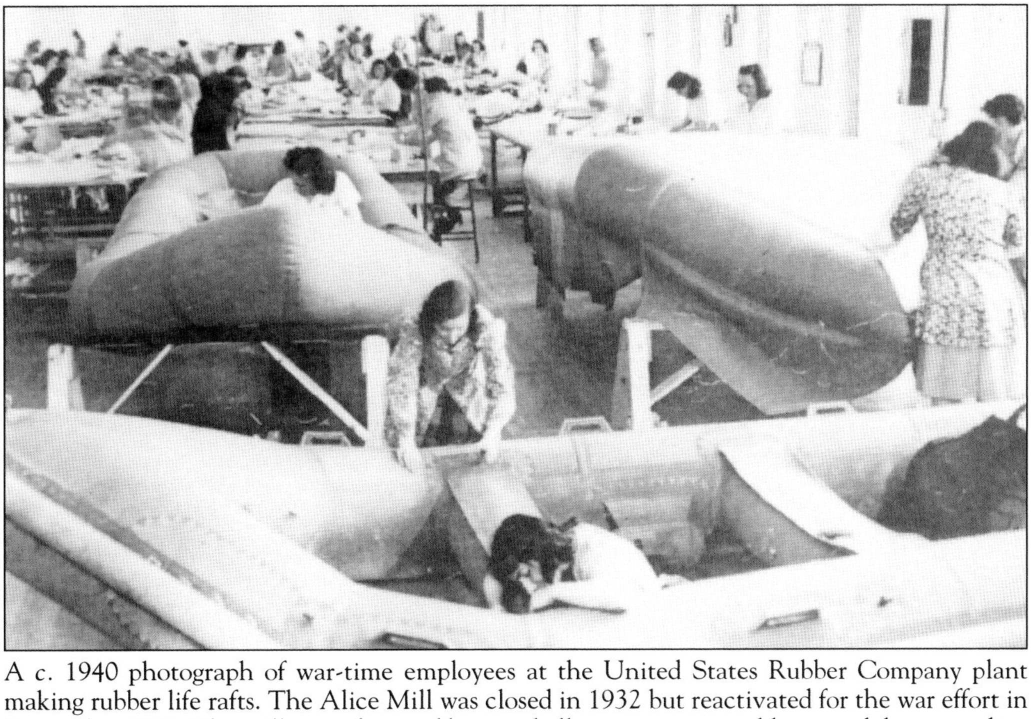

A *c.* 1940 photograph of war-time employees at the United States Rubber Company plant making rubber life rafts. The Alice Mill was closed in 1932 but reactivated for the war effort in September 1941. The mill manufactured barrage balloons, ten-man rubber attack boats, wading suits, and lifesaving suits. (Woonsocket Harris Public Library.)

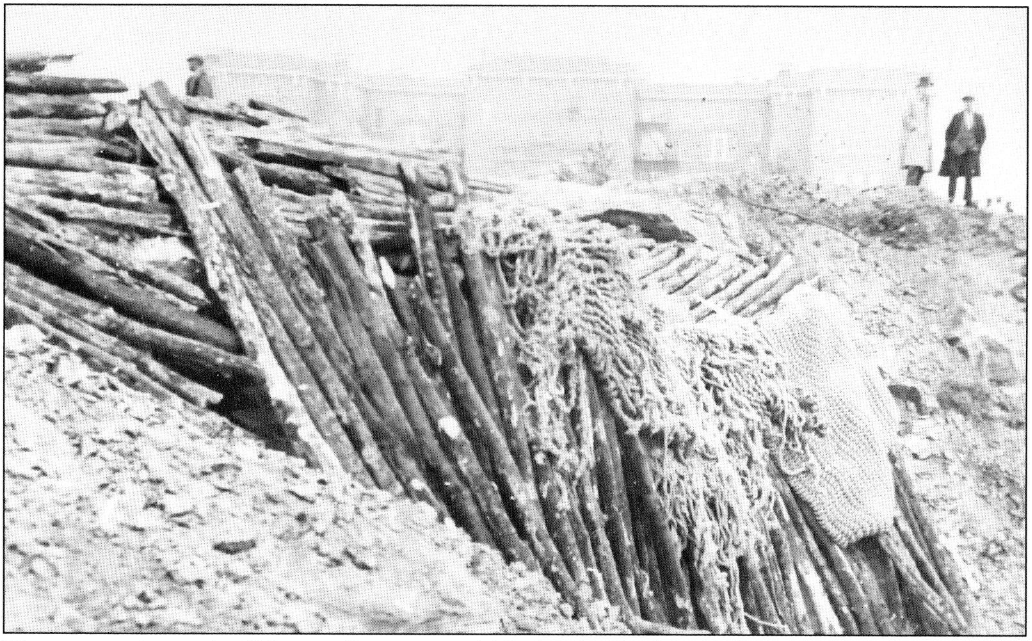

The quarry located off Logee Street, *c.* 1930. In the background is Mount Saint Charles Academy, designed by Walter Fontaine and built in 1924. It became a Catholic boys' high school with the support of L'Union Saint Jean-Baptiste and Monsignor Charles Dauray, pastor of the Church of the Precious Blood. (Mr. and Mrs. George C. Brin.)

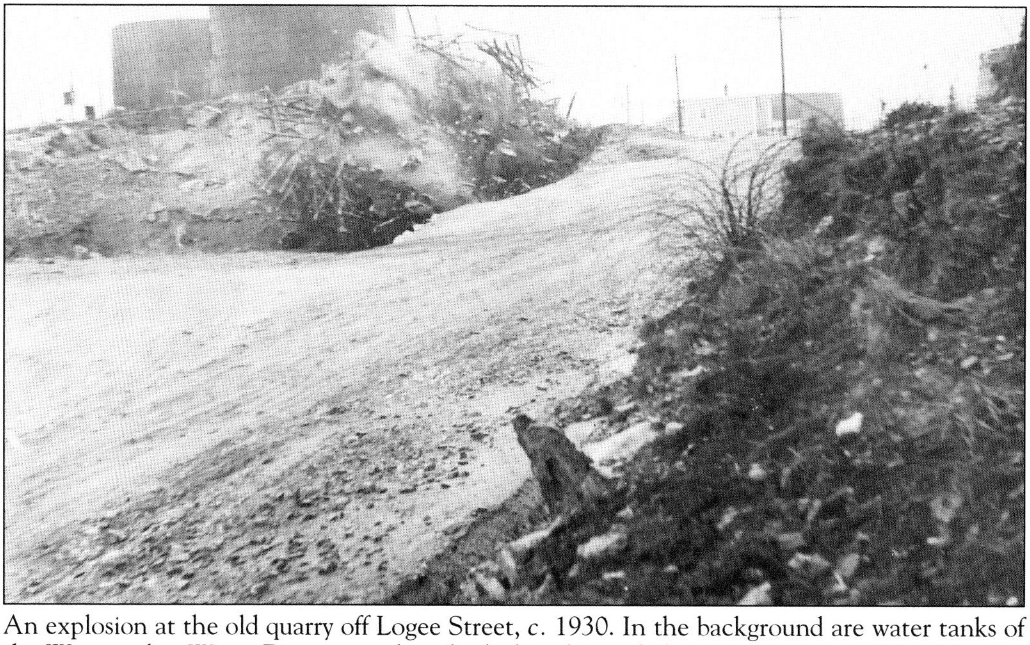

An explosion at the old quarry off Logee Street, *c.* 1930. In the background are water tanks of the Woonsocket Water Division and triple-deckers located along Logee Street. (Mr. and Mrs. George C. Brin.)

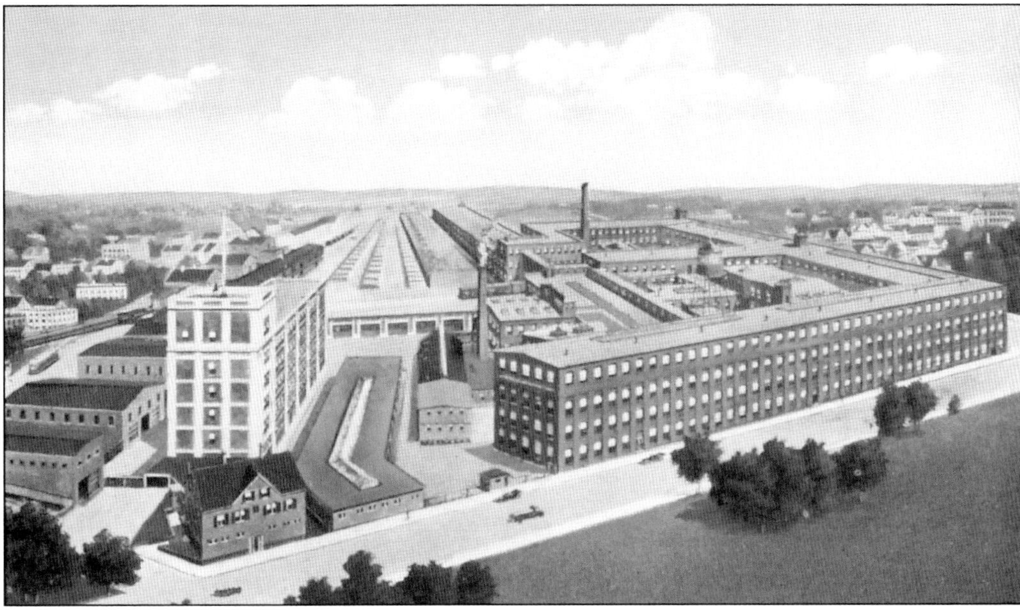

A postcard view of the Taft-Pierce Manufacturing Company, *c*. 1920. This factory complex along Mechanic Avenue dates from the 1860s as the site of Elliott's Lumber Yard and Planing Mill. The Wardwell Sewing Machine Company occupied the site by 1895. The Taft-Pierce Company purchased the property in 1910 and developed it into a world-class machine shop. (Mr. and Mrs. Robert C. Brin.)

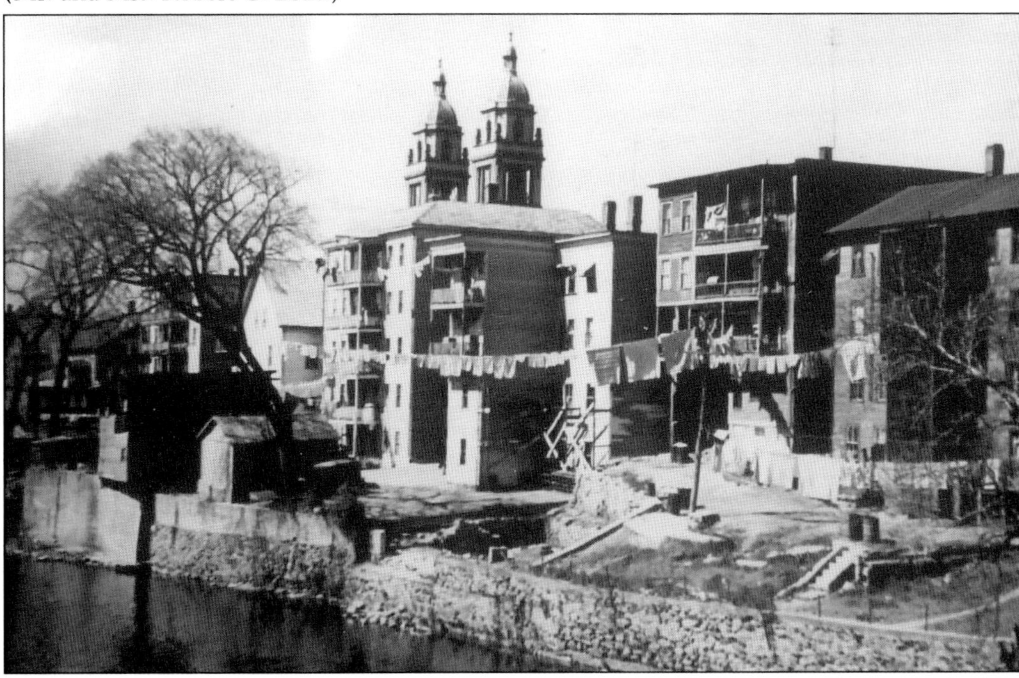

Tenement houses along the Blackstone River, *c*. 1940. These houses are along Cumberland Street. In the background, the towers of Saint Ann's Roman Catholic Church rise just above the houses. Between 1895 and 1925 tenement houses were the most common type of dwellings constructed.

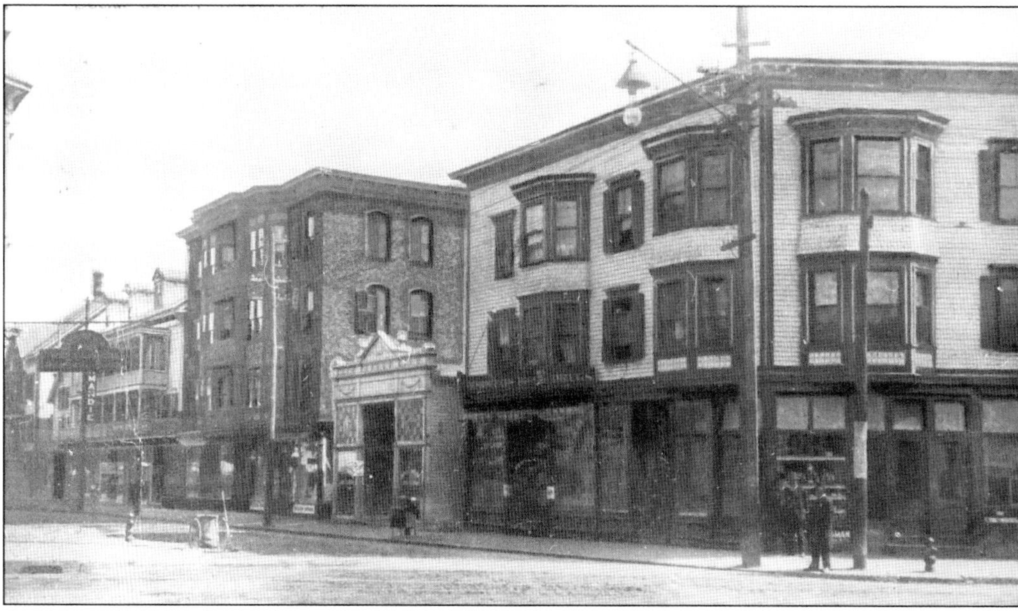

A postcard view of Social Corner, *c.* 1900. In the early twentieth century, this intersection of Social, Cumberland, and Rathbun Streets was the epicenter of the heavily French-Canadian Social District. Known as the Social "Coin," it became famous as the crossroads of this vital ethnic neighborhood. (Blackstone River Valley National Heritage Corridor Commission.)

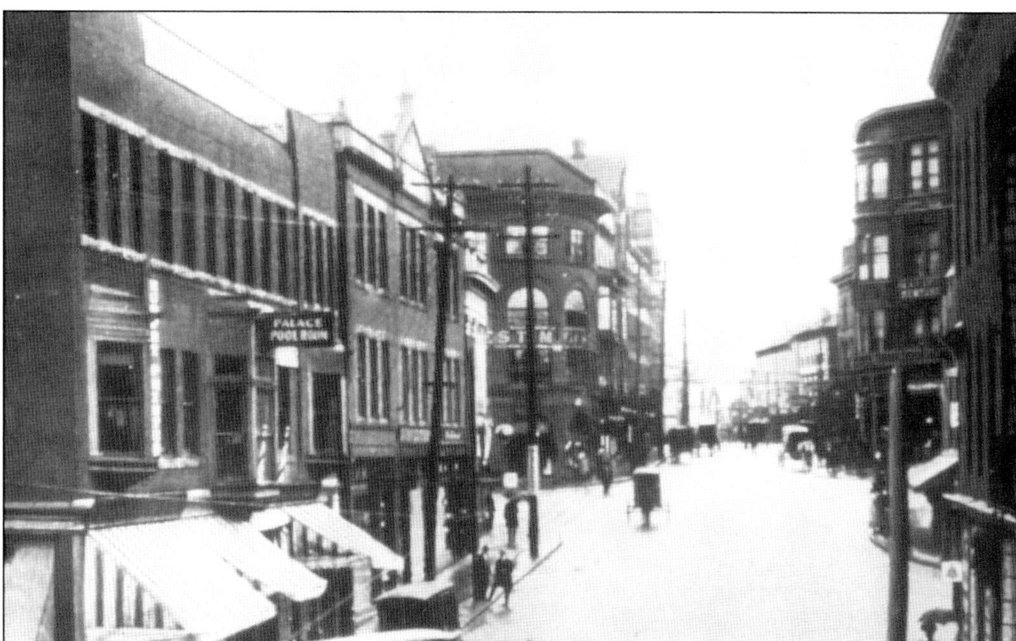

Depot Square, photographed from the railroad bridge overlooking Clinton Street, *c.* 1900. Included in this view, just left of the center, are the Unity Building, built *c.* 1886, and the first headquarters of L'Union Saint Jean Baptiste. Part of the Hope Building, built *c.* 1876, is at the extreme right. In the background are the McCarthy's Department Store building and the Longley Building.

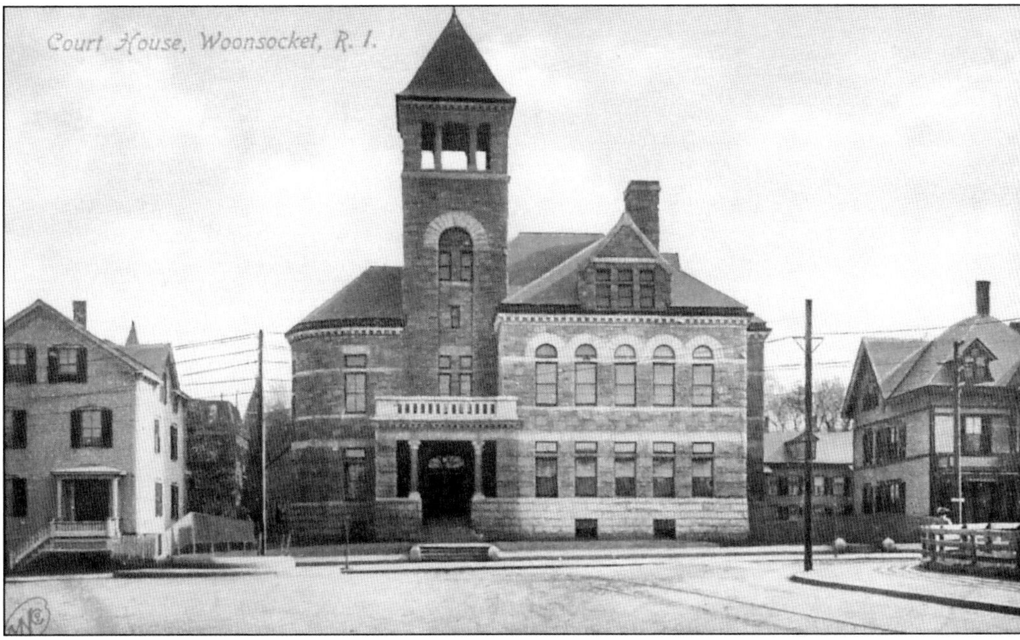

The Court House as seen in a postcard view, *c.* 1900. Designed by William Walker as a monumental structure and constructed in 1896, it complements the long vista down Court Street from Depot Square. It served as the location for sessions of the State Superior, Family, and District courts. (Mr. and Mrs. Robert C. Brin.)

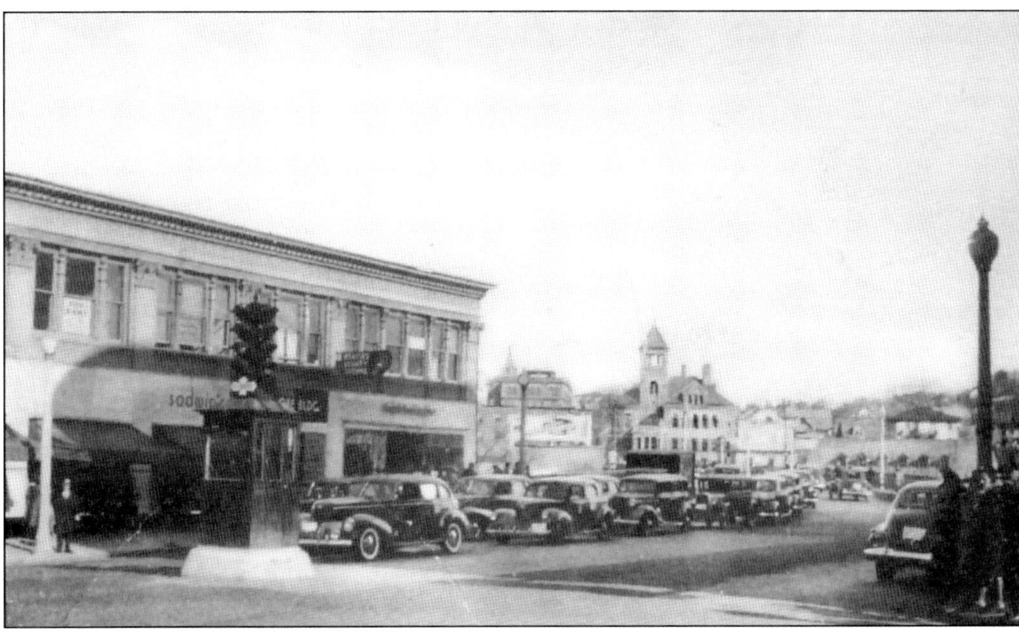

Flynn Square [Depot Square], *c.* 1940. The Globe Building, built *c.* 1900, is at left, while the Court House is in the distance. This scene is evidence that the area continued to be the center of Woonsocket's commercial activity during this era. (Mr. and Mrs. Robert C. Brin.)

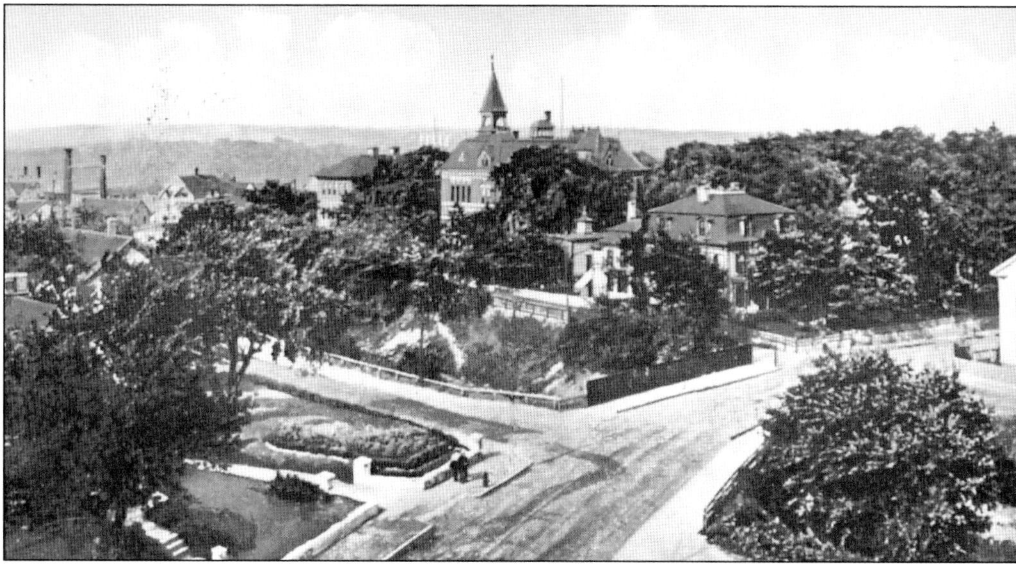

The old high school and surrounding area, photographed from the steeple of the First Baptist Church located on Blackstone Street, c. 1906. The bold tower marks the location of the Harris Public School, built in 1876 as the Woonsocket High School. William Walker, one of Rhode Island's leading late-nineteenth-century architects, designed it. (Mr. and Mrs. Robert C. Brin.)

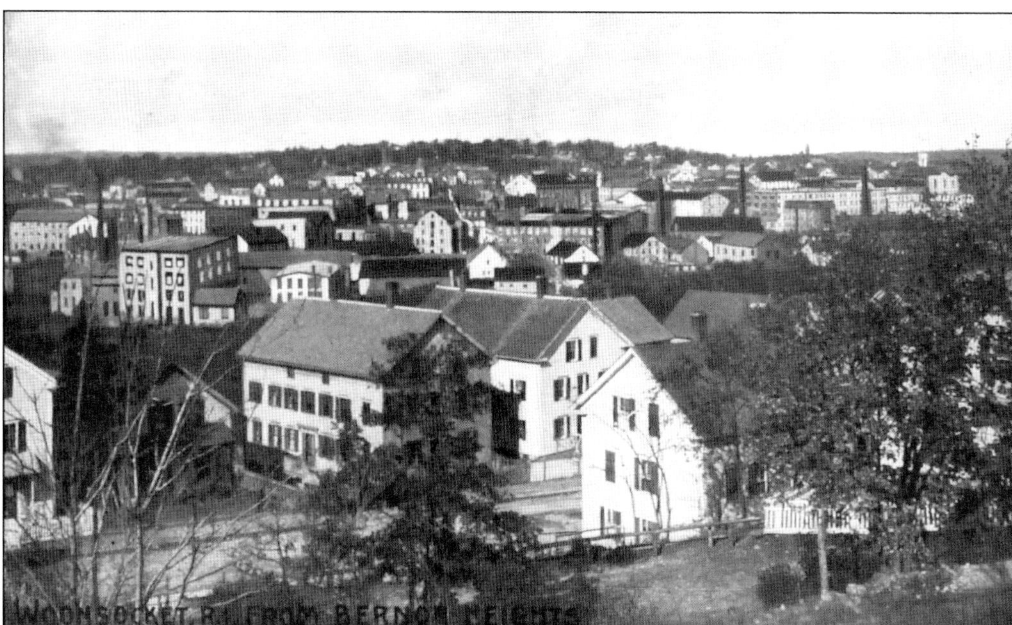

Bernon Village and the center of Woonsocket from Bernon Heights, c. 1912. Dan Daniels and Jonathan Russell established this village, originally known as Danville, in 1827. The mills associated with the village are of major historic and architectural significance, and have been placed on the National Register of Historic Places. (Mr. and Mrs. Robert C. Brin.)

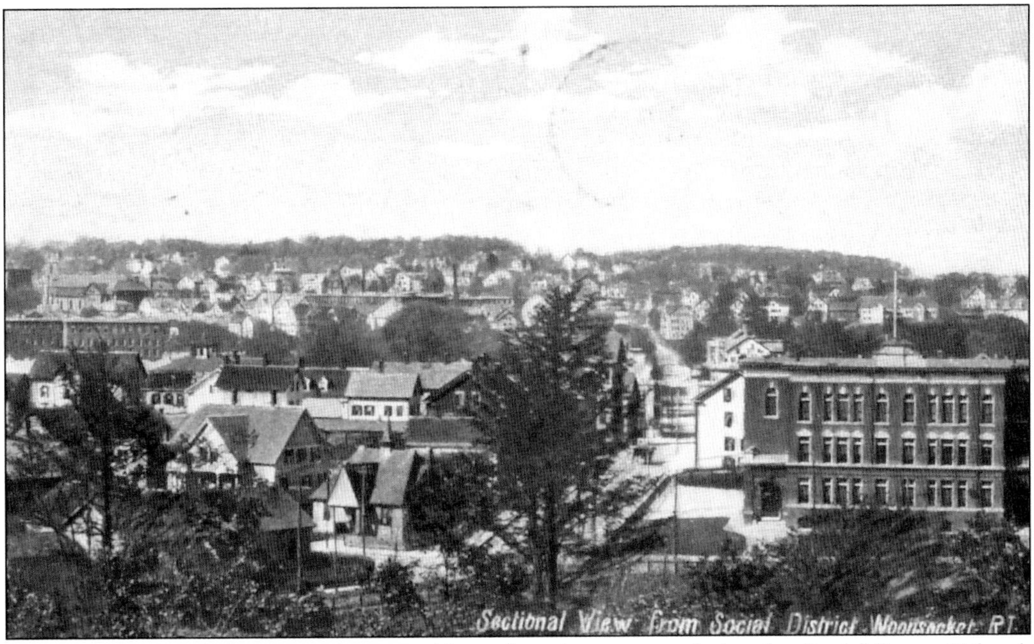

A *c.* 1908 view of the Social District. Note that the vista includes the Social Street School, constructed in 1902. The three-story schoolhouse, made of brick, has good terra-cotta ornamentation in the Renaissance style as part of the arched entrance porticoes. (Mr. and Mrs. Robert C. Brin.)

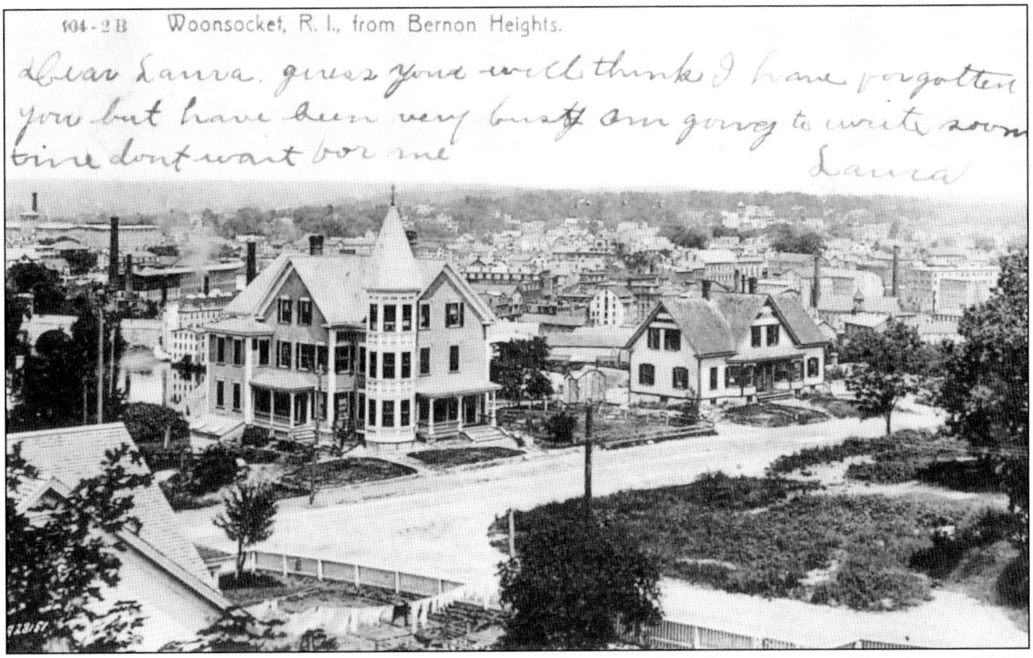

A panoramic view of the center of Woonsocket, photographed from Bernon Heights *c.* 1906. The houses in the foreground are on Grand Street. At left is the Globe [South Main Street] Bridge. (Mr. and Mrs. Robert C. Brin.)

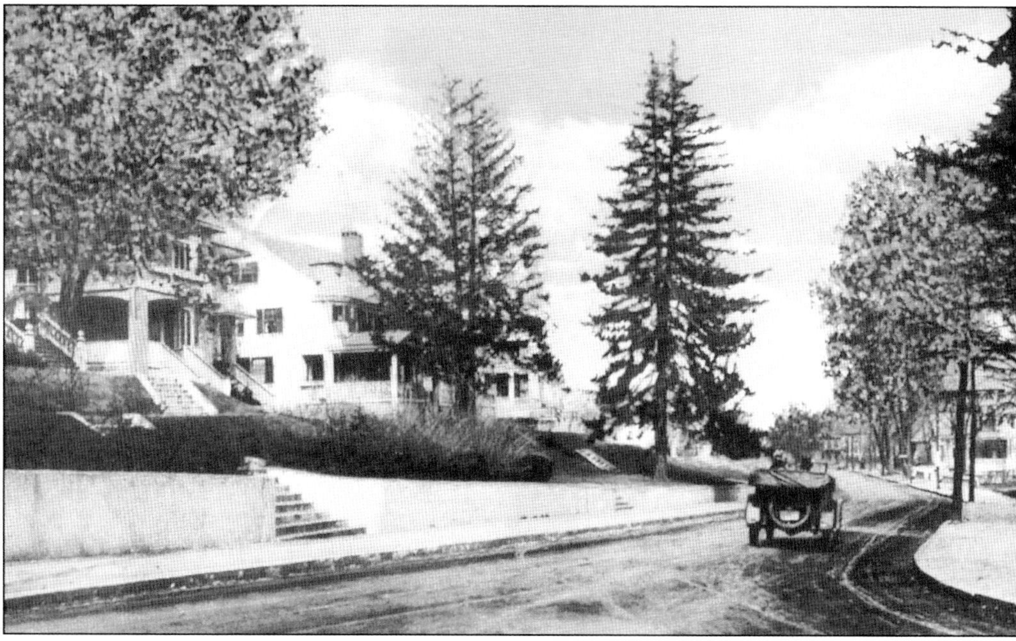

A postcard view of the intersection of Blackstone Street and Harris Avenue, c. 1920. In this view looking down Blackstone Street, Saint Michael's Ukrainian Catholic Church would be just off to the right. (Mr. and Mrs. Robert C. Brin.)

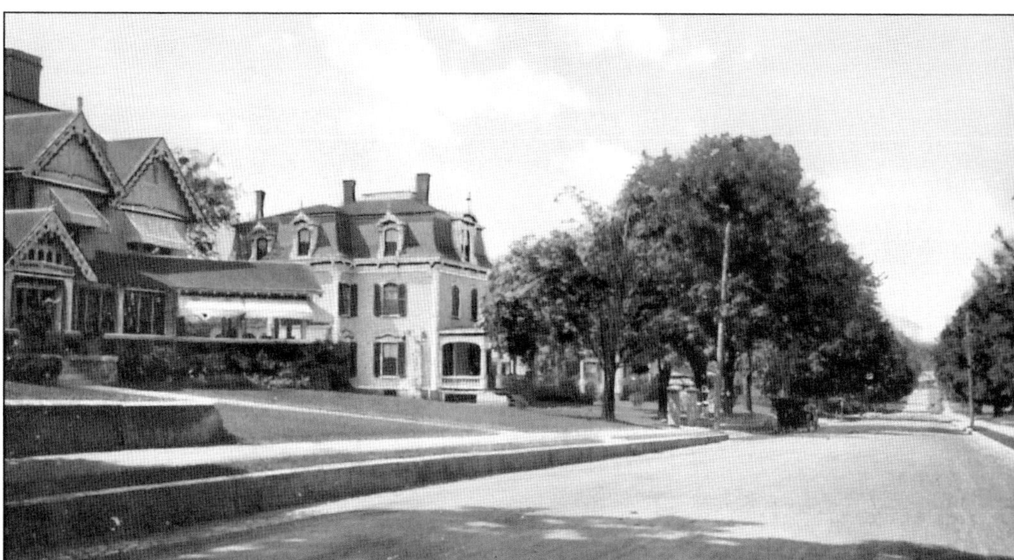

Prospect Street, c. 1920. The early twentieth century saw an expanding middle class in Woonsocket. Harris Avenue and Prospect, Winter, Spring, and Blackstone Streets were among those that developed into tree-shaded suburbia. (Mr. and Mrs. Robert C. Brin.)

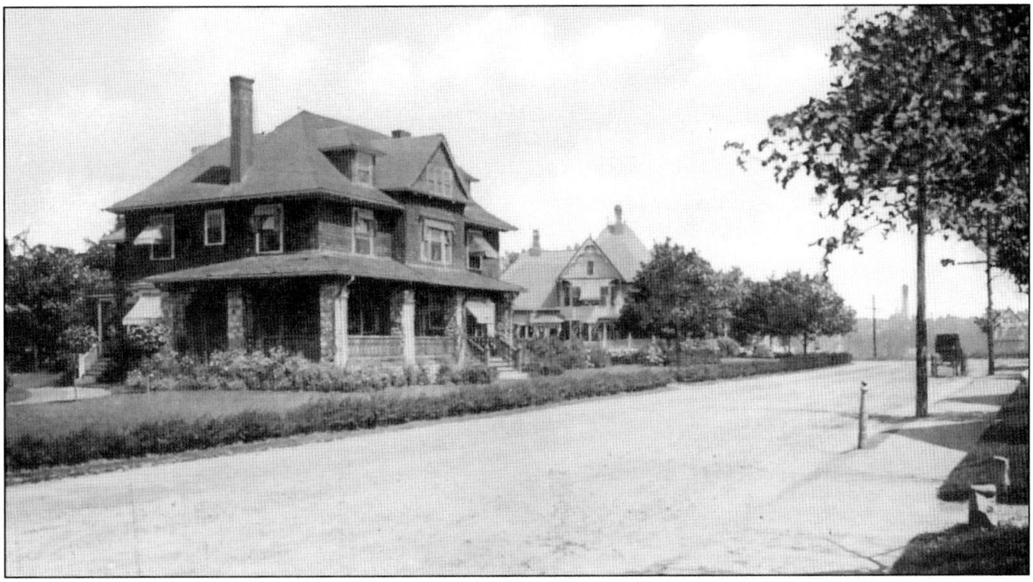

West Park Place, *c.* 1910. The house on the left was the home of Henry Rousseau, a pharmacist at Rousseau and Brown Drugstore on Main Street. This large two-and-one-half-story house, built *c.* 1908, has a shingle-clad second story over a fieldstone first story. (Mr. and Mrs. Robert C. Brin.)

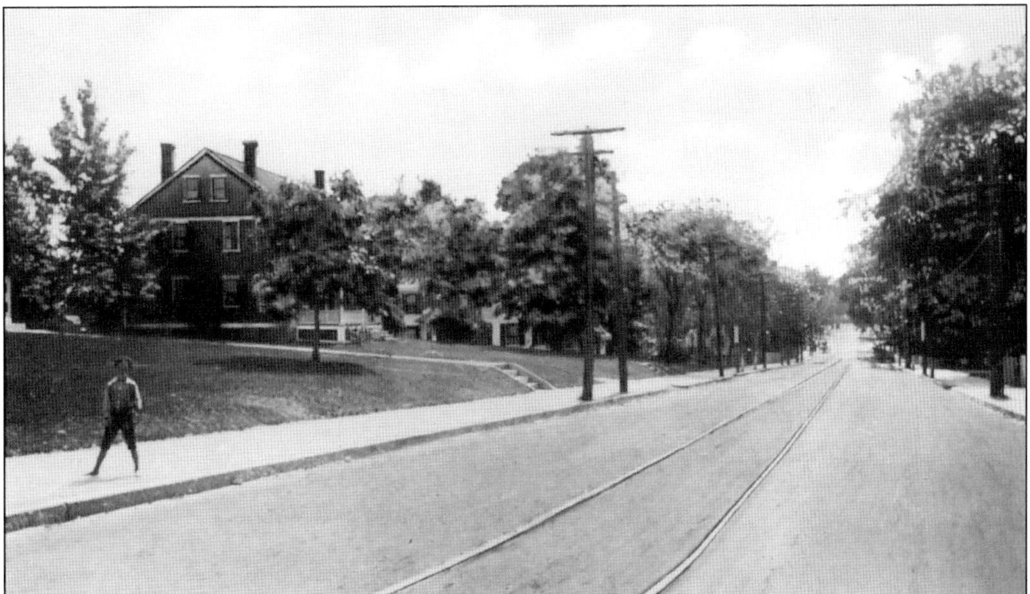

Providence Street in a postcard view, *c.* 1910. Photographed at the intersection of South Main Street, this is a view of the suburban neighborhood. The former Globe Congregational Church is just off to the left of the photograph. (Mr. and Mrs. Robert C. Brin.)

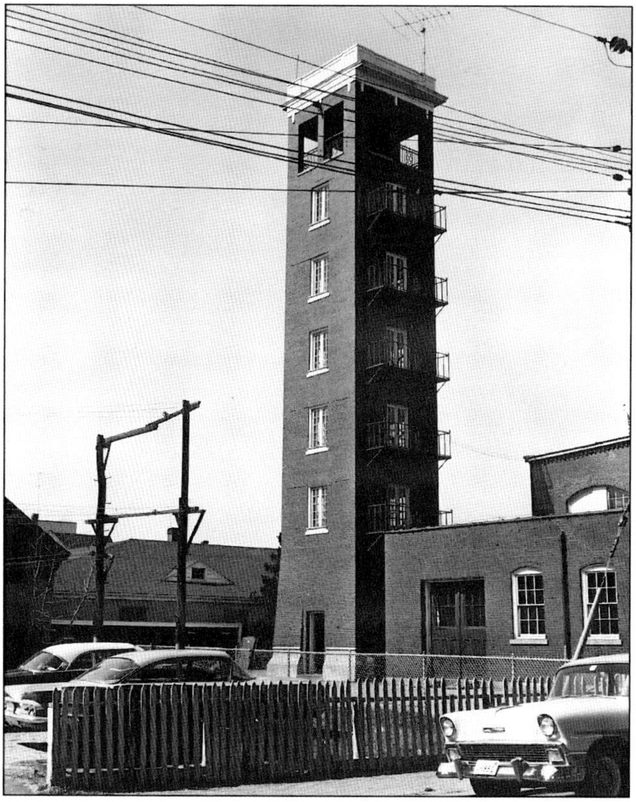

The 85-foot training and hose-drying tower flanking Woonsocket Fire Station Number Five, *c.* 1960. The handsome two-story brick firehouse, constructed in 1912, is on Social Street. Woonsocket Fire Chief Augustin J. Cote requested the building of this seven-story hose-drying tower in 1927. Today, the Woonsocket Housing Authority calls Station Five home. (Mr. and Mrs. Aram Archambault.)

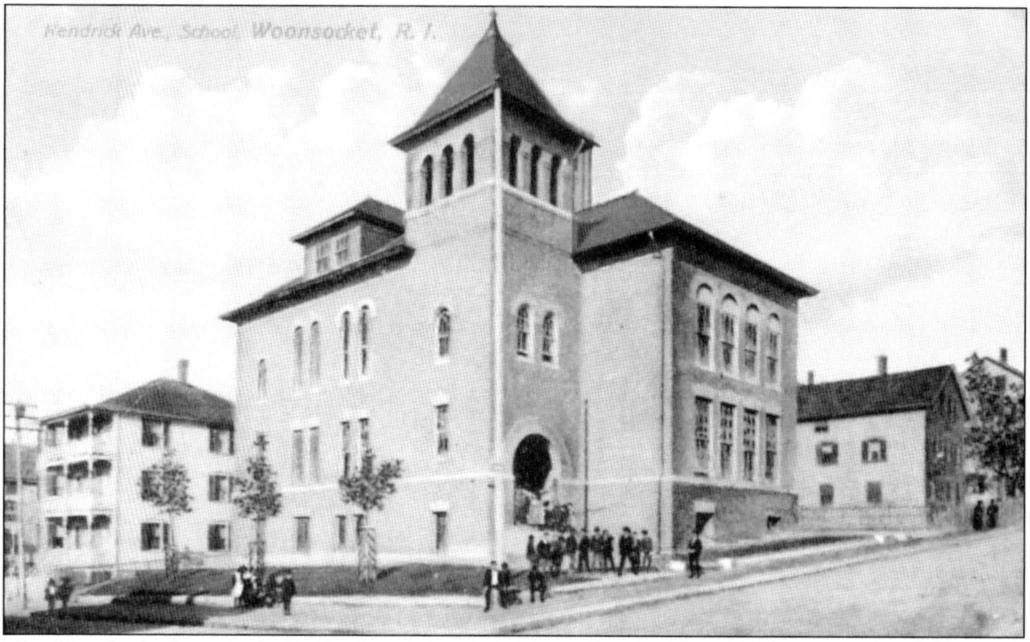

The Kendrick Avenue School, *c.* 1900. The Boston firm of Forbush and Hathaway designed this building. Built in 1895 and constructed of brick, this is a fine two-story school, accented by a tower and "Pompeiian brick" trim. (Mr. and Mrs. Robert C. Brin.)

Four

Bridge over Working Waters

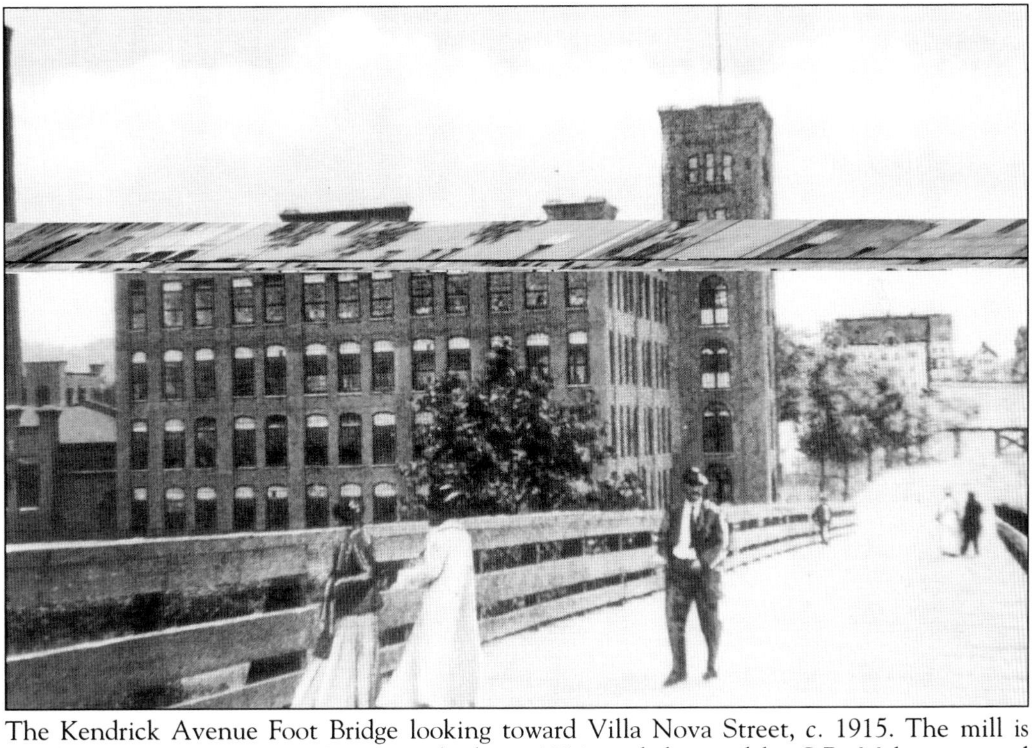

The Kendrick Avenue Foot Bridge looking toward Villa Nova Street, *c.* 1915. The mill is the former River Spinning Company, built in 1894, and designed by C.R. Makepeace and Company. They were mill engineers for W.F. and S.C. Sayles. One hundred and fifty employees manufactured woolen and merino yarns based on the French system. Later, the complex became the home to the Florence Dye Works. (Woonsocket Harris Public Library.)

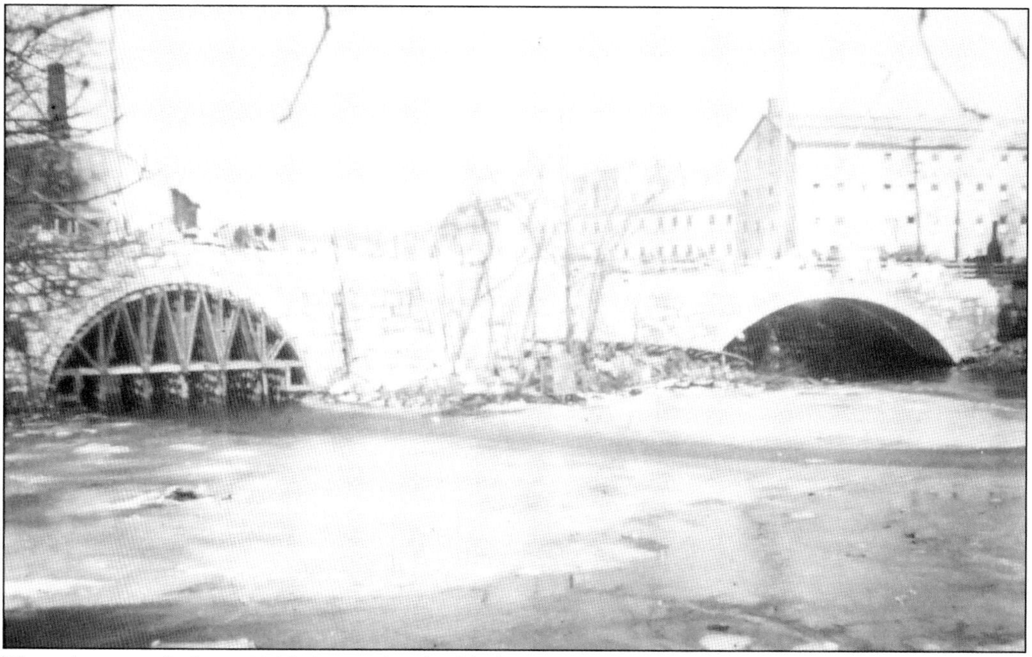

This photograph from 1903 shows the doubled, stone arched Globe Bridge under construction. Note that one arch is finished while the other still has the "falsework" supports. Since 1736 a span over the Blackstone River has existed at this location. Woonsocket was a highway stop during the colonial era, and Boston-bound travelers would have crossed the river at this location. (Woonsocket Harris Public Library.)

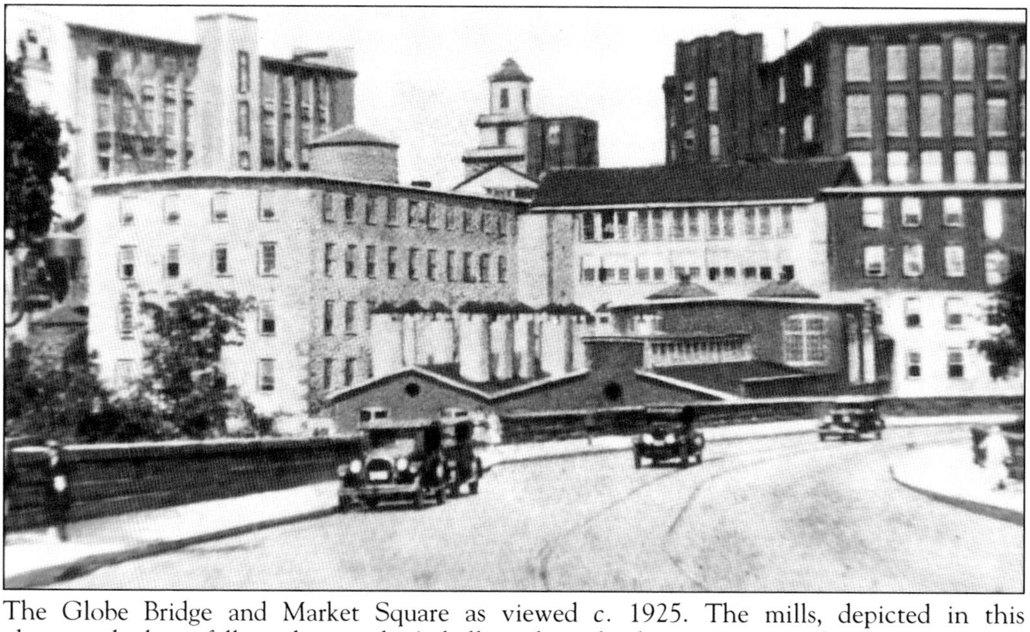

The Globe Bridge and Market Square as viewed *c.* 1925. The mills, depicted in this photograph, later fell to the wrecker's ball, and in the late 1960s a parking plaza costing $200,000 took their place. In 1996 this area has again undergone a revitalization that now showcases the falls and acts as a splendid gateway to Main Street. (Woonsocket Harris Public Library.)

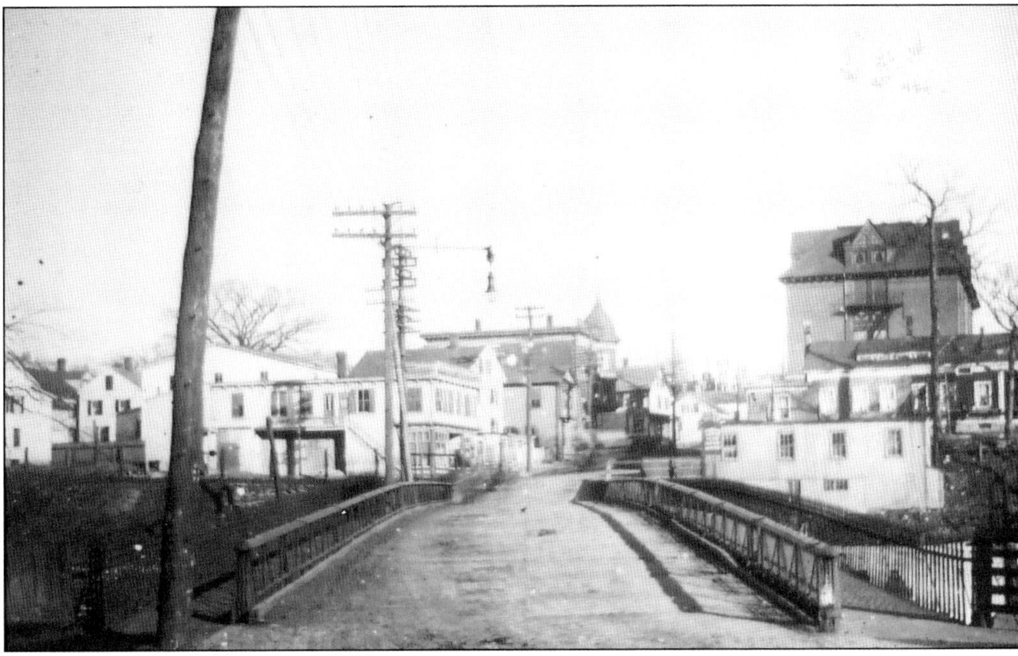

The Bernon Street Bridge, as photographed by Charles S. Lawton *c.* 1910. To the right of the center is the former home of the Jolicoeur Furniture Company. It was a three-and-one-half-story commercial block, constructed *c.* 1893 of brick with wood trim. It began its life as the meeting hall of the International Order of Odd Fellows. (Woonsocket Harris Public Library.)

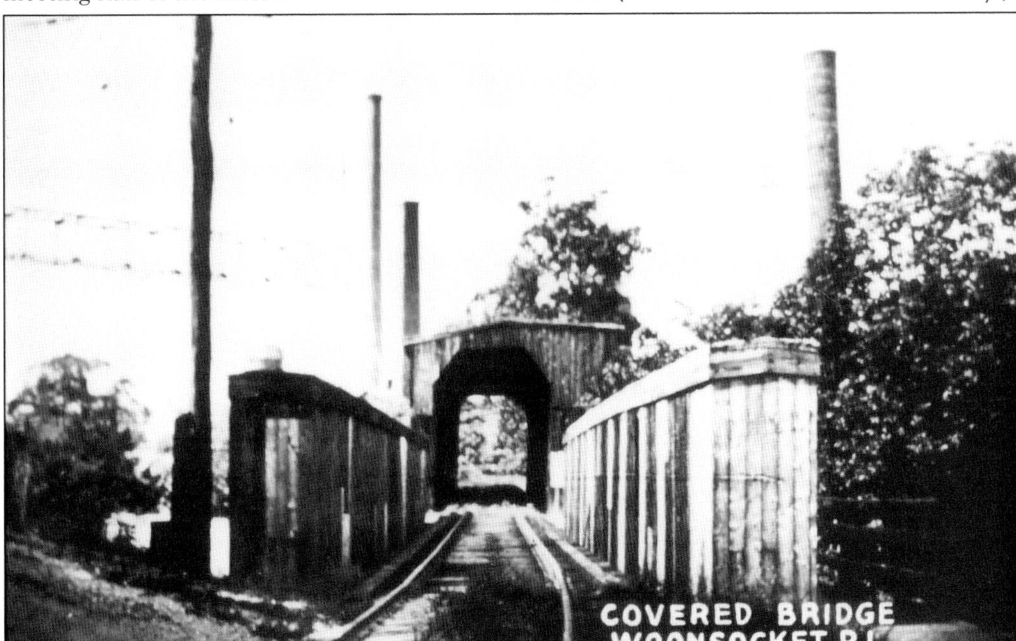

An interesting 1910 view of the old covered railroad bridge over the Blackstone River. The bridge, built in 1898, was part of a railroad spur. It ran from the main line of the Providence and Worcester Railroad, in the Hamlet Village, and ended in the Social District. (Woonsocket Harris Public Library.)

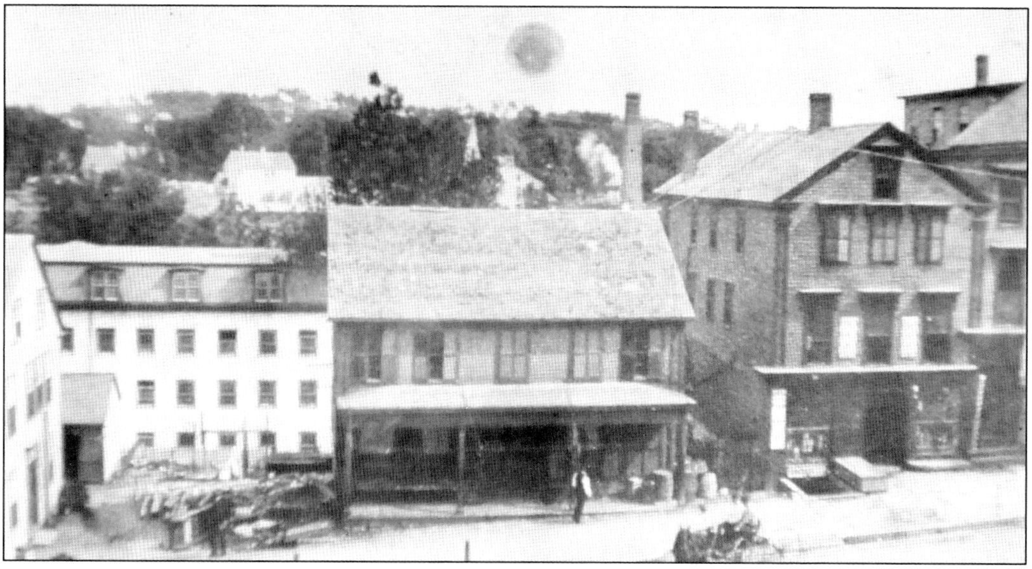

A *c.* 1894 photograph of the buildings which would be moved or torn down for the Court Street Bridge access. The New York firm of Dean and Westbrook was chosen to be the main contractor of the project. Construction began from the Hamlet Avenue end in 1893. (Woonsocket Harris Public Library.)

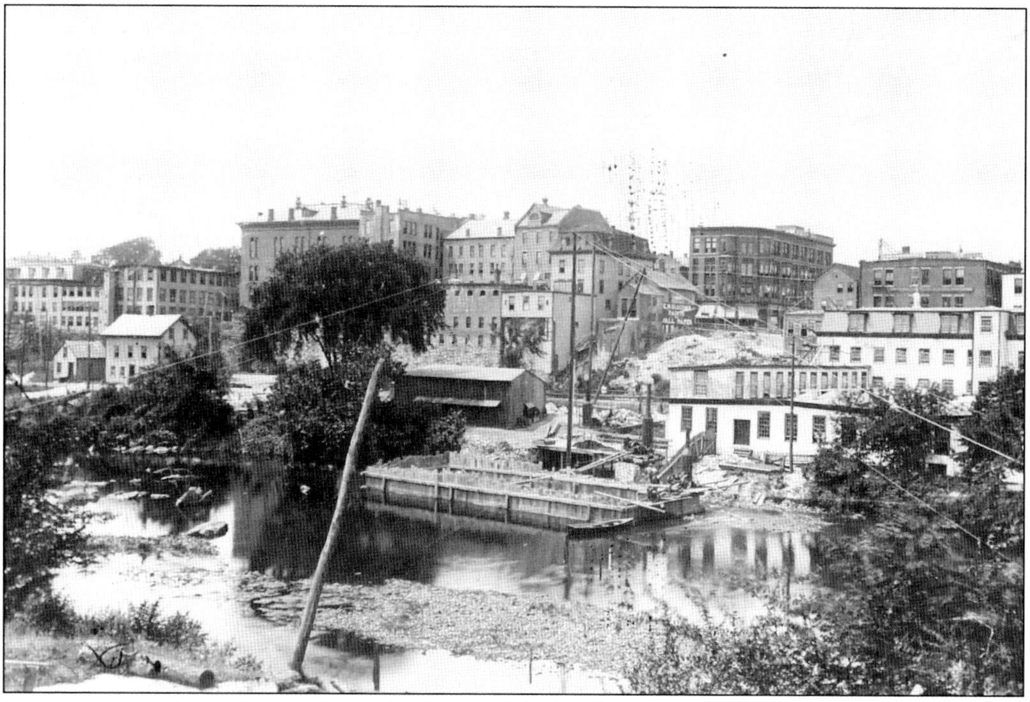

Construction of the Court Street Bridge, *c.* 1894. The view, looking toward Main Street, clearly shows some buildings already removed for access to the bridge. In the summer of 1894 it was reported in *The Patriot* that "work was lively all along the line." (Woonsocket Harris Public Library.)

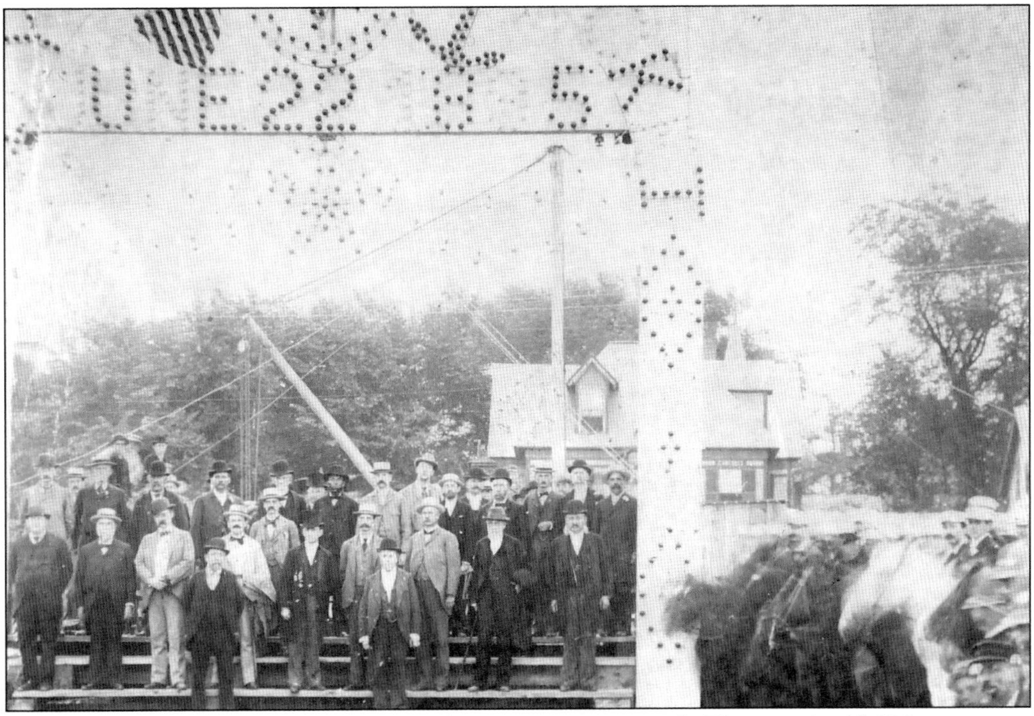

The opening of the Count Street Bridge on June 22, 1895. The nearly 15,000 spectators who attended the dedication ceremonies witnessed an electrical display. A huge arch with colored lights was the centerpiece that glowed "City of Woonsocket." (Woonsocket Harris Public Library.)

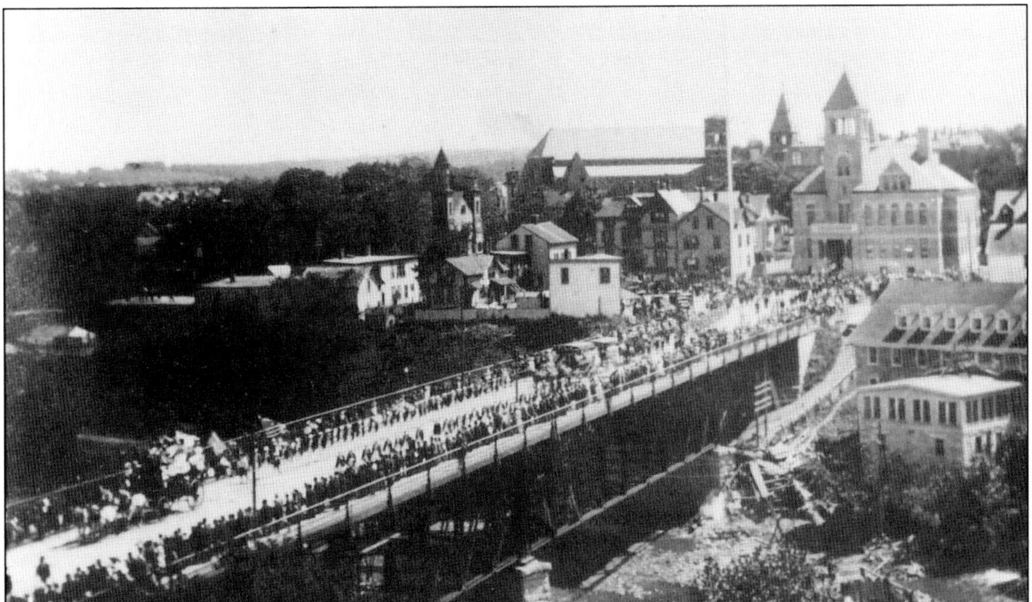

Woonsocket's Labor Day Parade, photographed by Charles S. Lawton on September 4, 1899, as it passes over the Court Street Bridge. When completed in 1895, the bridge had cost more than $300,000 and required 100,000 rivets and 40,000 bolts. (Woonsocket Harris Public Library.)

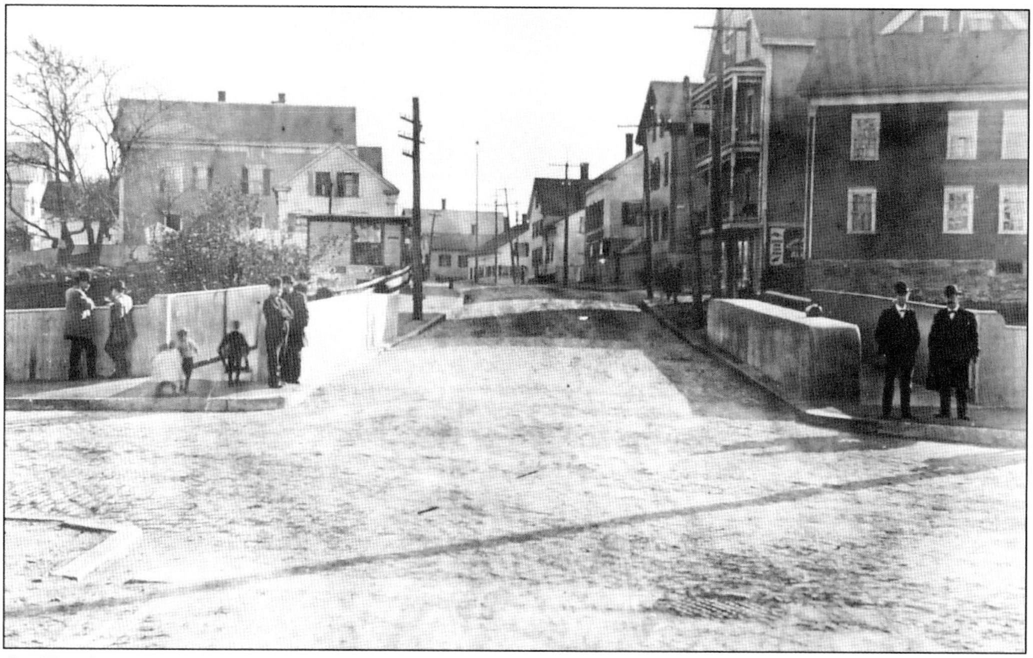

A Charles S. Lawton photograph of the Arnold Street Bridge in 1907. Constructed in that same year, it replaced the old wooden Arnold Street Bridge over the tracks of the Providence and Worcester Railroad. (Woonsocket Harris Public Library.)

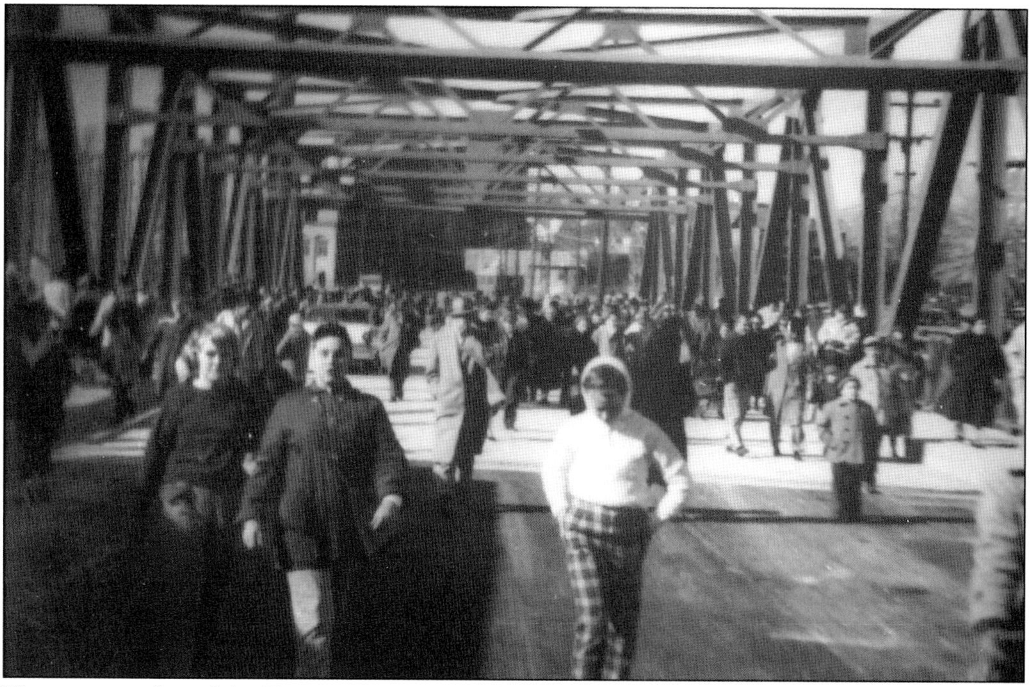

The opening day of the Fairmount Street Bridge, as captured on a chilly November 13, 1958. This new steel and concrete bridge replaced one destroyed in the hurricane and flood of 1955. Other bridges spanning the Blackstone and Mill Rivers replaced at this time were on Singleton, River, Sayles, Privilege, and East School Streets. (Woonsocket Harris Public Library.)

Five

The Butcher, the Baker, and the Candlestick . . . Worker

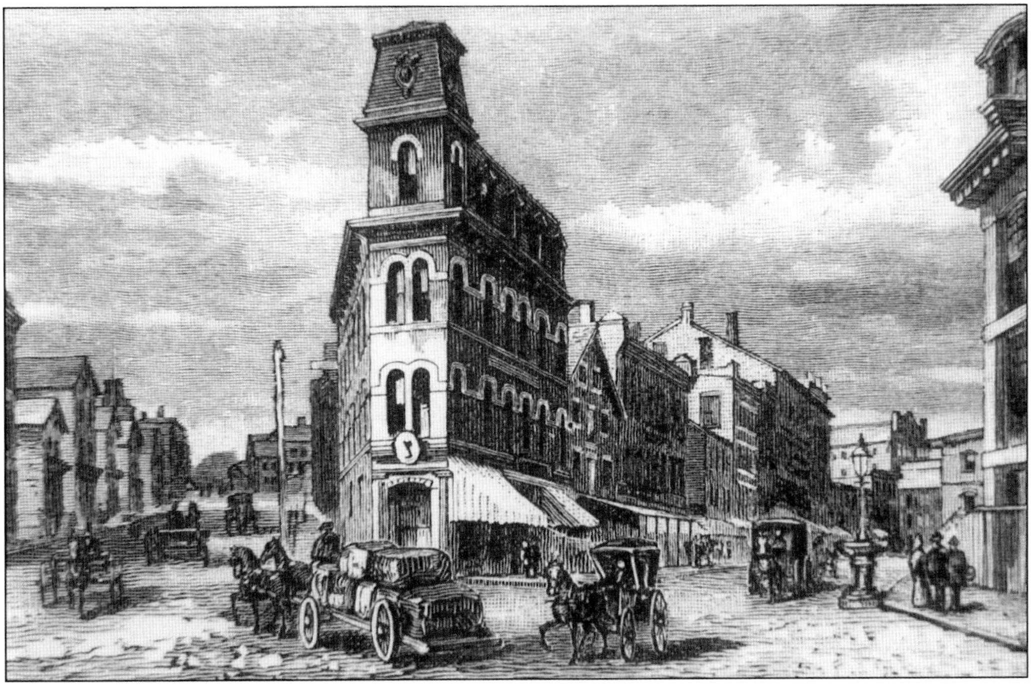

Market Square as sketched in 1886. This is the intersection of Arnold and Main Streets. Many buildings shown have either had their facades altered or demolished. On the extreme right of the scene is the former Lippitt Mill, later the Hanora Building, constructed in 1865. (Woonsocket Harris Public Library.)

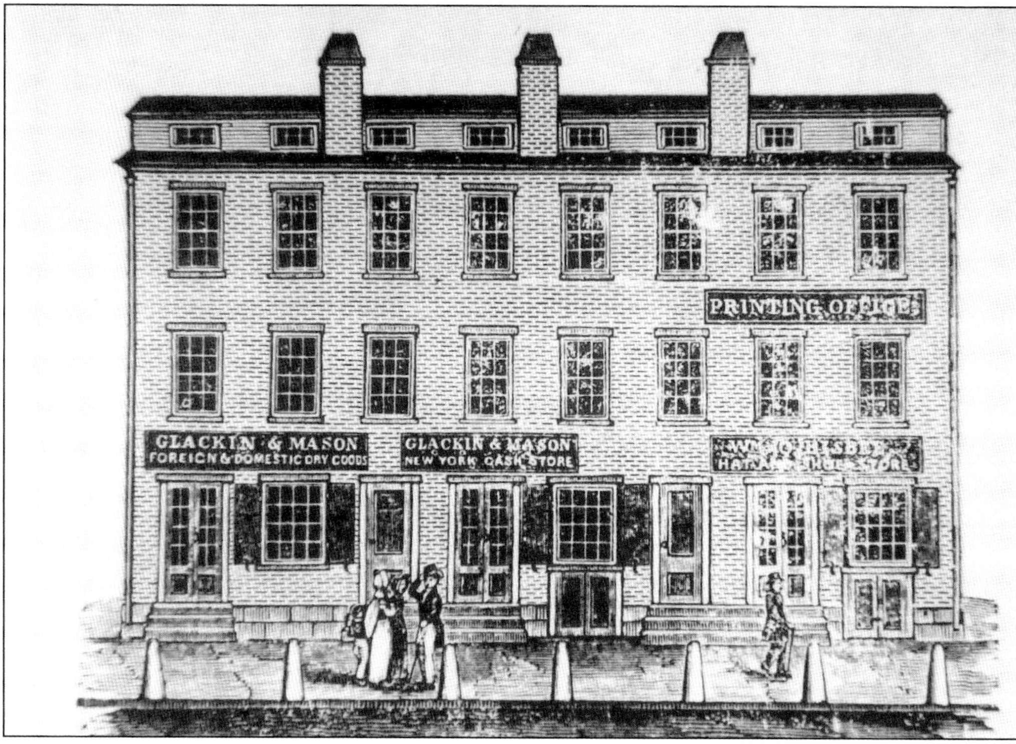

The Rathbun Block, which was located on Main Street, from an advertisement in *The Woonsocket Patriot* in 1848. Tenants who occupied storefronts in this building included Glackin and Mason, dealers in foreign and domestic dry goods, and William Hisbee, who operated a hat and shoe store. (Woonsocket Harris Public Library.)

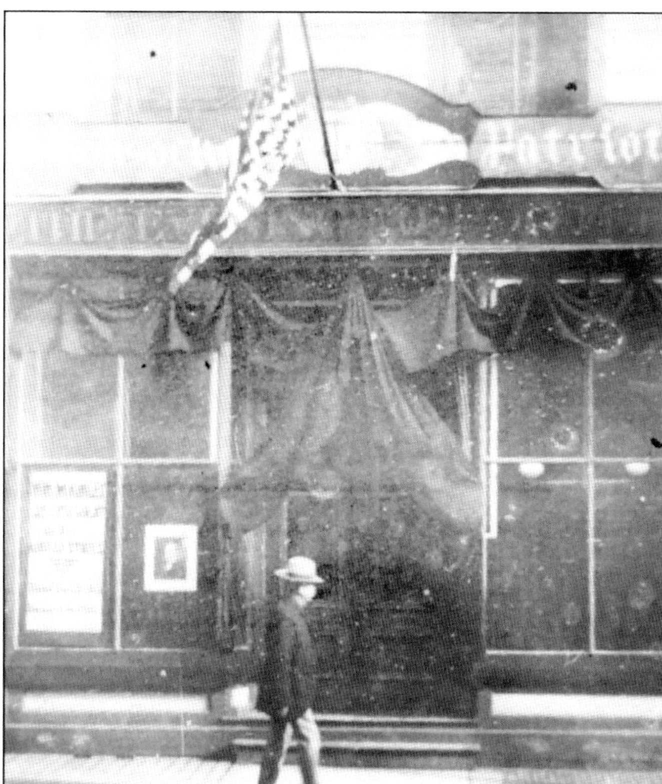

The offices of *The Woonsocket Patriot* and *The Evening Reporter* on Main Street, as photographed shortly after the assassination of President McKinley in 1901. Both newspapers were owned and published by Leroy B. Pease. (Woonsocket Harris Public Library.)

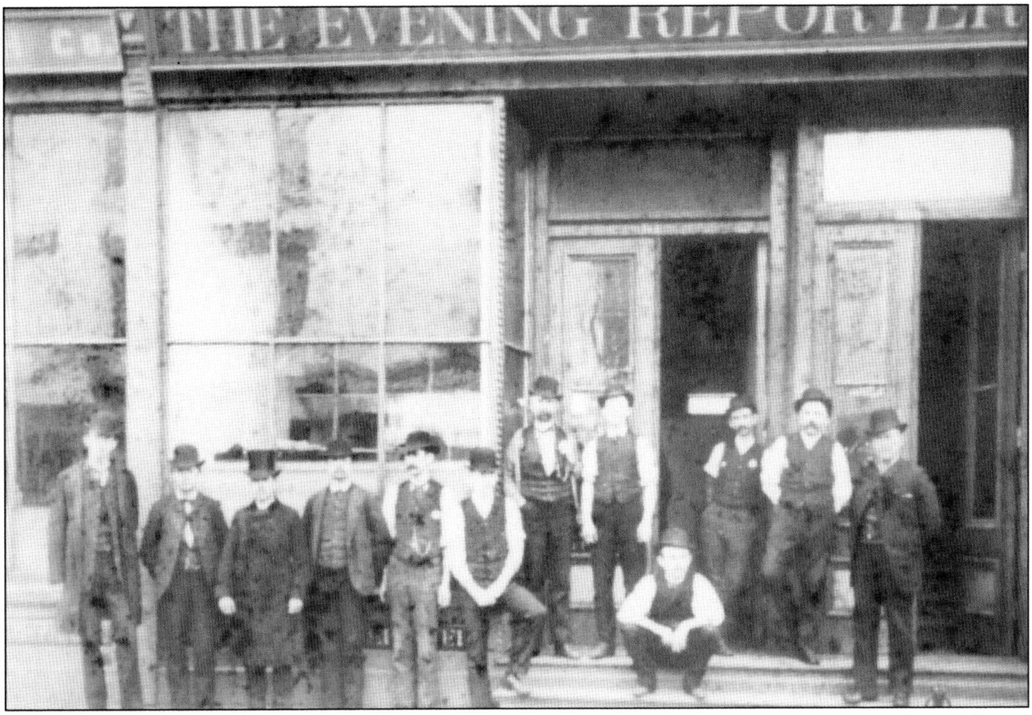

The crew of *The Evening Reporter*, captured on film *c.* 1890 on Main Street. Owned and published by Leroy B. Pease, the newspaper had a daily circulation in 1892 of 5,700 copies. In 1908, *The Call*, its rival, purchased *The Evening Reporter*. (Woonsocket Harris Public Library.)

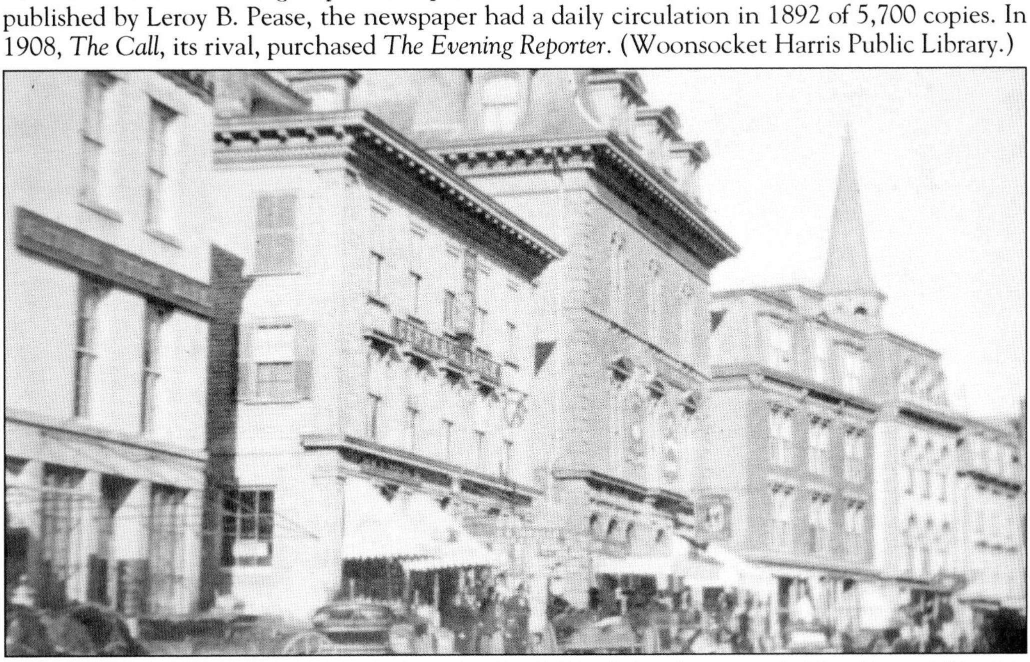

A *c.* 1890 view of Main Street including the Cook Block (in the center). The Central Block is to the left. The district between Market Square and Monument Square developed during the years 1870 to 1920 as the city's urban core. Here, the commercial institutions, including stores, banks, offices, and theaters, would reflect the aspirations of a community that was growing in affluence and self-confidence. (Woonsocket Harris Public Library.)

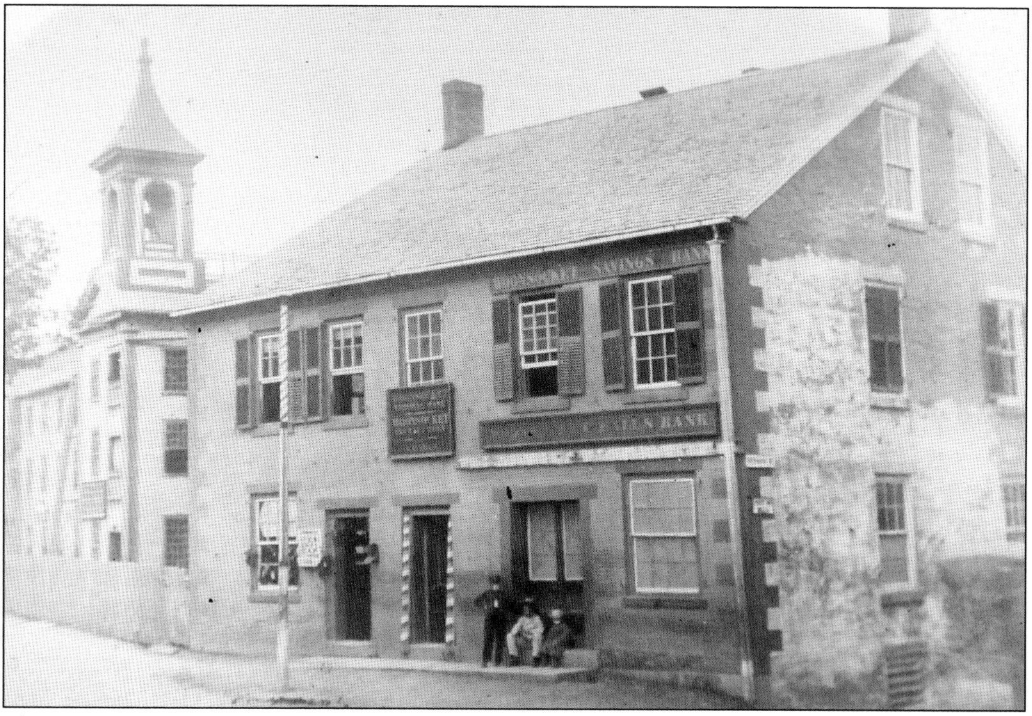

The original home of the Woonsocket Institution for Savings, *c.* 1860. Chartered in 1845, the bank, originally located in this building, was at the corner of Main and Bernon Streets. It would later relocate to Cook's Block on Main Street in 1867. (Woonsocket Harris Public Library.)

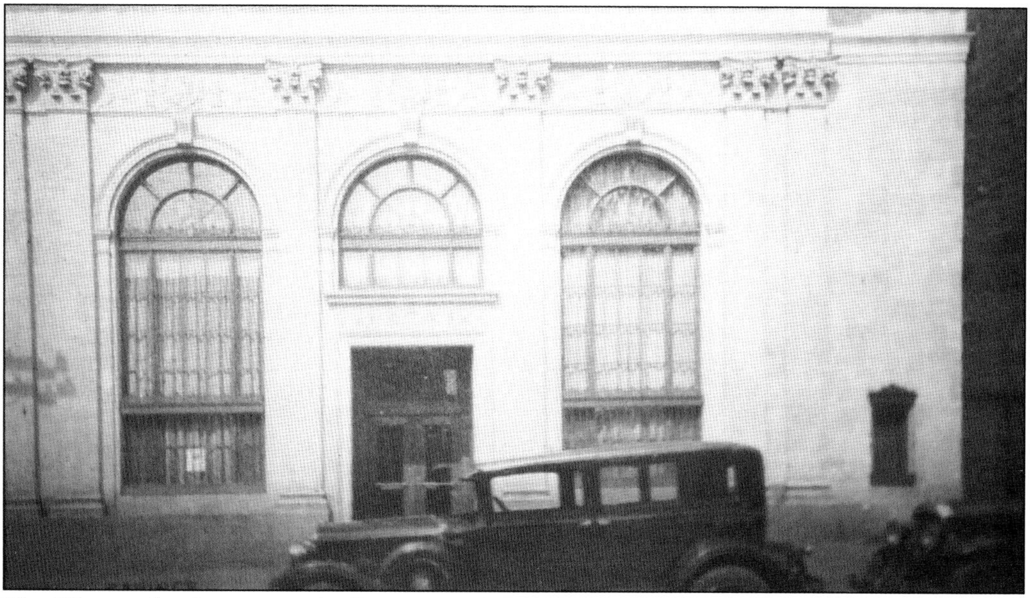

The Woonsocket Institution for Savings, on Main Street, *c.* 1930. Organized in 1845 at Market Square, the bank moved to the Cook Block on Main Street in 1867. Later it moved across the street to the ground level of the Harris Institute Building. In the late 1920s, under Aram J. Pothier's presidency, the bank constructed the building shown here at 144 Main Street. (Woonsocket Harris Public Library.)

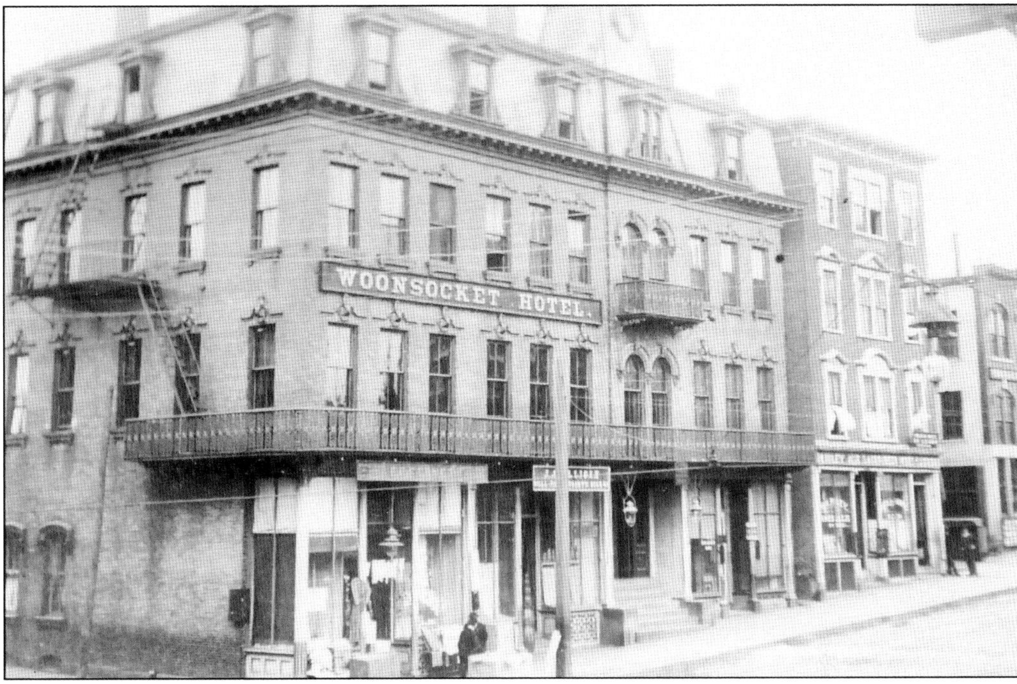

The Woonsocket Hotel, a Market Square landmark, *c.* 1900. In 1893, the city leaders rejected an offer to purchase the structure, for use as a city hall, for the sum of $55,000. (Woonsocket Harris Public Library.)

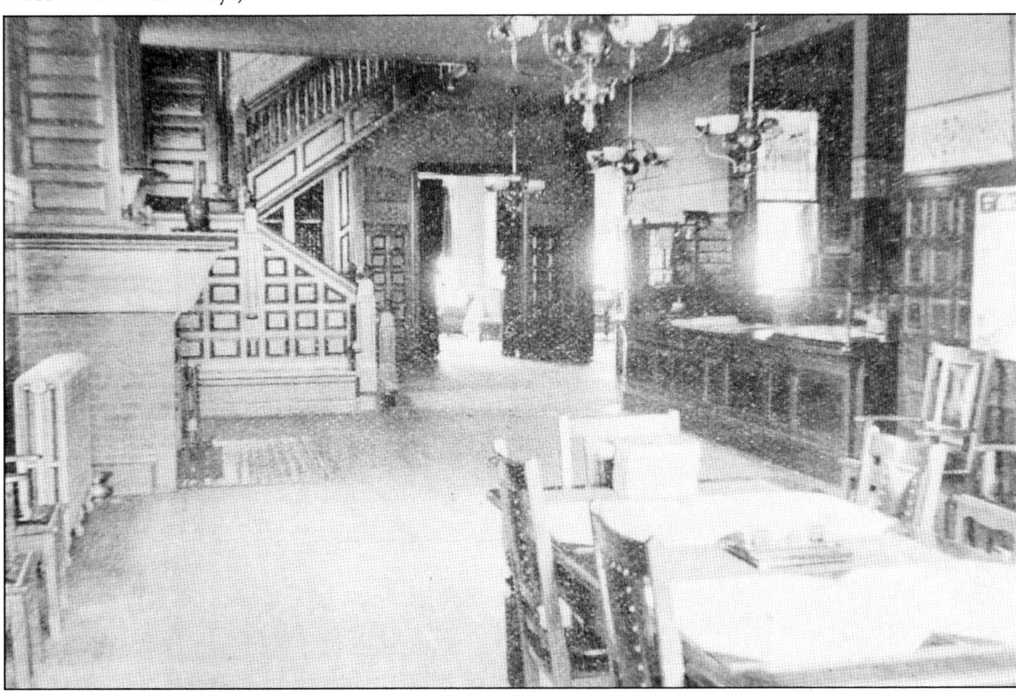

The main lobby of the Saint James Hotel, on Main Street, 1907. Constructed in 1892 by A.C. Brooks, it was the leading hostelry in Woonsocket for years. Fire destroyed this Main Street landmark in November 1986. (Woonsocket Harris Public Library.)

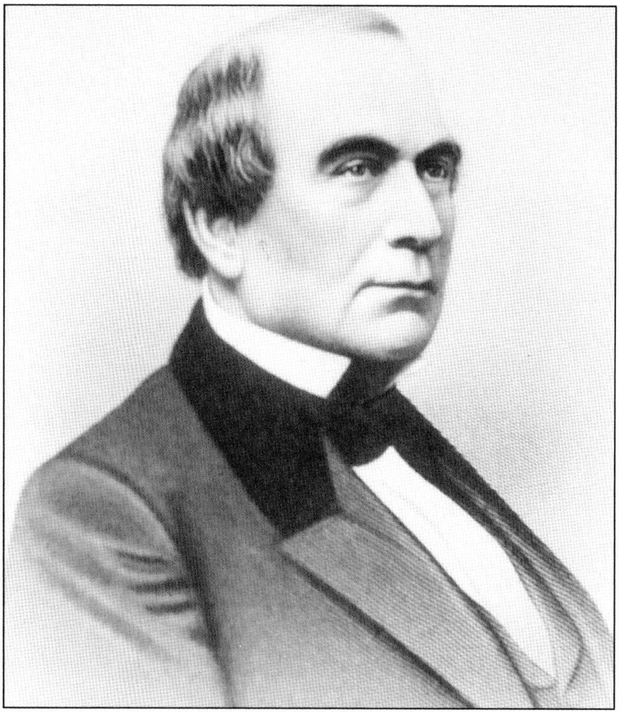

A portrait of Edward Harris (1801–1872,), Woonsocket's most prominent citizen in the nineteenth century. Born in the village of Limerock in Lincoln, Rhode Island, Harris entered the textile industry in Woonsocket by 1831. He was active in political and civic affairs, and constructed the Harris Block for use by the community. Harris also established the Harris Institute Library, and donated the land for the city's first high school and the Oak Hill Cemetery. (Woonsocket Harris Public Library.)

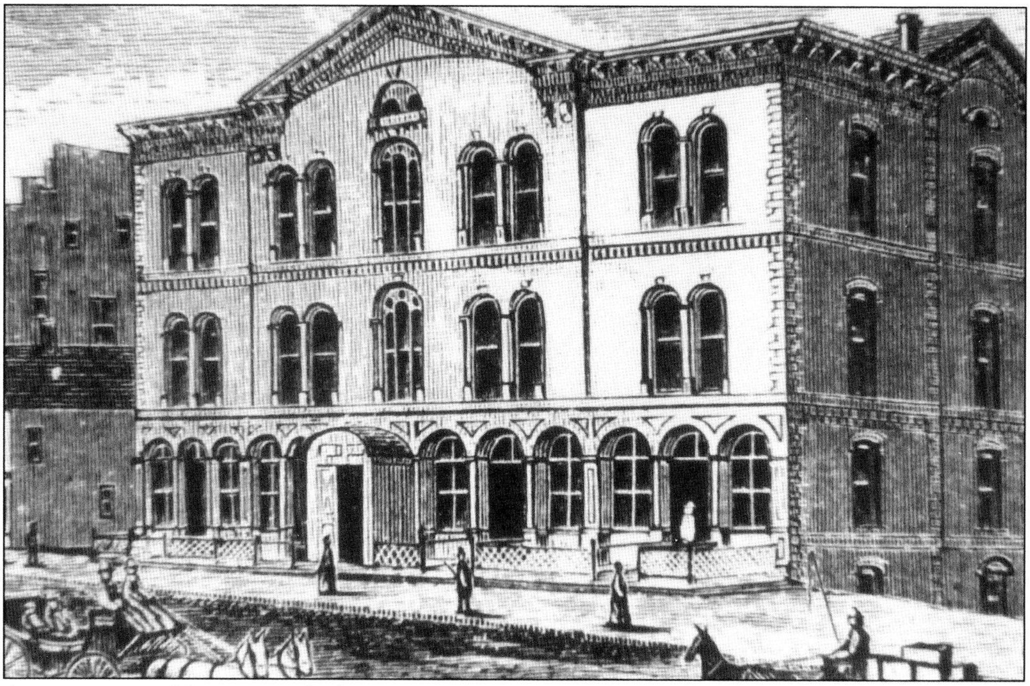

An engraving of the Harris Block on Main Street *c.* 1880. Constructed by Edward Harris in 1856, the Harris Block was Woonsocket's first major commercial building. Built in the Italianate style that was popular at the time, the block is three stories high. The structure included a meeting hall where Abraham Lincoln spoke in 1860, a library, and commercial stores. (Woonsocket Harris Public Library.)

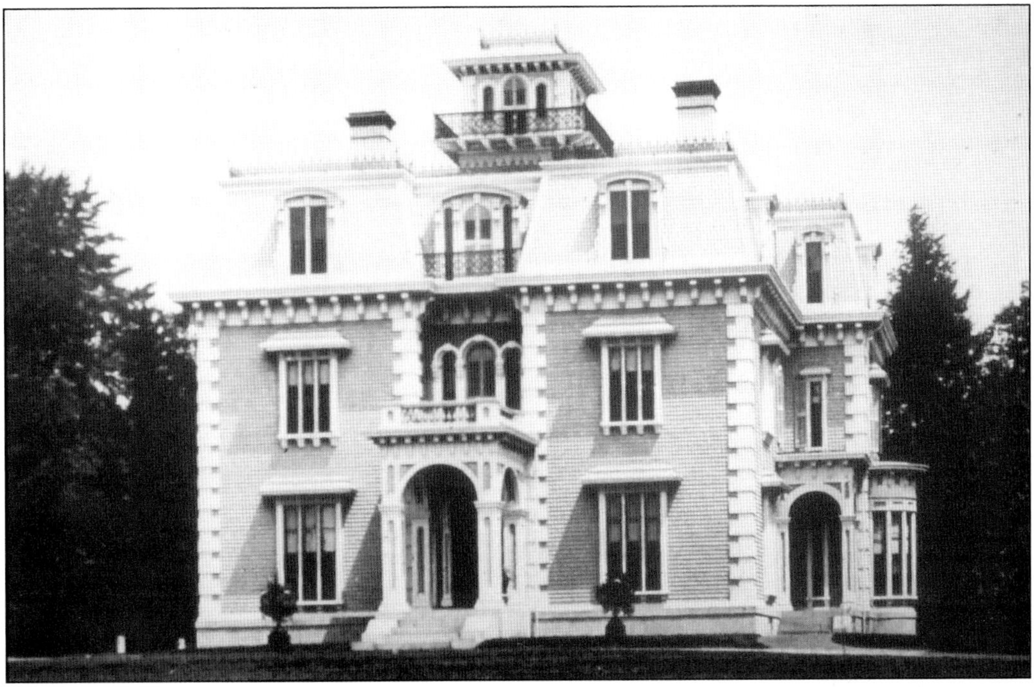

Edward Harris' mansion Oakley, built around 1855, with modifications to the roof about 1870, as photographed *c.* 1890. This stately home overlooked the city and was part of the Harris Estate, the largest in Woonsocket, which encompassed the entire North End. On March 8, 1860, Abraham Lincoln stayed overnight here after speaking in Harris Hall. (Woonsocket Harris Public Library.)

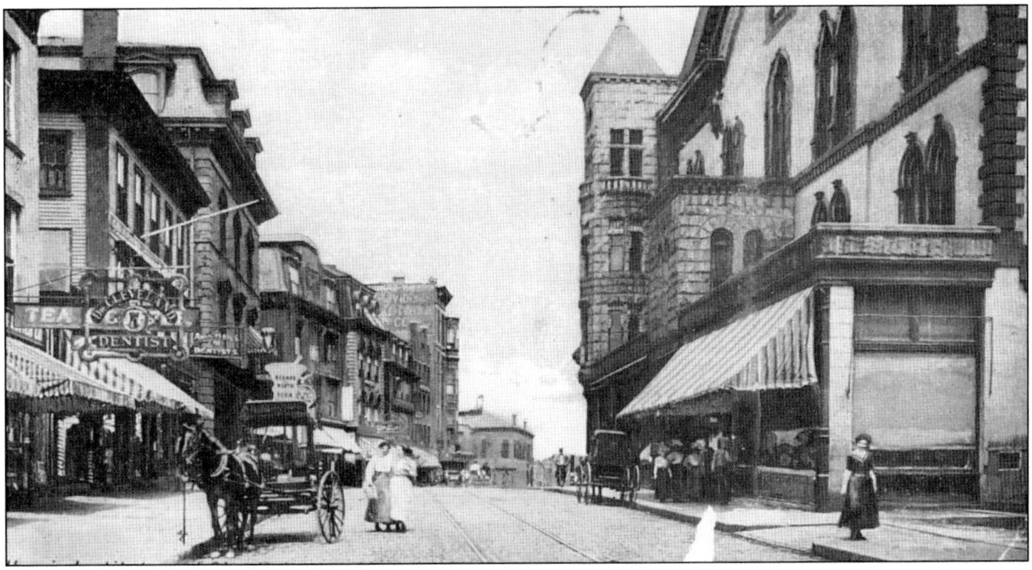

The Harris Institute and city hall on Main Street, *c.* 1910. Built by Edward Harris in 1856, the "Harris Block" is the oldest part of the building. In 1891 a rugged, granite-clad extension was added in a Richardsonian Romanesque style. In 1902, the officers of the Harris Institute offered the complex to the city for use as a city hall. The city council accepted the offer. (Mr. and Mrs. Robert C. Brin.)

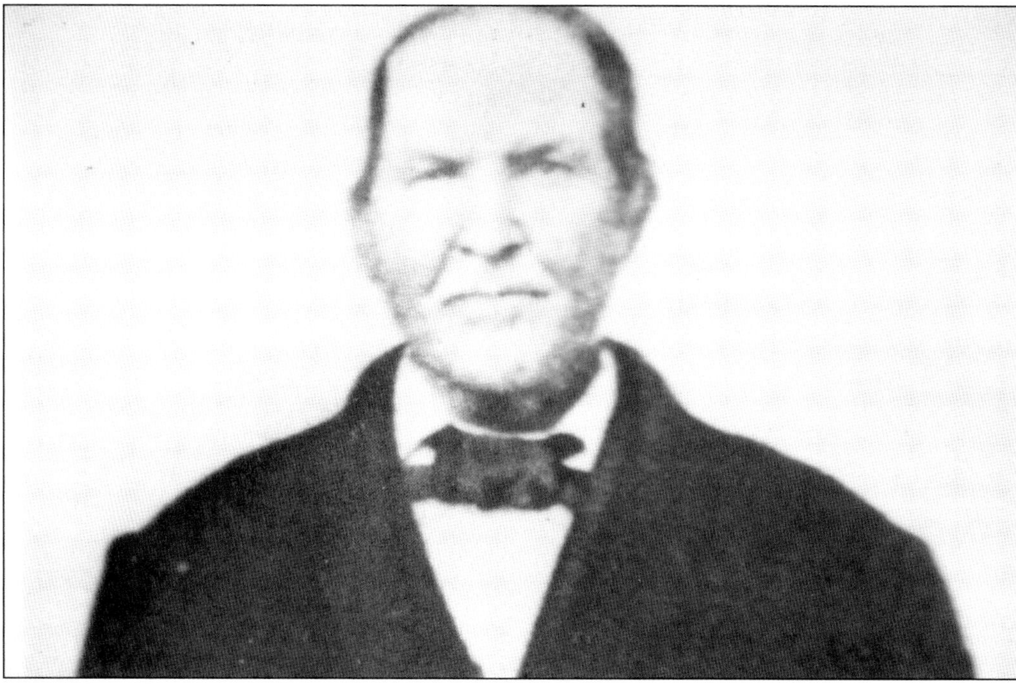

Michael Reddy, considered Woonsocket's first Irish immigrant, c. 1870. Reddy came to the city during the construction of the Blackstone Canal in 1826. He purchased land on Front Street in 1840 from the Woonsocket Company and built a house. Reddy also owned "Logee Hill Farm," located near his home. He organized the first Catholic service in the area, and helped establish a permanent Catholic church in the city in the 1840s. (Woonsocket Harris Public Library.)

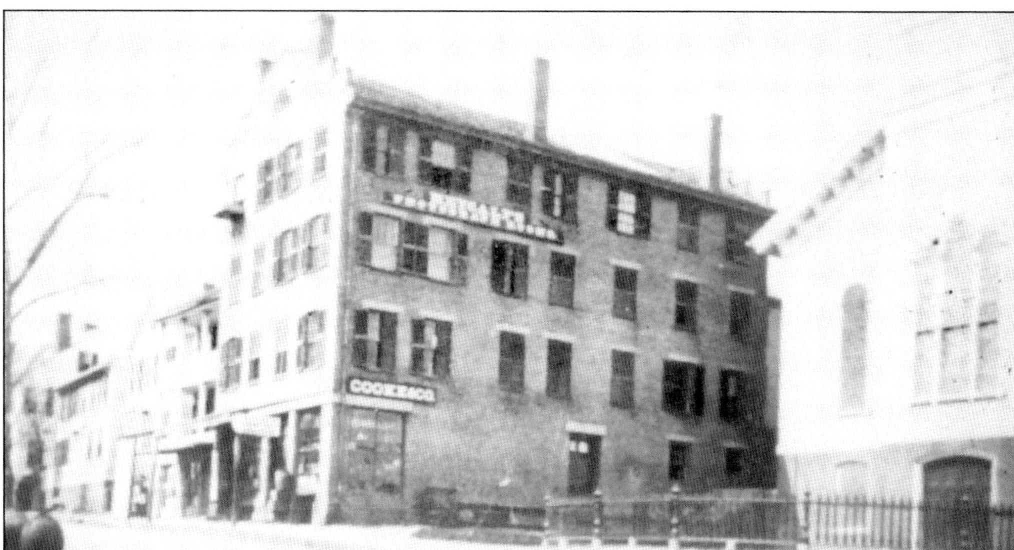

The Bryant Block, constructed in 1849 on Main Street, c. 1870. Most residents will remember that the Joseph Brown Drug Store was later located in this building. The church to the right in the photograph is the First Baptist Church, originally located at the corner of Main and High Streets. (Woonsocket Harris Public Library.)

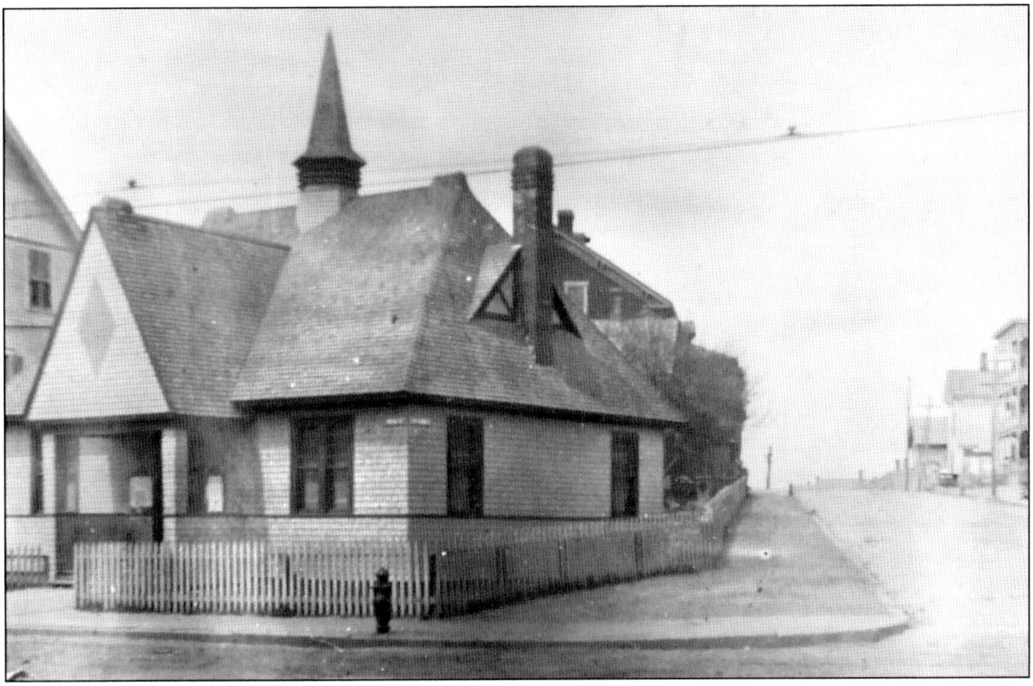

The Fifth Ward Club, at the corner of Social and East School Streets, as seen through the lens of Charles S. Lawton, *c.* 1900. Voters abolished the ward system that had dominated Woonsocket's political scene since 1888, with the passage in November 1952 of the Home Rule Charter. (Woonsocket Harris Public Library.)

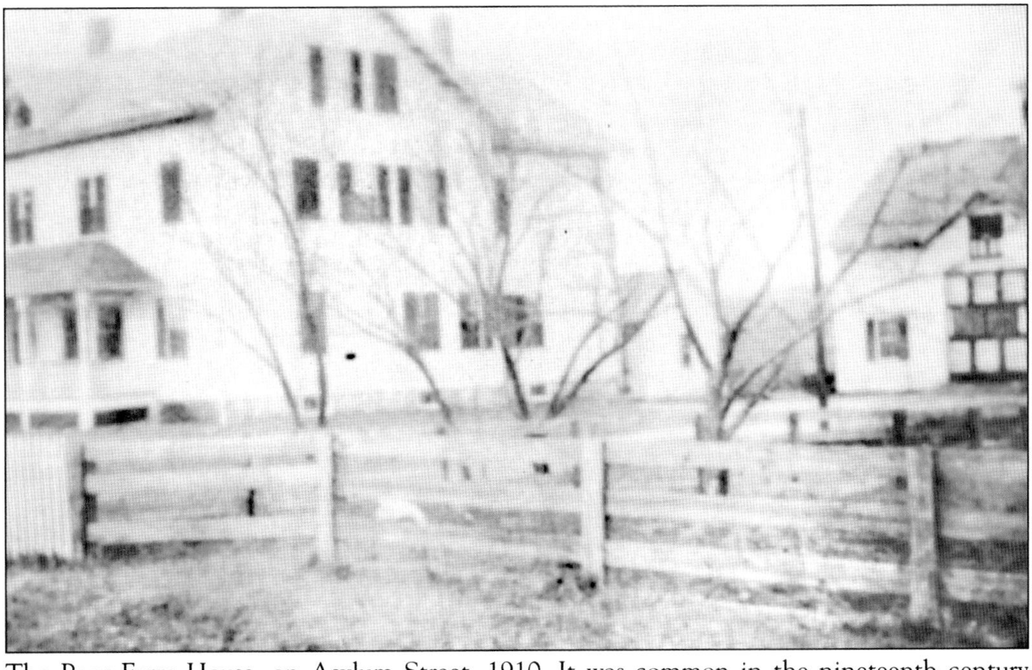

The Poor Farm House, on Asylum Street, 1910. It was common in the nineteenth century for communities such as Woonsocket to establish "Poor Houses" to help the less fortunate. (Woonsocket Harris Public Library.)

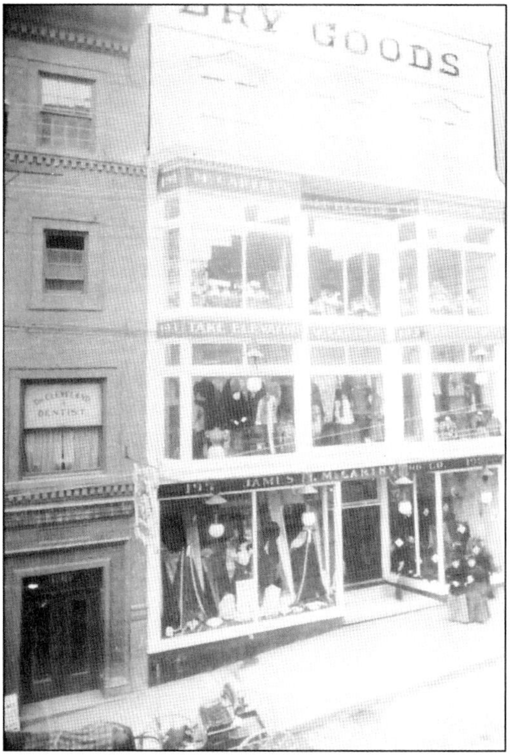

The original McCarthy's store on Main Street, *c.* 1890. James M. McCarthy, who founded this establishment in 1889, would guide it to become "Woonsocket's Largest Store." McCarthy's, which featured forty-five specialty departments, was a fixture on Main Street until the store relocated to the Walnut Hill Plaza in the 1960s. (Woonsocket Harris Public Library.)

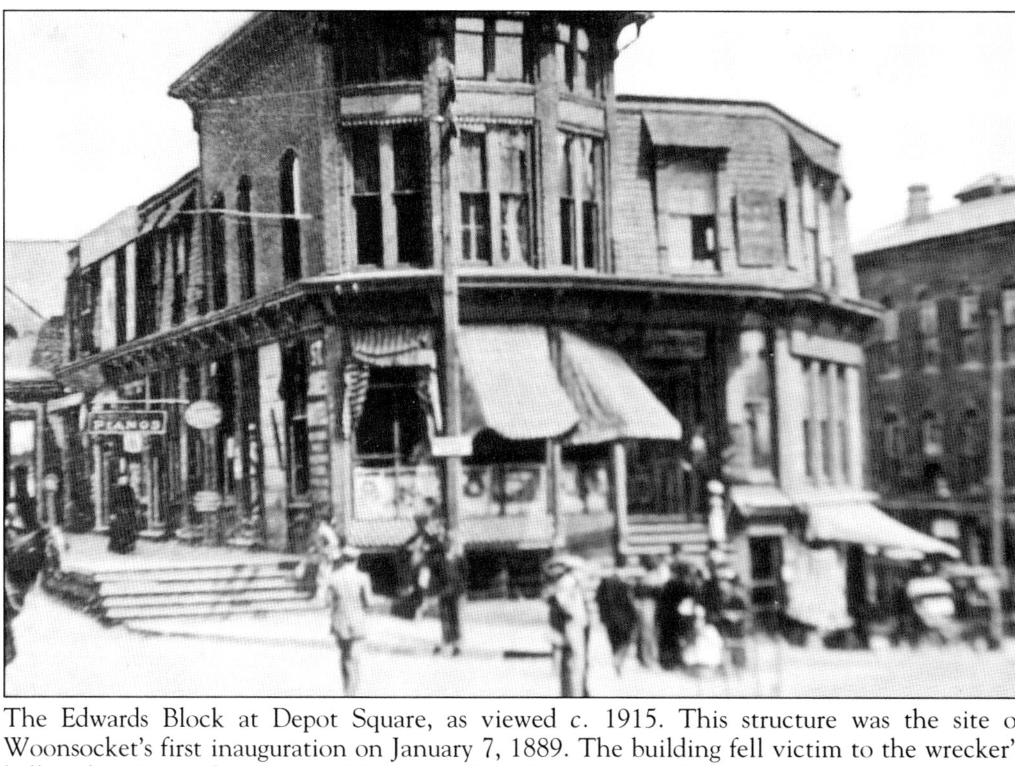

The Edwards Block at Depot Square, as viewed *c.* 1915. This structure was the site of Woonsocket's first inauguration on January 7, 1889. The building fell victim to the wrecker's ball in the 1960s. The Hope Building is to the right. (Woonsocket Harris Public Library.)

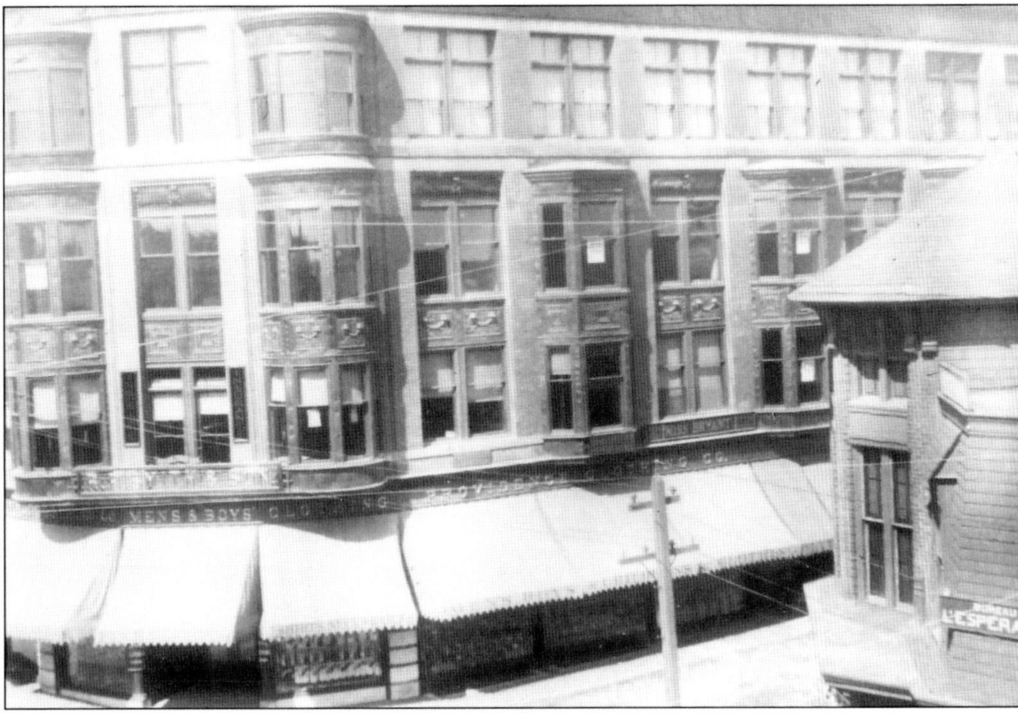

The Longley Building, *c.* 1890. This four-story brick retail and office block, built in 1890 at the corner of Main and High Streets, includes bay windows. The Providence Clothing Company, a clothing store for men and boys, occupied the first floor, while offices occupied the second and third. The fourth floor included a large hall that was available for community events. (Woonsocket Harris Public Library.)

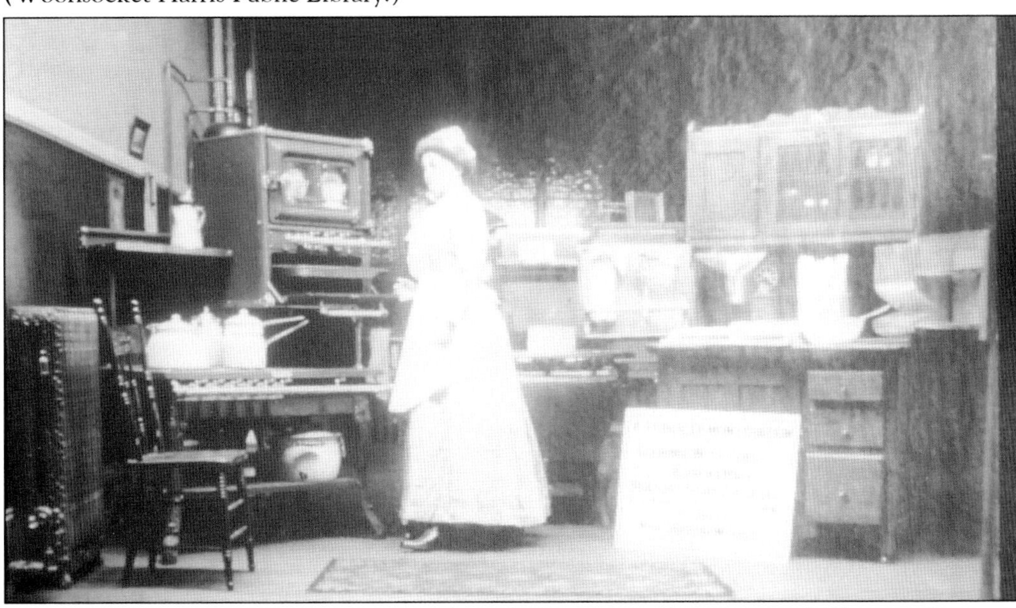

Old-fashioned kitchen appliances in the Blackstone Valley Gas and Electric Company Showroom, *c.* 1930s. The showroom was in the Unity Building, on Main Street, at this time. (Woonsocket Harris Public Library.)

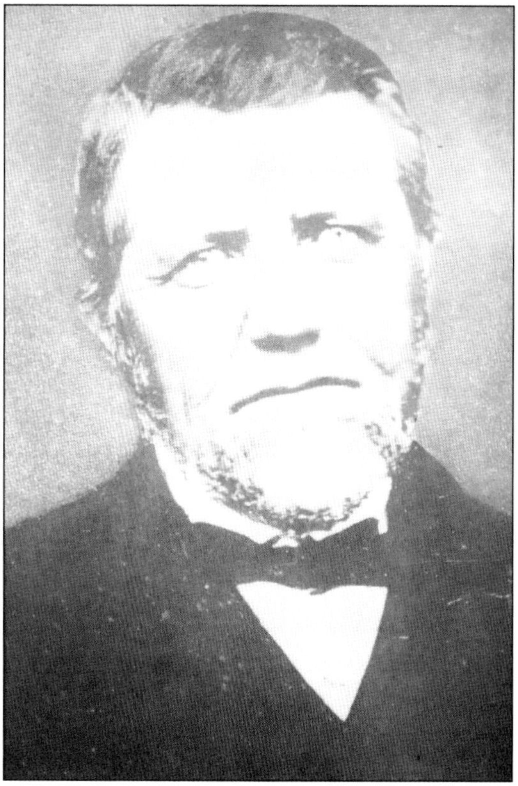

Francois Proulx (1815–1884), a mill agent for George Ballou, *c.* 1860. Proulx is considered the first French-Canadian settler in Woonsocket. (Woonsocket Harris Public Library.)

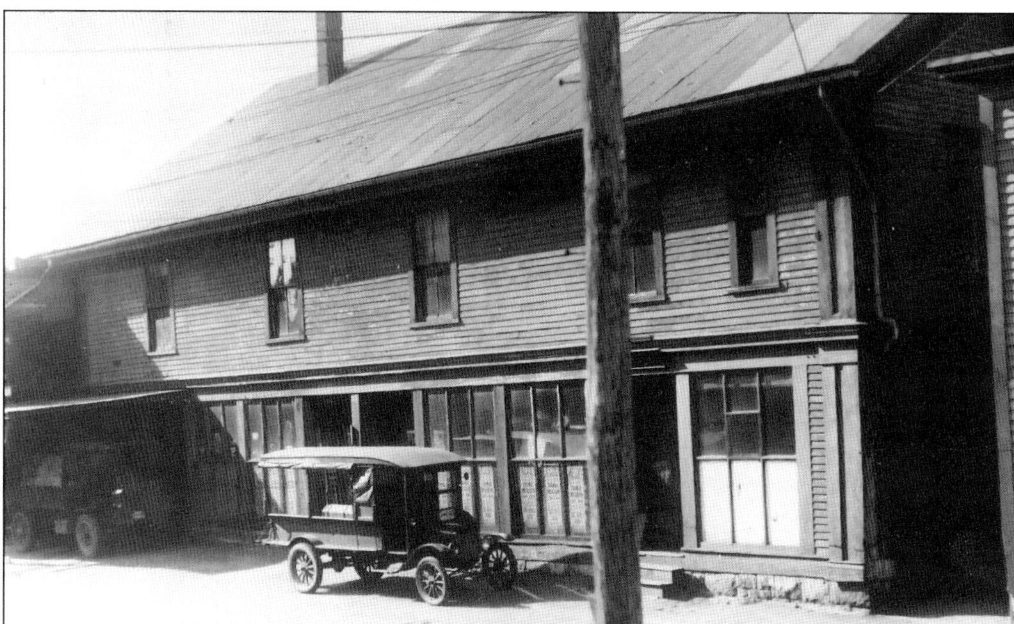

Bouvier Hall, *c.* 1925. Located at 115 High Street, Bouvier Hall was the scene of many political and social gatherings. When the "L'Union Saint-Jean-Baptiste d'Amerique" was founded in 1900, they used this building as their first headquarters. The wrecker's ball demolished the hall in 1960. (Woonsocket Harris Public Library.)

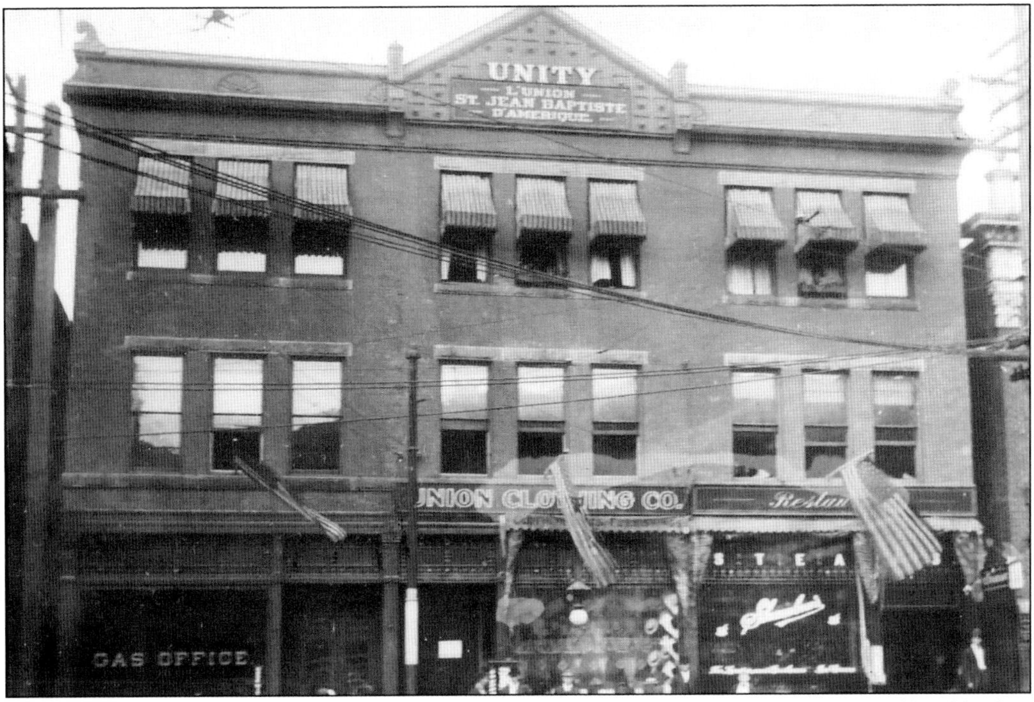

The Unity Building, built *c.* 1886, photographed *c.* 1900. This three-story brick office block is at the head of Clinton Street in Depot Square. L'Union Saint-Jean-Baptiste d'Amerique had its home office here from 1901 to 1927. (Woonsocket Harris Public Library.)

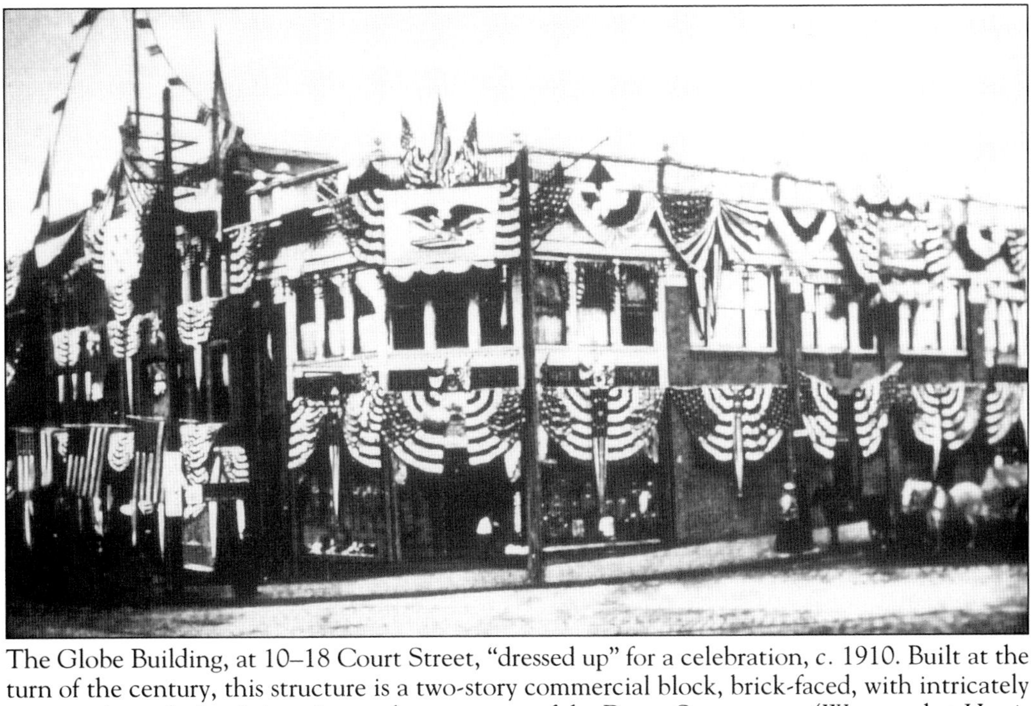

The Globe Building, at 10–18 Court Street, "dressed up" for a celebration, *c.* 1910. Built at the turn of the century, this structure is a two-story commercial block, brick-faced, with intricately patterned wood trim. It is an integral component of the Depot Square area. (Woonsocket Harris Public Library.)

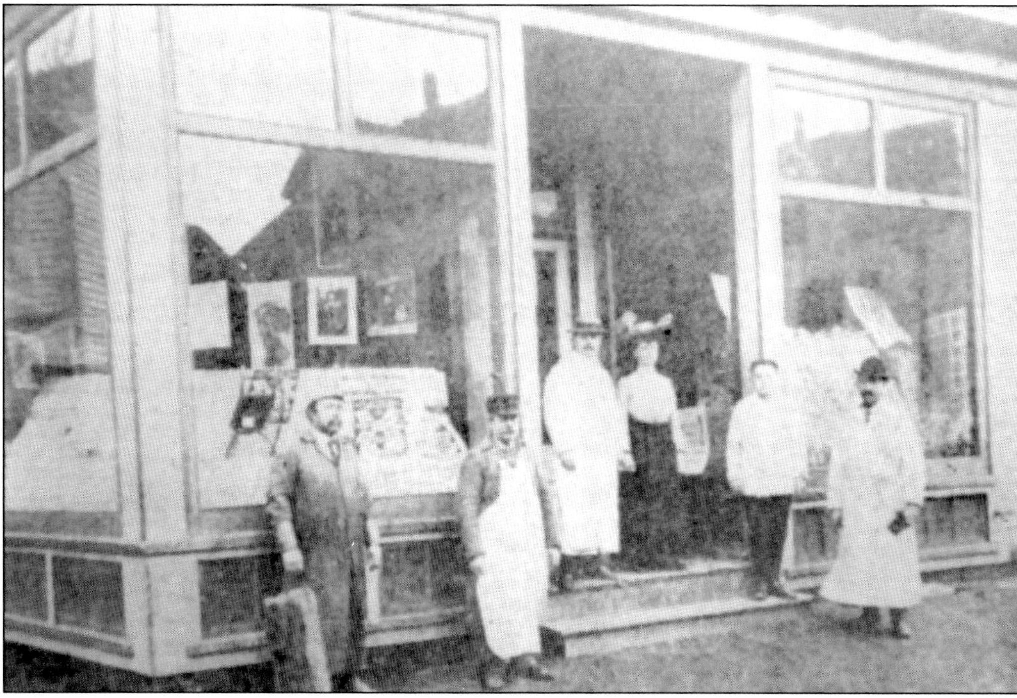

Bousquet's Market, located on Lincoln Street, *c.* 1910. The market, located in a section of Woonsocket that developed around the turn of the twentieth century, was a popular place. Residents who lived in the surrounding triple-deckers and worked in the Globe Company Mill patronized this market often. (Woonsocket Harris Public Library.)

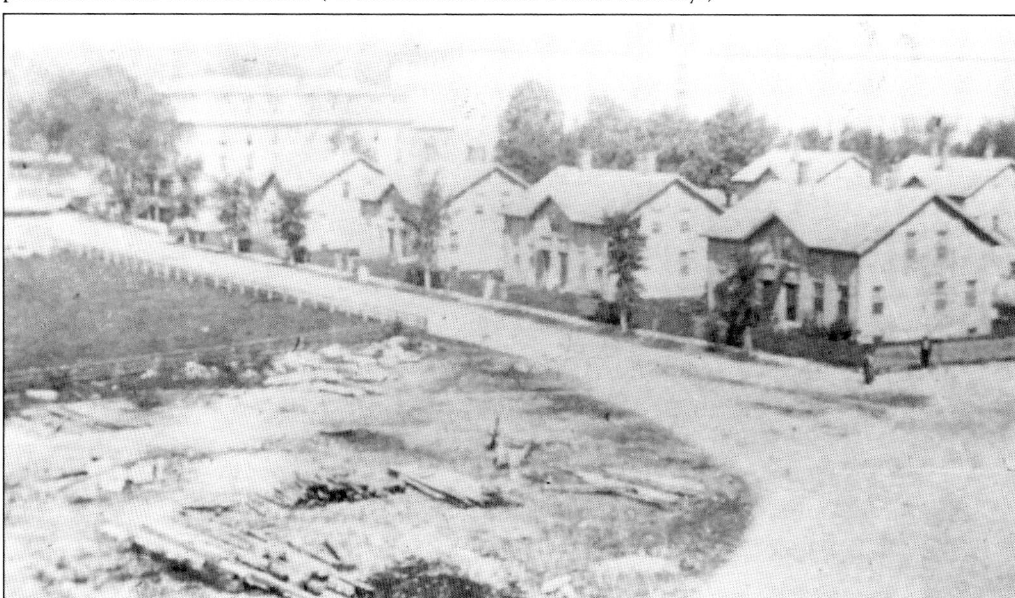

Nourse Village, located between Social and Clinton Streets, *c.* 1900. The village dates back to the 1880s, with the construction of the mill along Clinton Street. In the early 1970s the village, which contained many well constructed and historic buildings, was leveled as part of an urban renewal project. (Woonsocket Harris Public Library.)

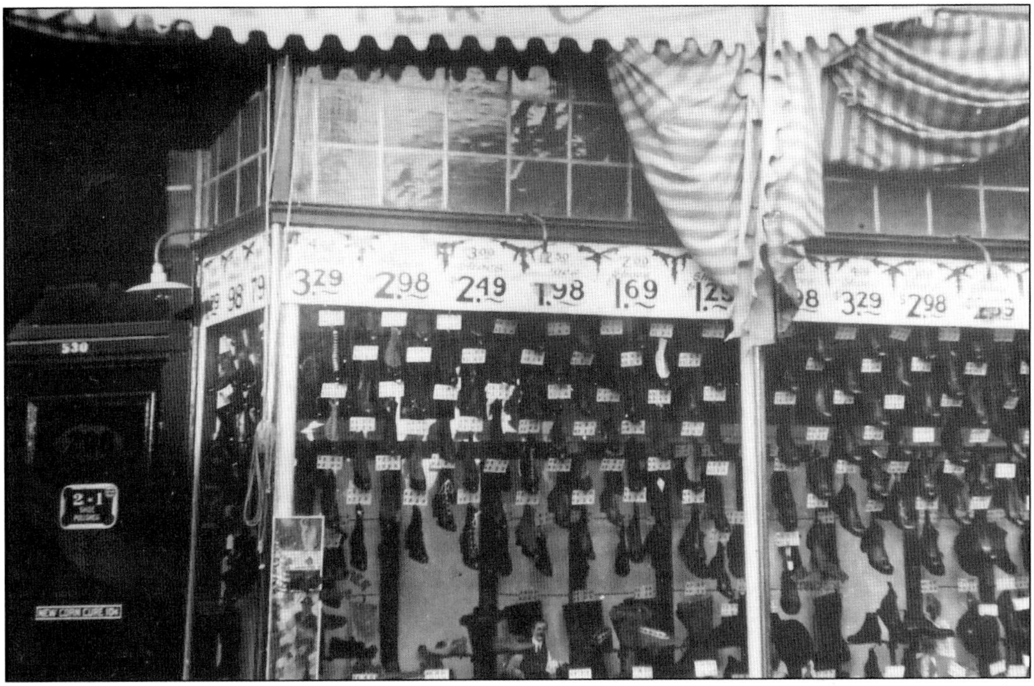

The Pelletier Brothers Shoe Store, at the corner of Social and Rathbun Streets, *c.* 1908. This establishment was at Social Corner. Called the Social "Coin," it was the epicenter of the heavily French-Canadian Social District. (Woonsocket Harris Public Library.)

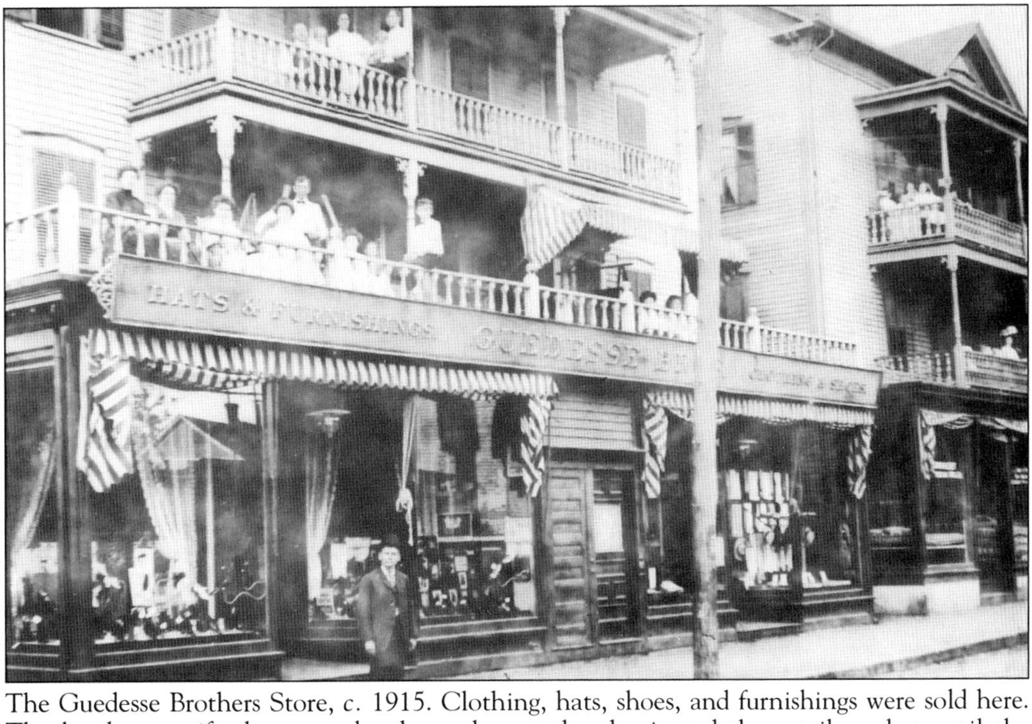

The Guedesse Brothers Store, *c.* 1915. Clothing, hats, shoes, and furnishings were sold here. The brothers typify the many local merchants who dominated the retail market until the encroachment of national chain stores in the 1920s. (Woonsocket Harris Public Library.)

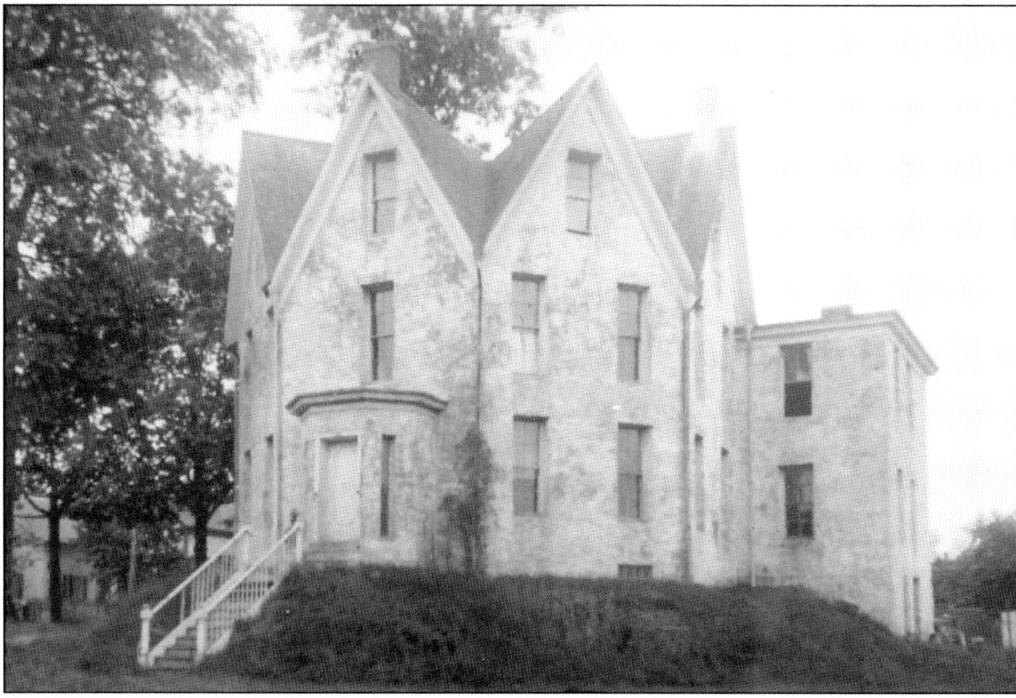

The Sabin Pond House at the corner of Bernon and Grove Streets, *c.* 1900. Sabin Pond, a local manufacturer, built this structure *c.* 1849. The very unusual single family home was a two-and-a-half-story octagonal house, stonewalled, with a gable-roof. It was demolished in the mid-1980s. (Woonsocket Harris Public Library.)

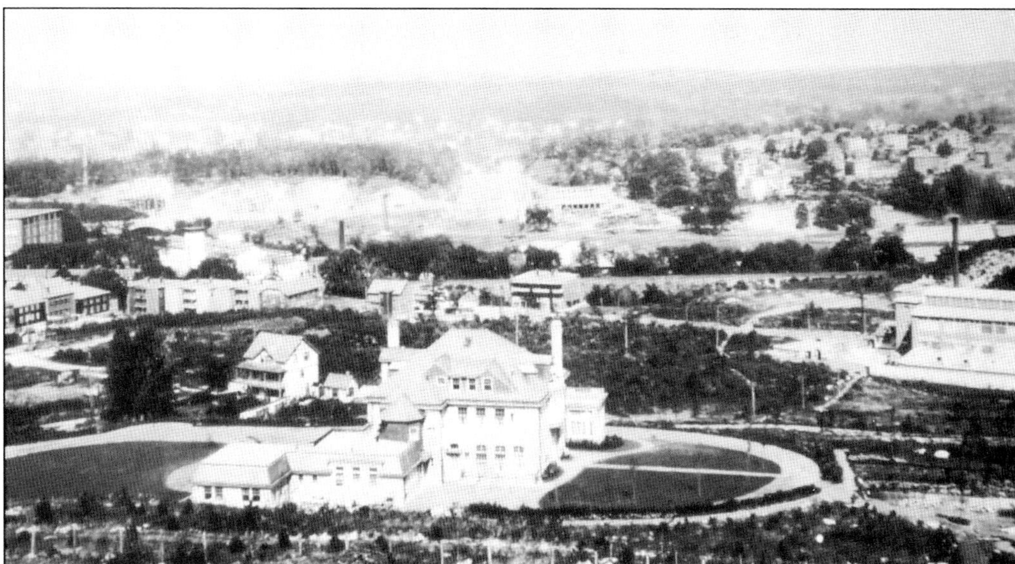

The Lepoutre Mansion, as seen from Mount Saint Charles Academy, *c.* 1920s. Auguste Lepoutre, who founded the Lafayette Worsted Company, built this mansion in 1923. The mansion later became the home of the Club Canadien, and was remodeled again to become Mercy Hospital. Today this structure forms the centerpiece of the Mount Vernon Apartments. (Woonsocket Harris Public Library.)

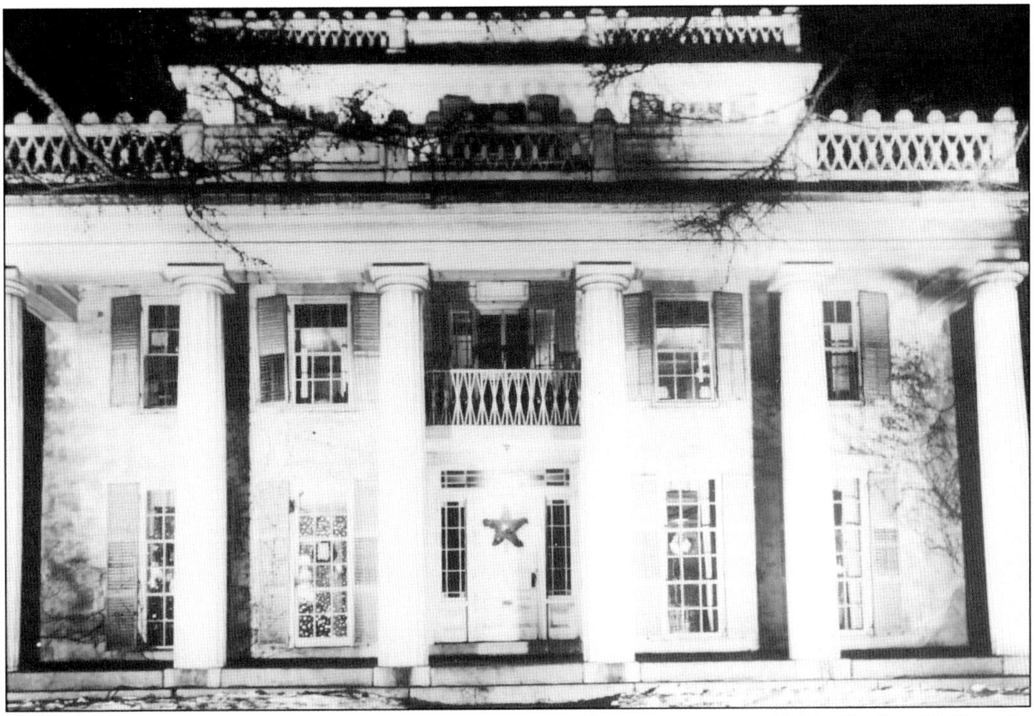

The Old Stone House, on South Main Street, in a night time scene in 1930. Cephas Holbrook, the proprietor of the Woonsocket Hotel, built this grand Greek Revival dwelling *c.* 1835. The two-and-one-half-story stone structure had a monitor-on-hip-roof and a full colossal Doric portico across the front. George C. Ballou, the owner of the Globe Mills, called it home by the year 1850. (Woonsocket Harris Public Library.)

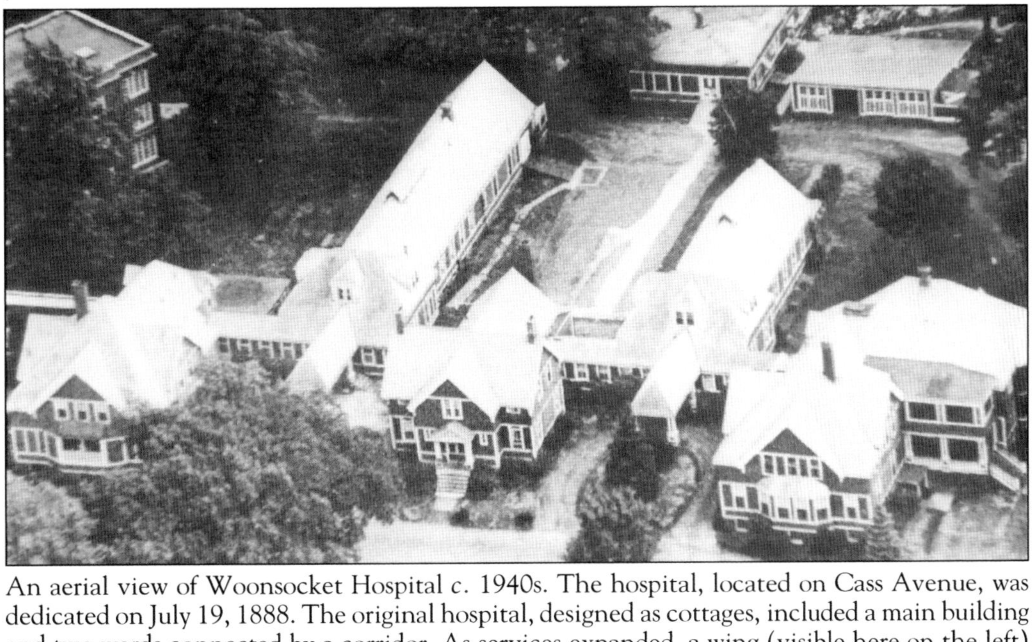

An aerial view of Woonsocket Hospital *c.* 1940s. The hospital, located on Cass Avenue, was dedicated on July 19, 1888. The original hospital, designed as cottages, included a main building and two wards connected by a corridor. As services expanded, a wing (visible here on the left) was added in 1926 to replace obsolete buildings. (Woonsocket Harris Public Library.)

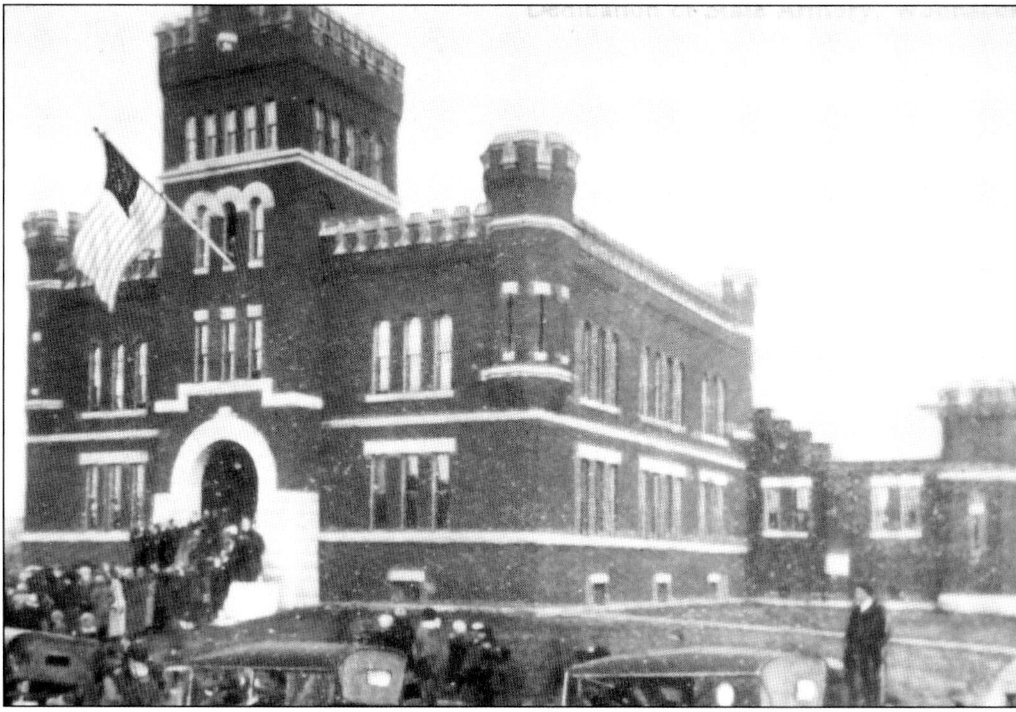

The dedication of the Woonsocket Armory on South Main Street, January 31, 1913. Designed by William Walker and built in 1912, this armory was Woonsocket's third. It is a stone-trimmed, brick castle-like structure. (Woonsocket Harris Public Library.)

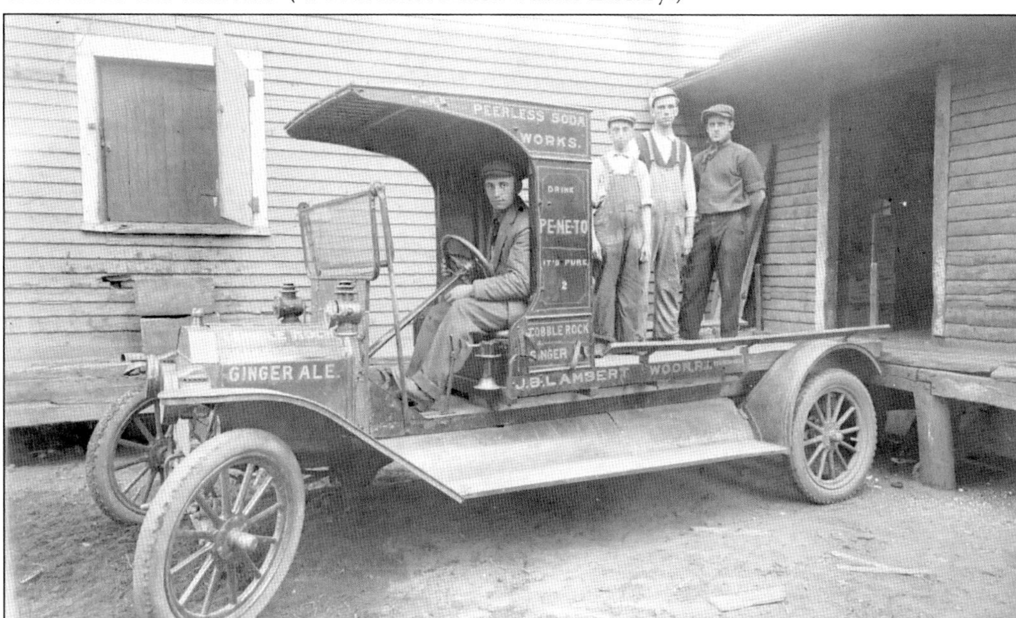

Delivery truck #2 of the Peerless Soda Works *c.* 1915. The soda company, owned by J.B. Lambert, made a variety of carbonated beverage drinks. (Blackstone River Valley National Heritage Corridor Commission.)

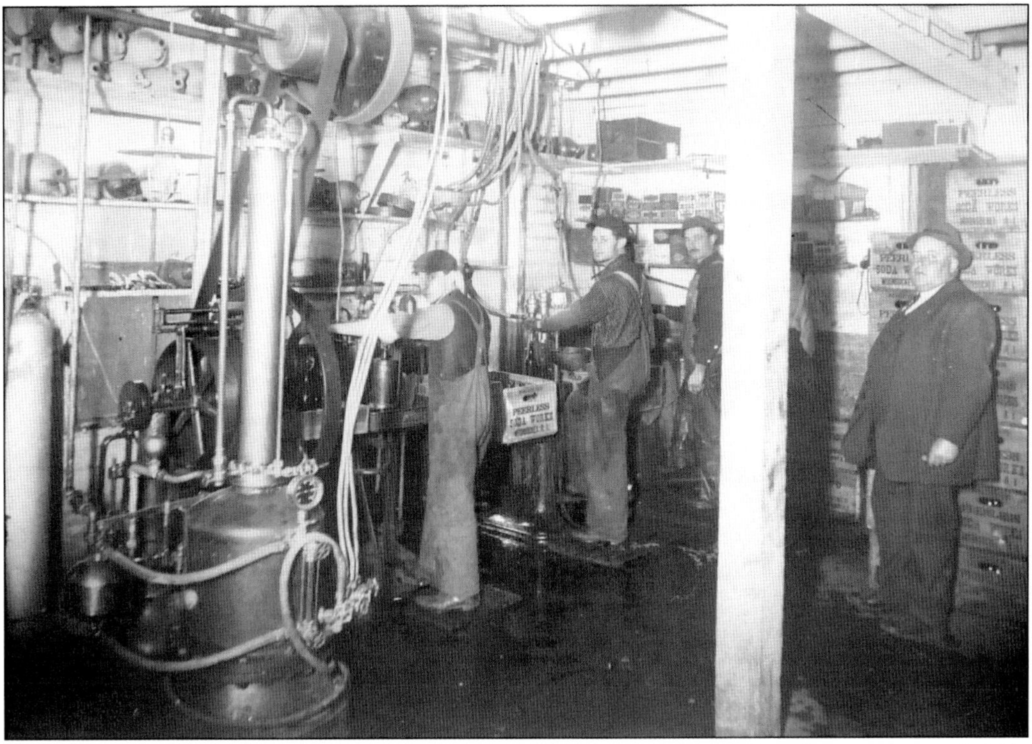

A view inside the Peerless Soda Works in Woonsocket *c.* 1915. The firm, known for its Cobble Rock Ginger Ale, was popular with local residents. (Blackstone River Valley National Heritage Corridor Commission.)

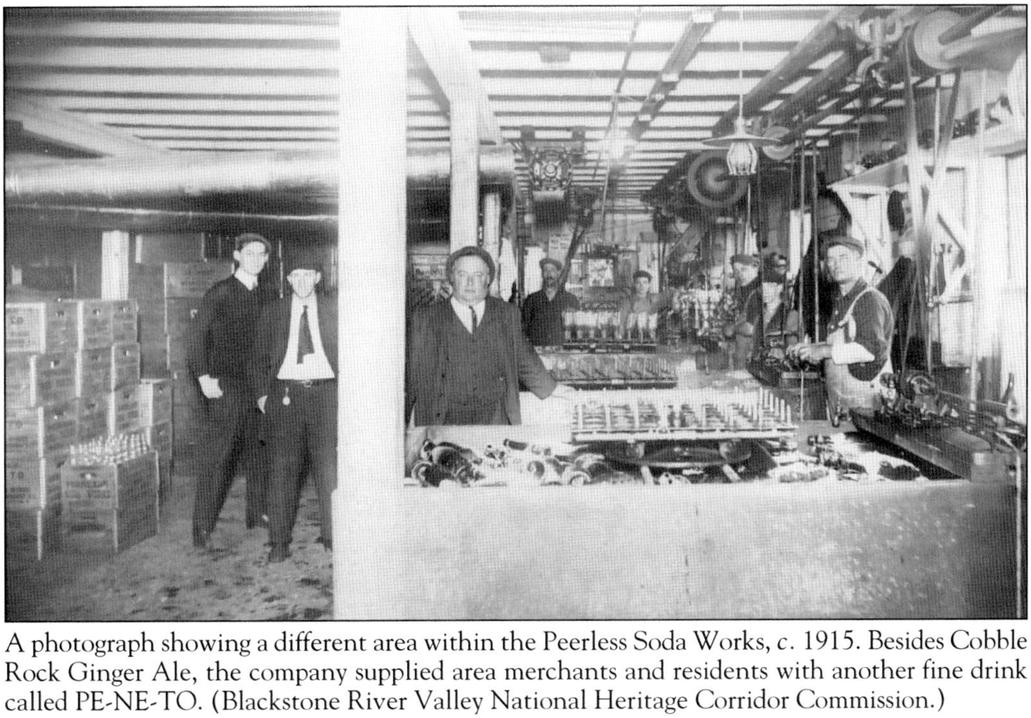

A photograph showing a different area within the Peerless Soda Works, *c.* 1915. Besides Cobble Rock Ginger Ale, the company supplied area merchants and residents with another fine drink called PE-NE-TO. (Blackstone River Valley National Heritage Corridor Commission.)

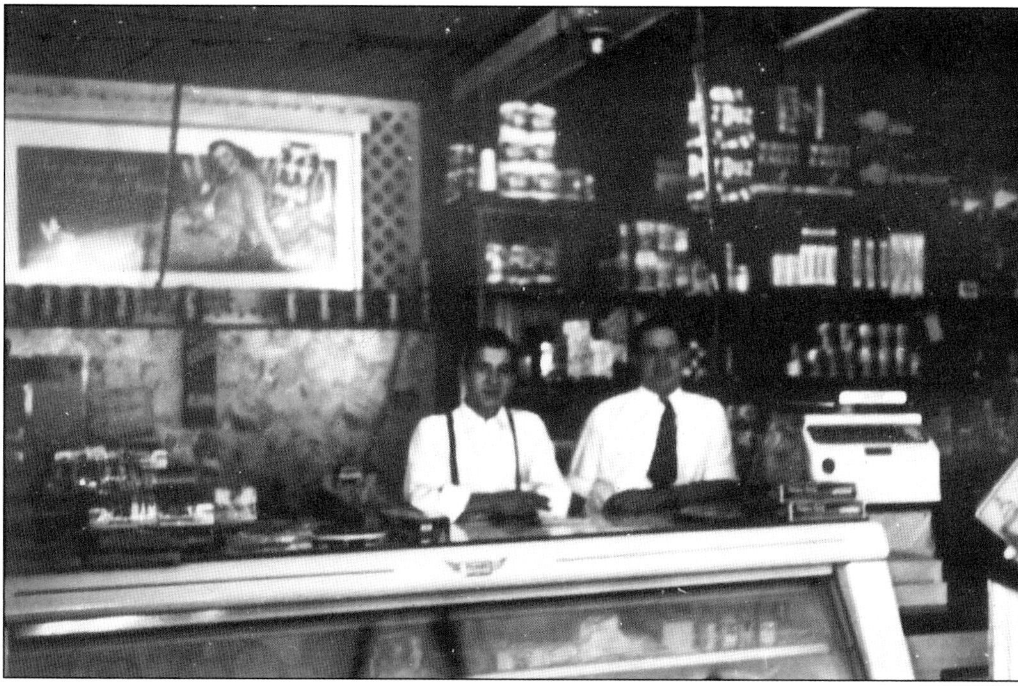

The interior of Plouffe's Variety Store, *c.* 1940. It was common throughout the many neighborhoods of Woonsocket to find small stores, such as Plouffe's, providing a variety of items including foodstuffs, tobacco products, candy, etc.

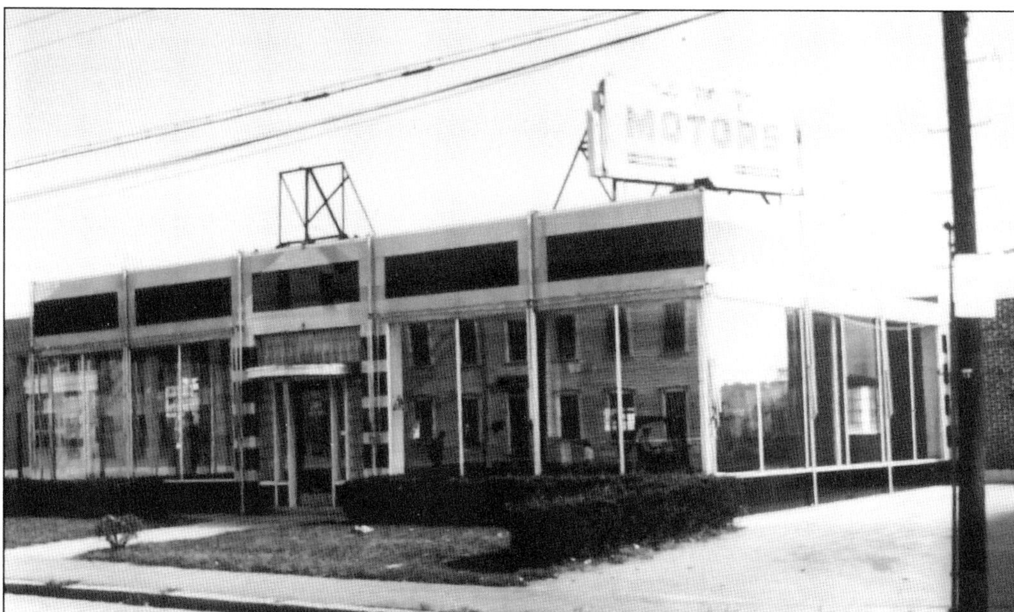

A frontal view, *c.* 1950, of Jay Motors, located on Pond Street. The rise in the standard of living, which many workers in the manufacturing sector experienced, allowed them to purchase automobiles. Small dealerships such as Jay Motors catered to the rise in the middle class in the city. Today this structure houses the offices of the Rhode Island Department of Employment and Training. (Woonsocket Harris Public Library.)

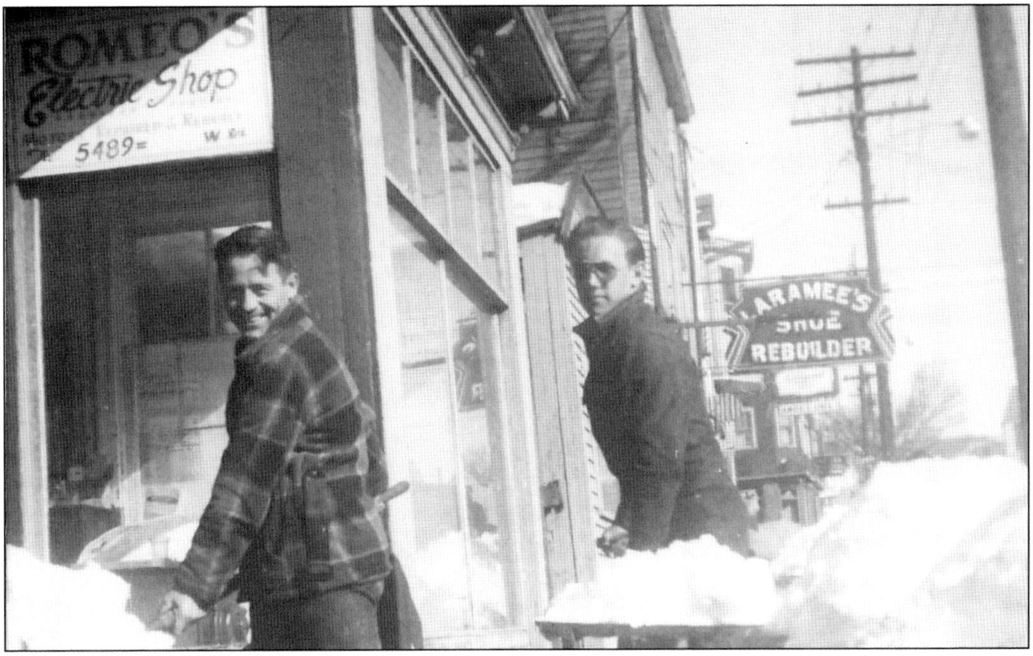

An outside view of the Bernon Street electric repair shop of Romeo Brousseau, after a winter snow storm, c. 1956. The shop was in a building near the Bernon Street Bridge. Behind these enthusiastic "snow removers" is Laramee's Shoe Rebuilding shop. The "fellow" on the left is Amadee Brin. (Mr. and Mrs. George E. Brin.)

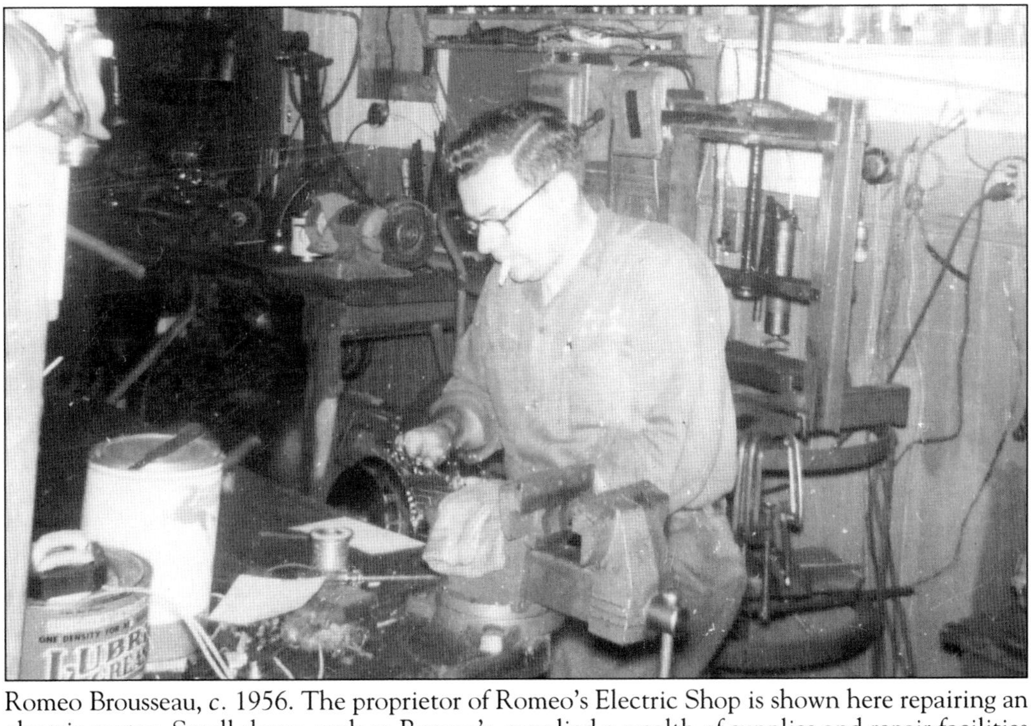

Romeo Brousseau, c. 1956. The proprietor of Romeo's Electric Shop is shown here repairing an electric motor. Small shops, such as Romeo's, supplied a wealth of supplies and repair facilities to the many mills in Woonsocket. (Mr. and Mrs. George E. Brin.)

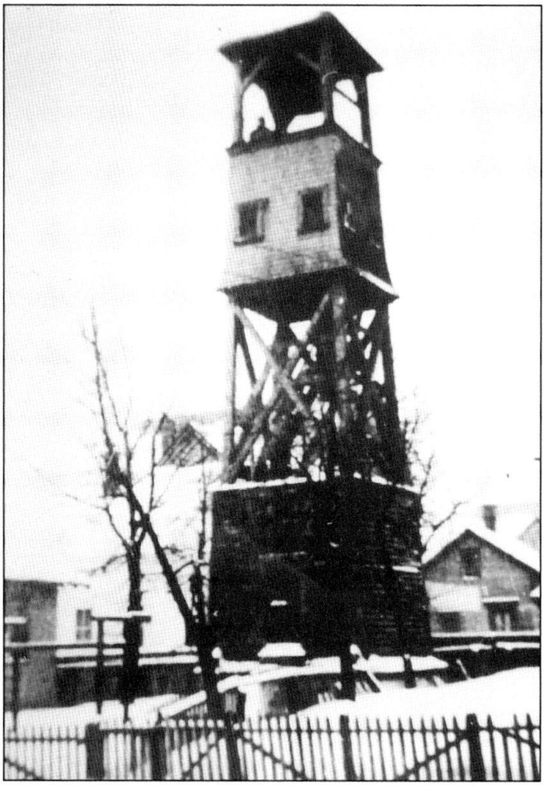

The Boyden Street Fire Tower, 1915. The tower contained a fire bell that was sounded in the event of a fire. Instead of keeping a vigilant eye out for fires from the tower, a modern electric fire alarm system would replace this antiquated signaling method. (Woonsocket Harris Public Library.)

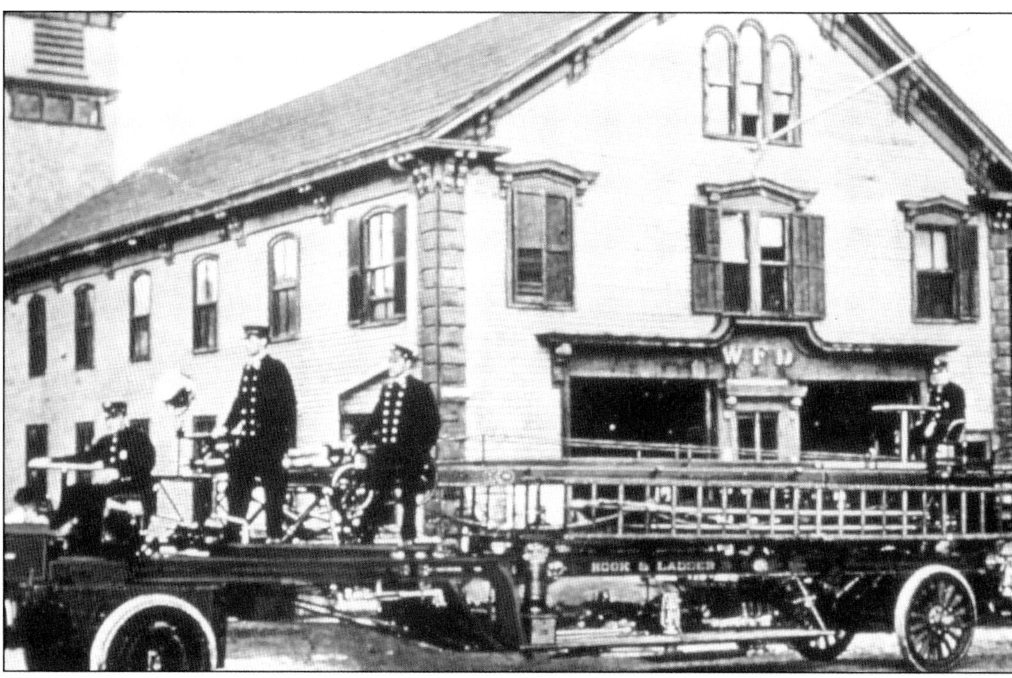

Woonsocket Fire Department Station #3 on North Main Street *c*. 1915. In front of the station is an early motorized hook and ladder truck. A modern structure replaced this station in 1926. (Woonsocket Harris Public Library.)

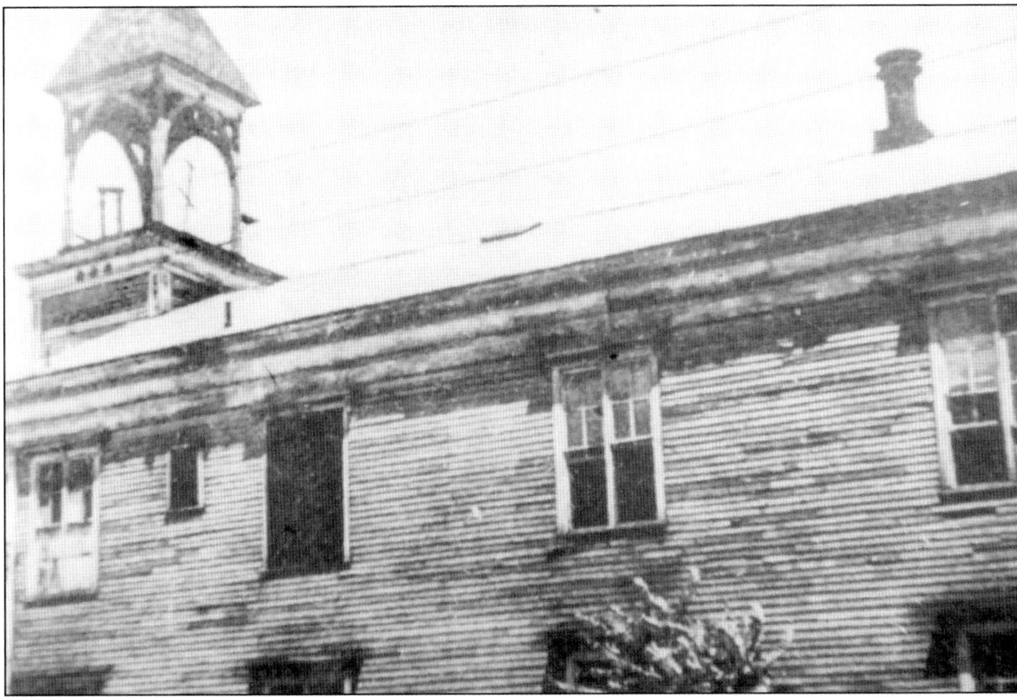

Woonsocket Fire Department Station #1, on Armory Street, 1952. This structure, built c. 1840s, was Woonsocket's first armory. (Woonsocket Harris Public Library.)

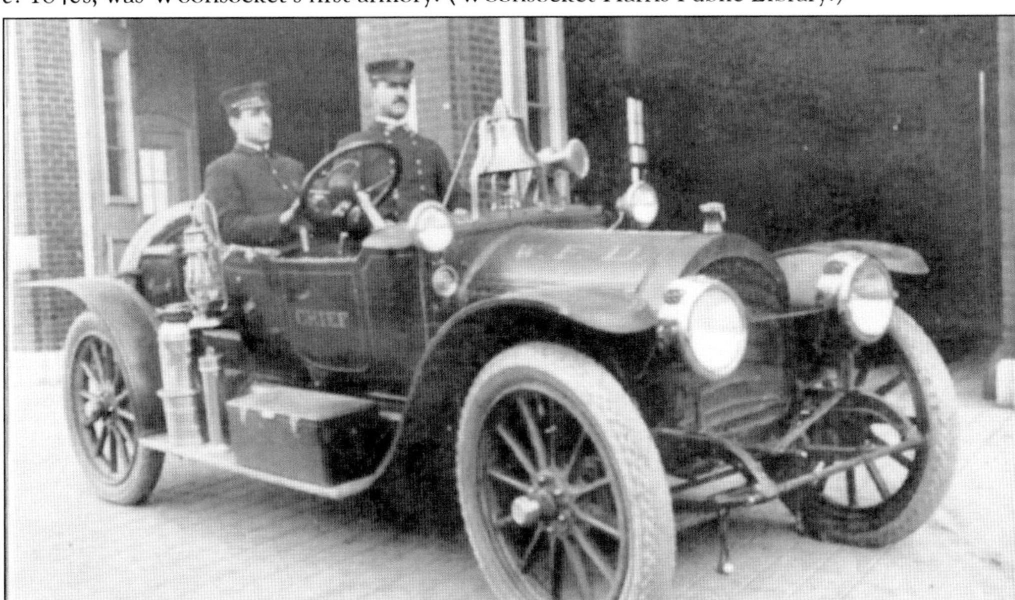

Chief Augustin J. Cote and his aide Levi Sutherland in front of Woonsocket Fire Station #5 on Social Street. Affectionately known as "Gus" Cote, Augustin was Woonsocket's fire chief from 1908 to 1954. He transformed the fire department into a professional firefighting force, and was responsible for the replacement of the horse-powered equipment with modern motorized vehicles. When he retired in April 1954, Cote estimated that he had responded to about 20,000 alarms in his career. (Mr. and Mrs. Aram Archambault.)

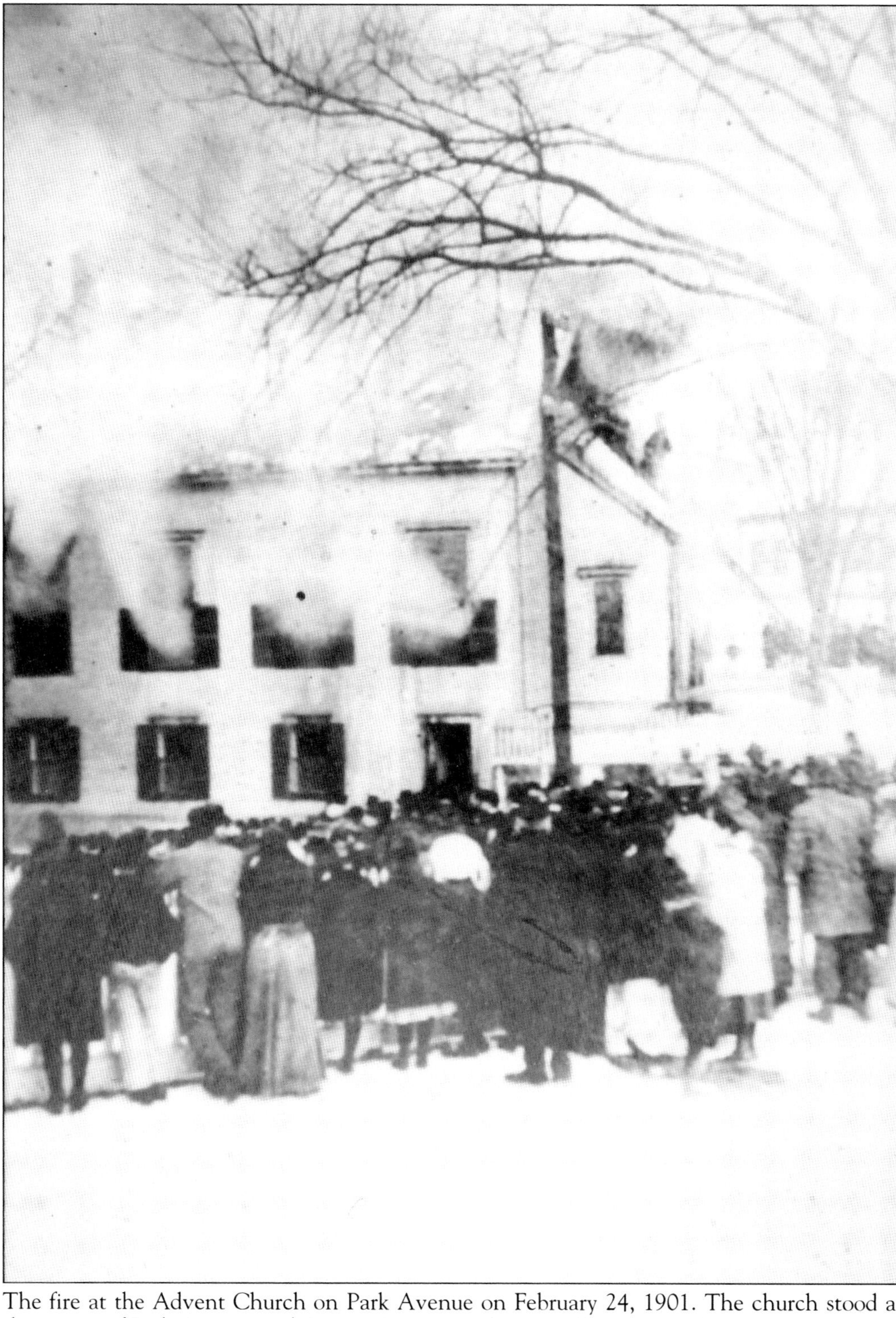

The fire at the Advent Church on Park Avenue on February 24, 1901. The church stood at the corner of Park Avenue and Greene Streets. Today a small apartment house sits on the site. (Woonsocket Harris Public Library.)

Deputy Fire Chief Elie A. Belrose with two little fellows during Fire Prevention Week on October 8, 1965. The tots, Anthony (left) and Joseph Miller, accidentally set fire to a mattress at their home at 83 Summer Street. (Mr. and Mrs. Aram Archambault.)

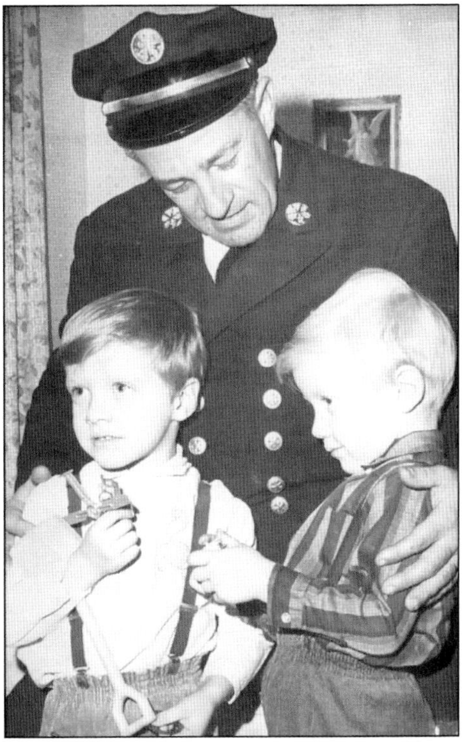

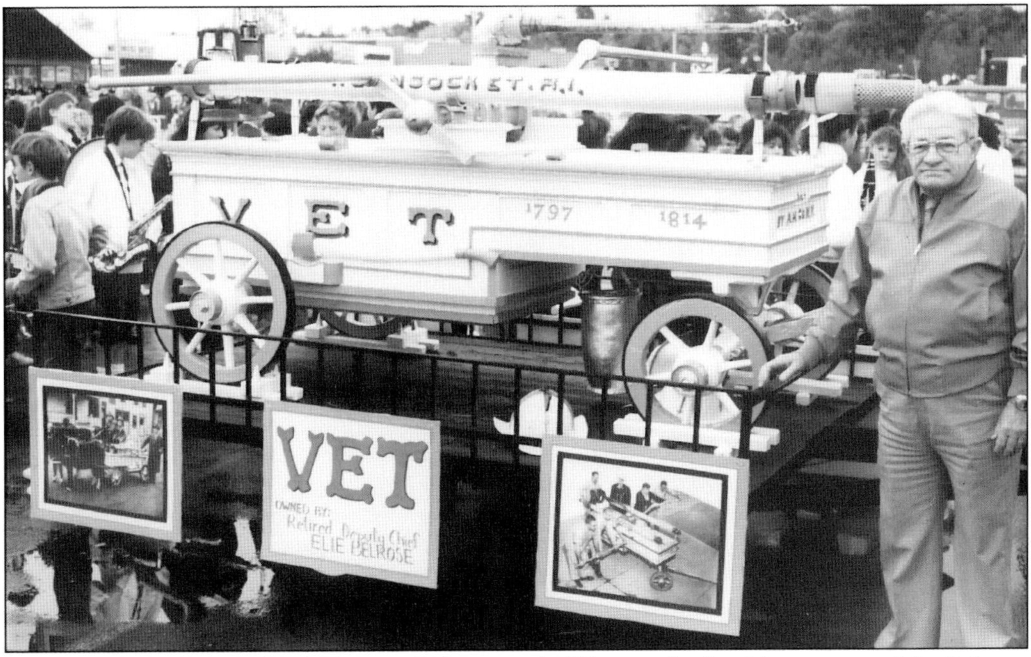

Retired Deputy Fire Chief Elie A. Belrose with Woonsocket's oldest piece of firefighting equipment at the 1987 Autumnfest celebration. Built in 1797, it was a "Bucket Engine." Pulled by man or horse, it functioned as a cart to carry many bucket loads of water at a time to a fire. Conversion of the "Vet" in 1814 made it a "Suction Pump." Installation included a holding tank, man-powered pump, and hoses. (Mr. and Mrs. Aram Archambault.)

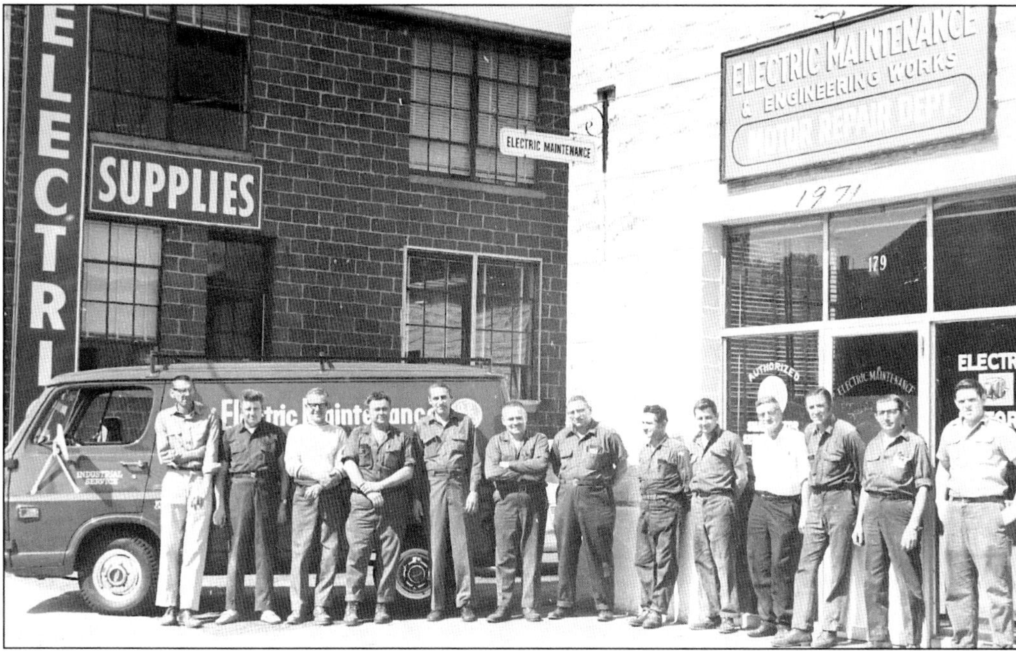

The crew from Electric Maintenance and Engineering Works in front of the company's shops on Railroad Street in 1971. Known throughout the area for their expertise in electrical appliance and motor repair, the firm serviced both residential and industrial customers. Today the electrical supplies division is on Cumberland Hill Road. The only individual identified is George E. Brin, sixth from left. (Mr. and Mrs. George E. Brin.)

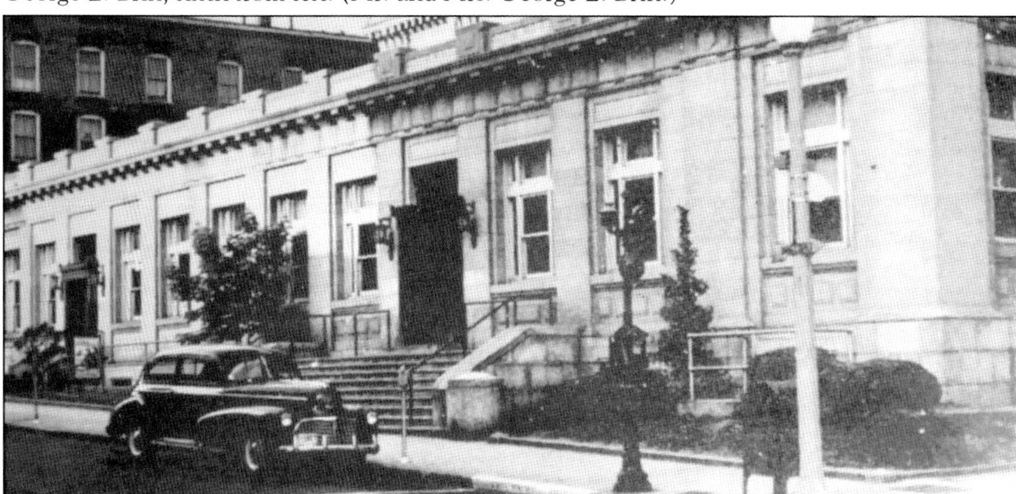

The Old Woonsocket Post Office at the corner of Main and Federal Streets, 1948. The original section of the post office, constructed between 1910 and 1912, is in a fine Beaux Arts classical style. An addition, built *c.* 1930, repeated the detailing of the original building. The post office served the public at this location until 1976, when construction of a more modern facility took place at the corner of Social and Worall Streets. The Woonsocket YMCA later acquired the property, constructed a new Olympic-size swimming pool, and added a covered walkway on Federal Street. Today this is the Ann W. Hack Community Pool and Building. (Woonsocket Harris Public Library.)

Six

We Gather Together . . . Workers and Mill Owners

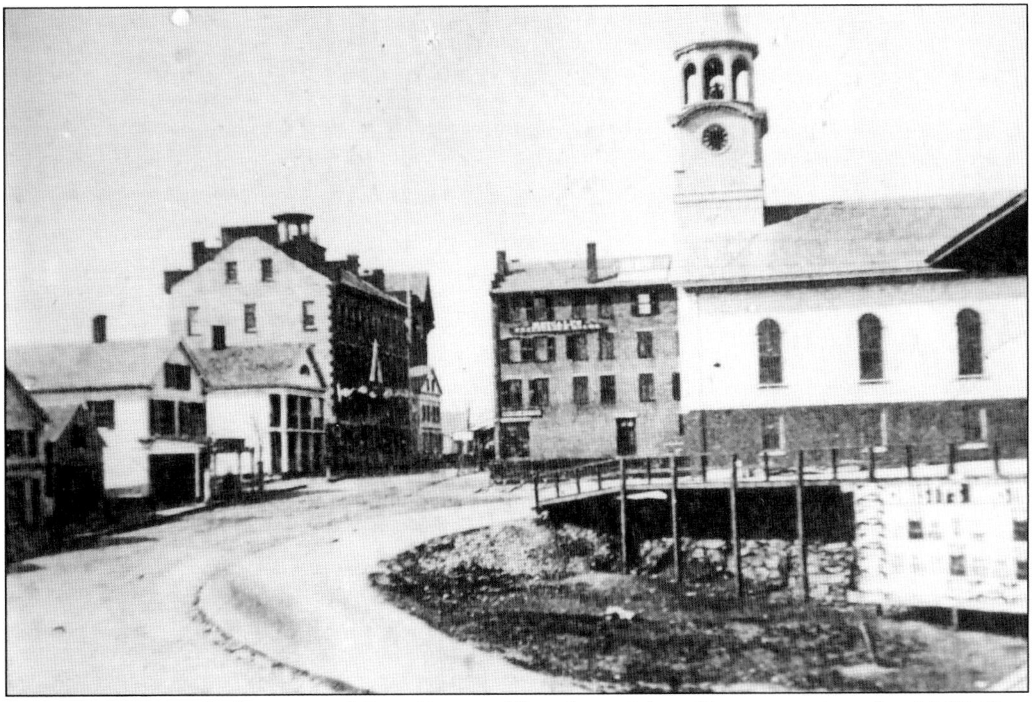

Depot Square, with the original First Baptist Church on Main Street, as viewed *c.* 1860. One of Woonsocket's first churches, it remained in the busy downtown area until 1892, when construction of a new edifice took place on Blackstone Street. Today the Longley Building sits on this site. (Woonsocket Harris Public Library.)

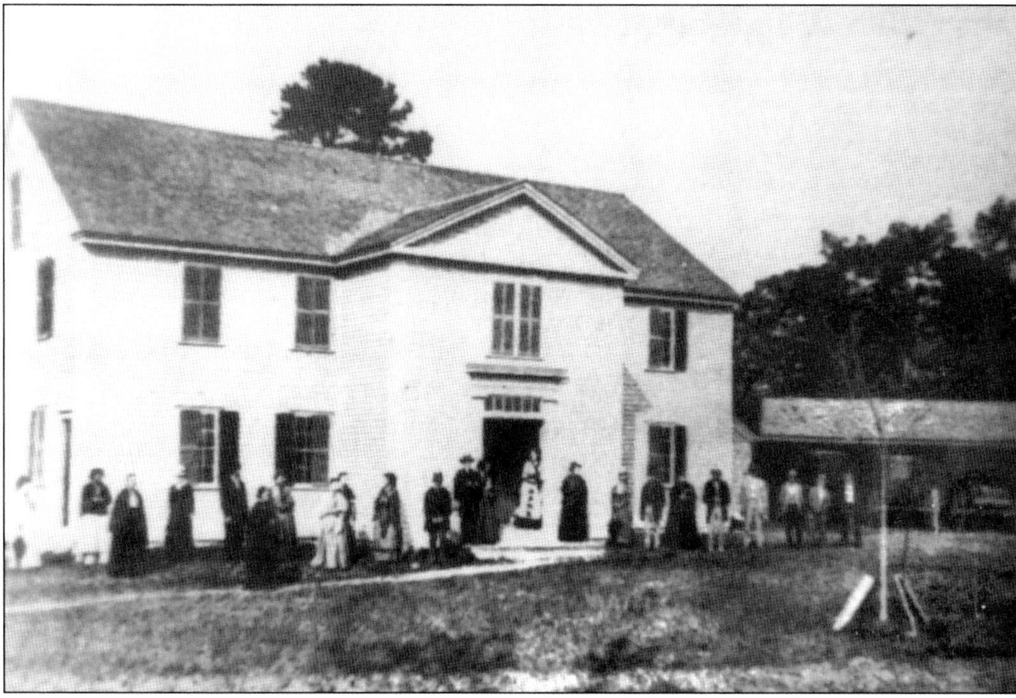

The original Friends Meeting House, on Great Road, built *c.* 1720 and photographed *c.* 1860. This structure, built by John Arnold and other Quakers, was the first religious building in northern Rhode Island. This building reflects a remarkable simplicity for its time. The meetinghouse burned in 1881 and was replaced with the present structure. (Woonsocket Harris Public Library.)

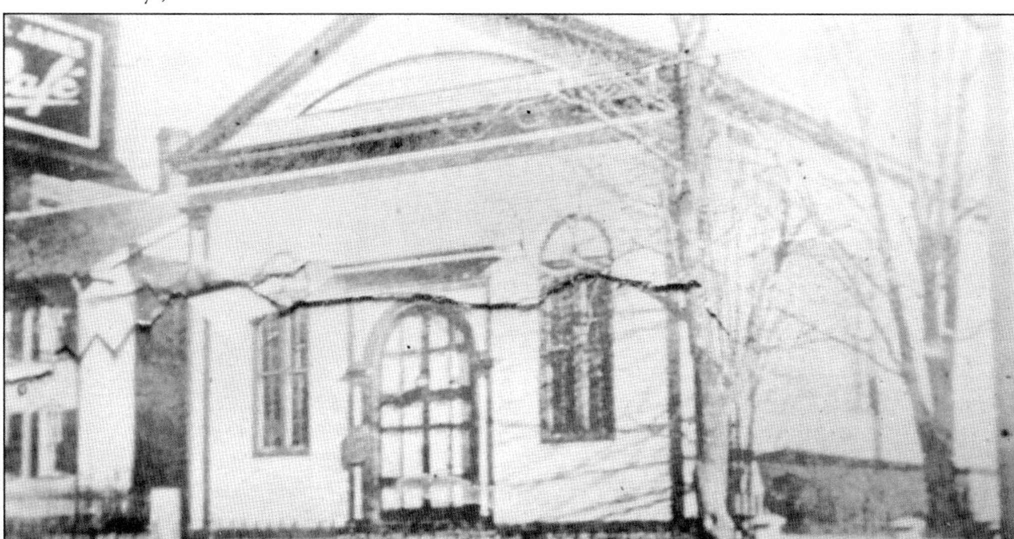

The former Methodist Meeting House on Main Street, 1900. Many Protestant Churches originally located their houses of worship along Main Street. Realizing that the commercialization of their immediate vicinity was not conducive to worship, most relocated to the growing suburbs. Today the Methodist church can be found on Federal Street. (Woonsocket Harris Public Library.)

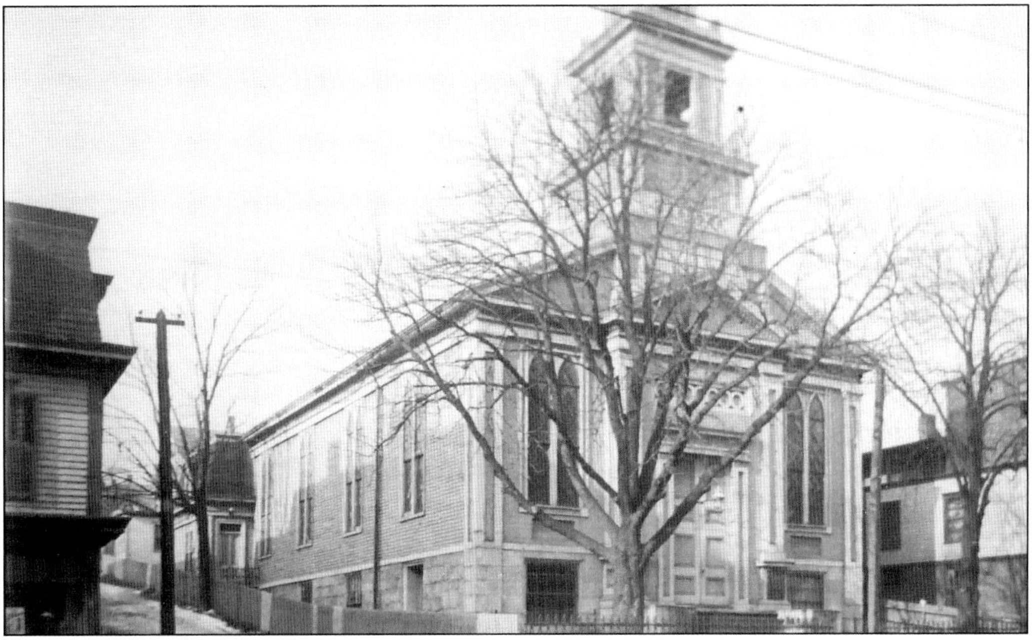

The former Universalist church at the corner of Main and Church Streets, *c.* 1920s. The Woonsocket Universalist Society sold this property in 1919, when they voted to build a modern church away from the congested business-theater district. Today the corner of Earle and Snow Streets is home to the First Universalist Church. (Woonsocket Harris Public Library.)

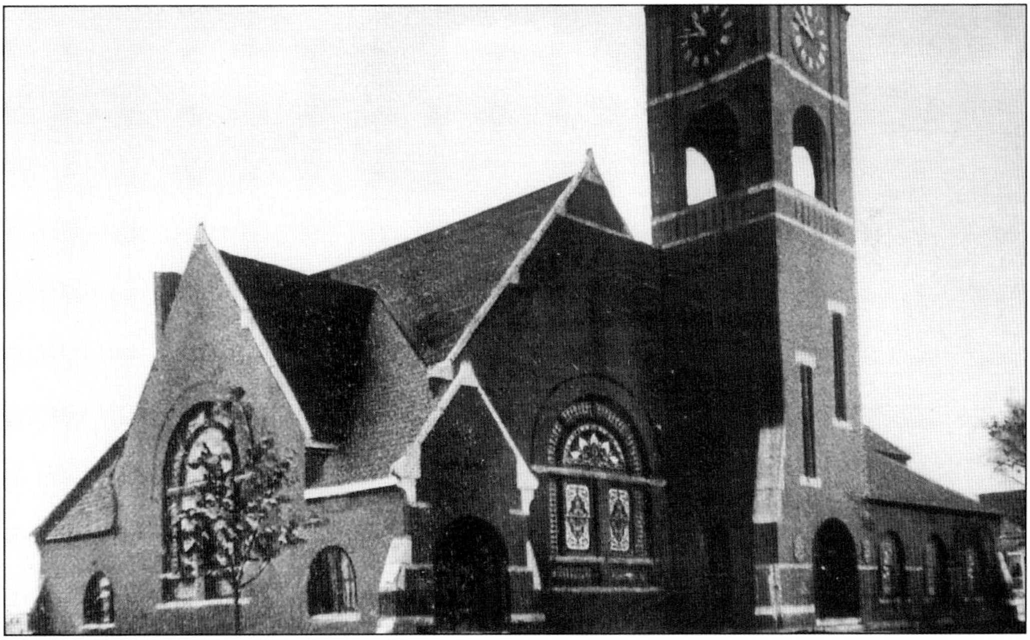

The First Baptist Church on Blackstone Street, *c.* 1915. An architect from Manchester, New Hampshire, by the name of Butterfield was the designer. The Darling Brothers of Worcester, Massachusetts, built the church in 1891 for the sum of about $29,000. It is a handsome brick church, with remarkable fine stained-glass windows, and accentuated by a 60-foot spire. (Woonsocket Harris Public Library.)

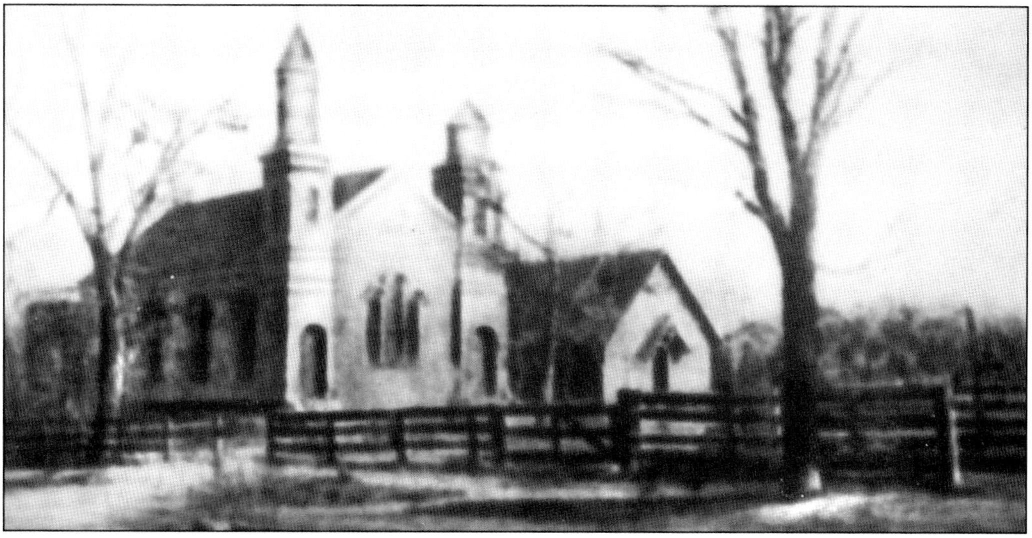

The original Saint James Episcopal Church, on Hamlet Avenue, 1872. "Saint James Church at Woonsocket Falls, Smithfield" was incorporated in 1832 and the original building was dedicated on May 16, 1833. Extensive renovations occurred in 1938, and on January 1, 1939, the "new" Saint James Church was dedicated. In the early nineteenth century the six original Protestant churches built their houses of worship in the center of Woonsocket. Today, Saint James Church is the only one still located on its original site in the central part of the city. (Woonsocket Harris Public Library.)

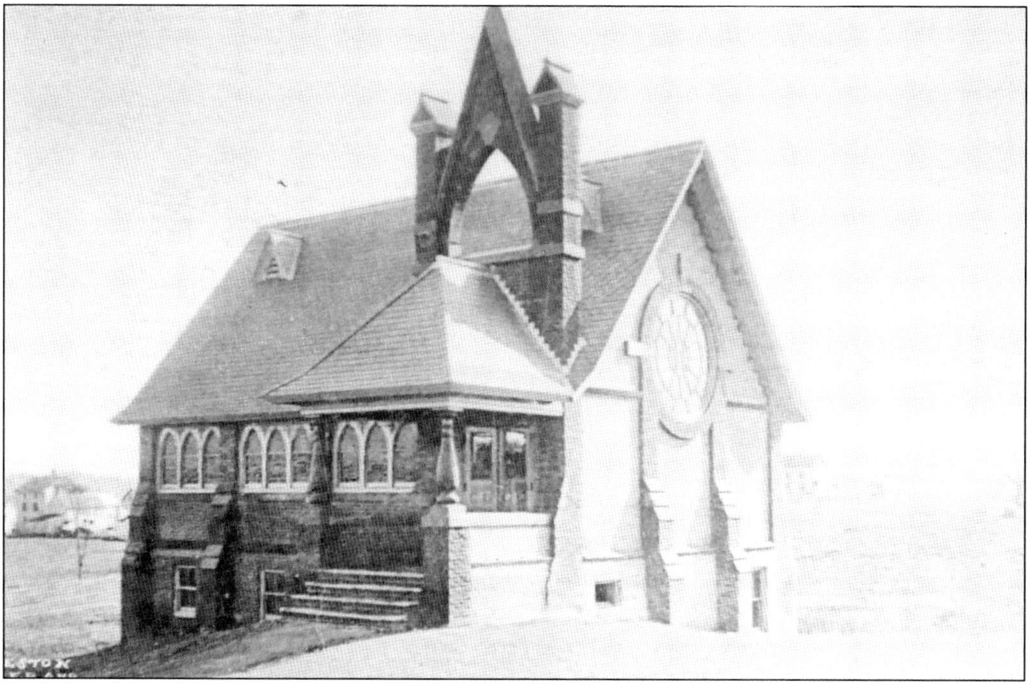

Saint Andrew's Chapel, a mission church of Saint James Episcopal Parish, *c.* 1890s. Constructed in 1894–95 at the corner of Seventh Avenue and Fairmount Street, this picturesque chapel served the newly developing Fairmount neighborhood. The chapel opened with a service of Holy Communion on August 11, 1895. (Woonsocket Harris Public Library.)

The Globe Congregational Church, on South Main Street, as seen through the lens of Charles S. Lawton in 1888. Constructed in 1842, at the corner of South Main and Pleasant Streets, it was destroyed by fire in December 1904. (Woonsocket Harris Public Library.)

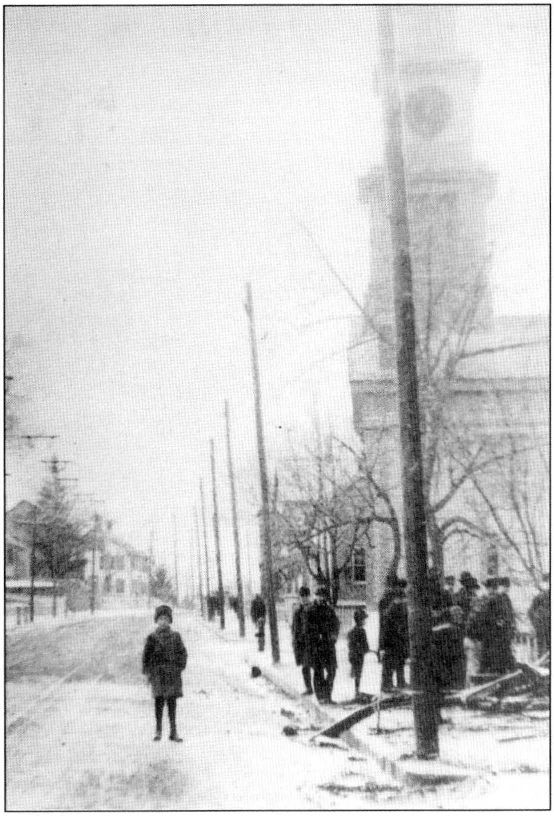

A Charles S. Lawton photograph of the "new" Globe Congregational Church, at the corner of South Main and Providence Streets, *c.* 1900. The church, built in 1900 through the generosity of Harriet R. Ballou, is in the Jacobean style, with leaded windows glazed with translucent glass. The Congregational parish, organized in 1834, remained in Woonsocket until 1974, when it consolidated with a congregation in Slatersville, North Smithfield. Today the Saint James Baptist Church occupies this house of worship. (Woonsocket Harris Public Library.)

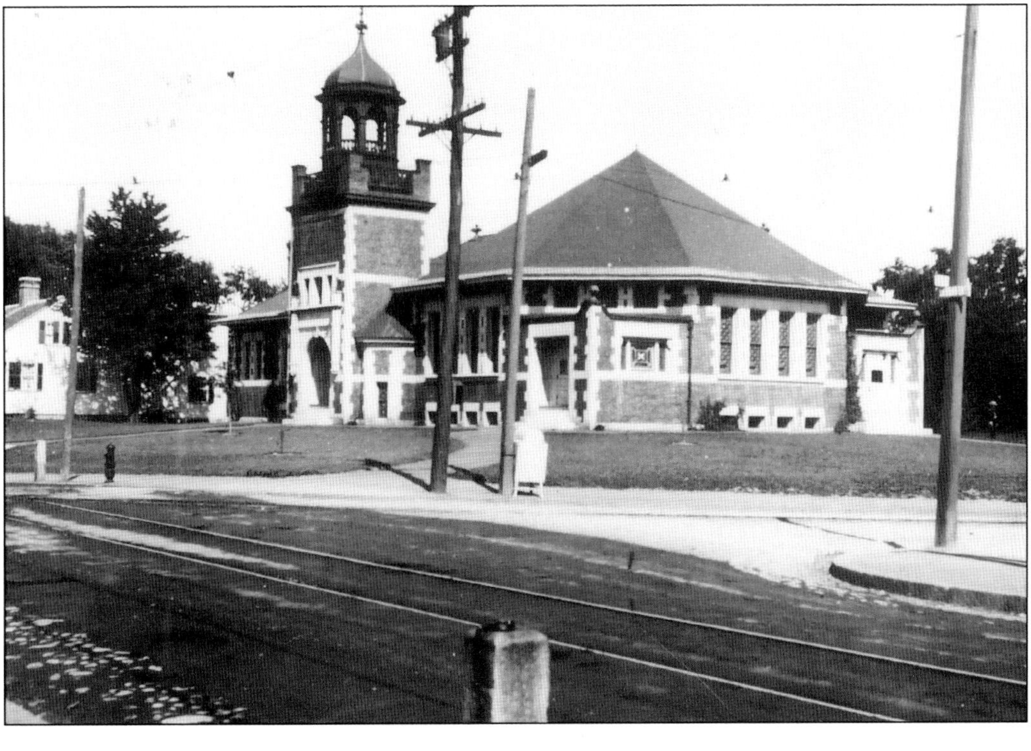

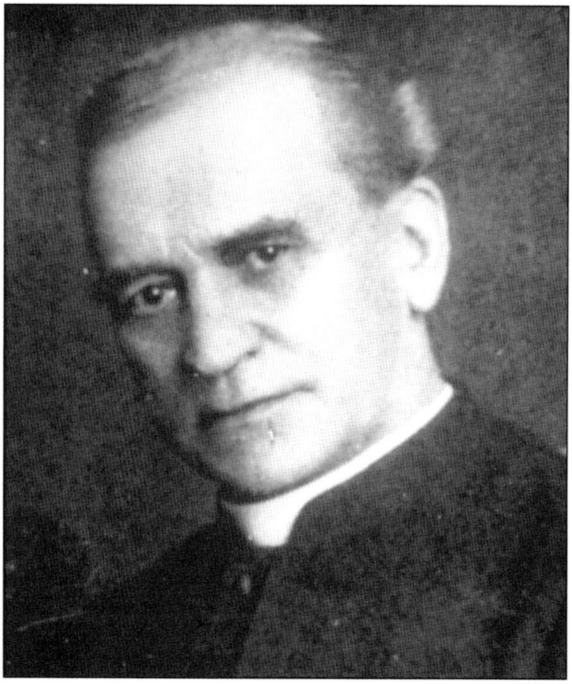

A 1920 photograph of Monsignor Charles Dauray, the longtime pastor of Precious Blood Church. He arrived in Woonsocket in 1875 and set about to establish a model parish. The complex would have a large church, a rectory, convent-school, high school for young women, an orphanage, home for the aged, and an academy for boys. The rank of Pronotary Apostolic was bestowed on Monsignor Dauray in 1929. (Woonsocket Harris Public Library.)

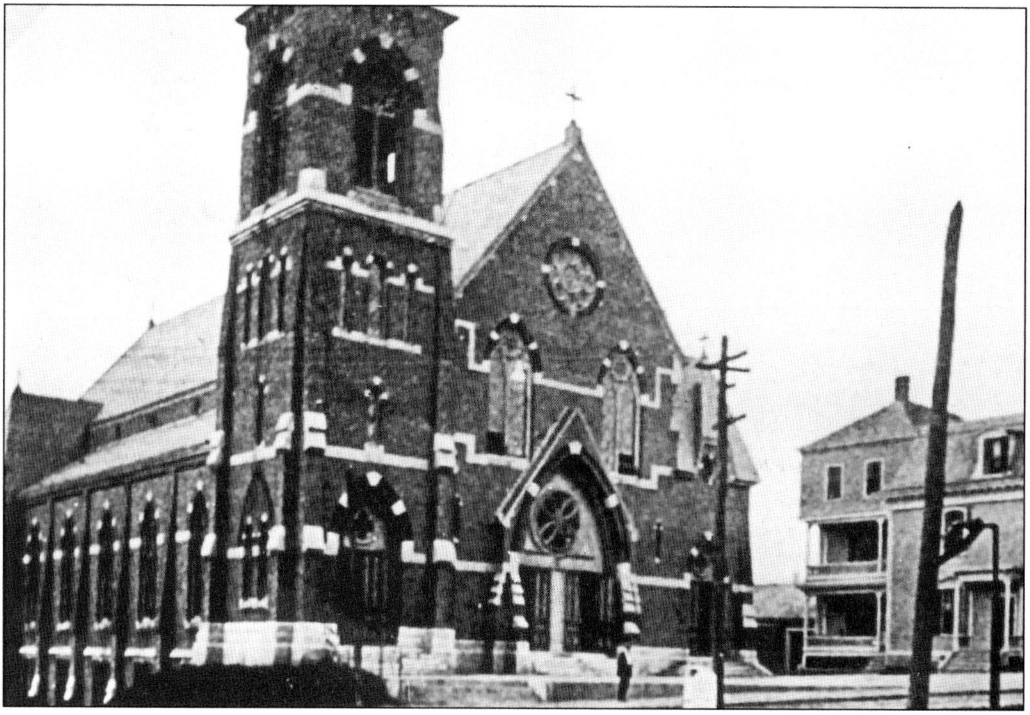

The Church of the Precious Blood on Carrington Avenue, 1900. This parish, organized in 1874, was the first Roman Catholic Church set aside to minister to the French-Canadian population of Woonsocket. The present church, designed by W.F. Fontaine and Sons, was dedicated on July 17, 1881. The rebuilding of the handsome copper-trimmed belfry with its eight-foot gold-leafed cross was completed in 1909. (Woonsocket Harris Public Library.)

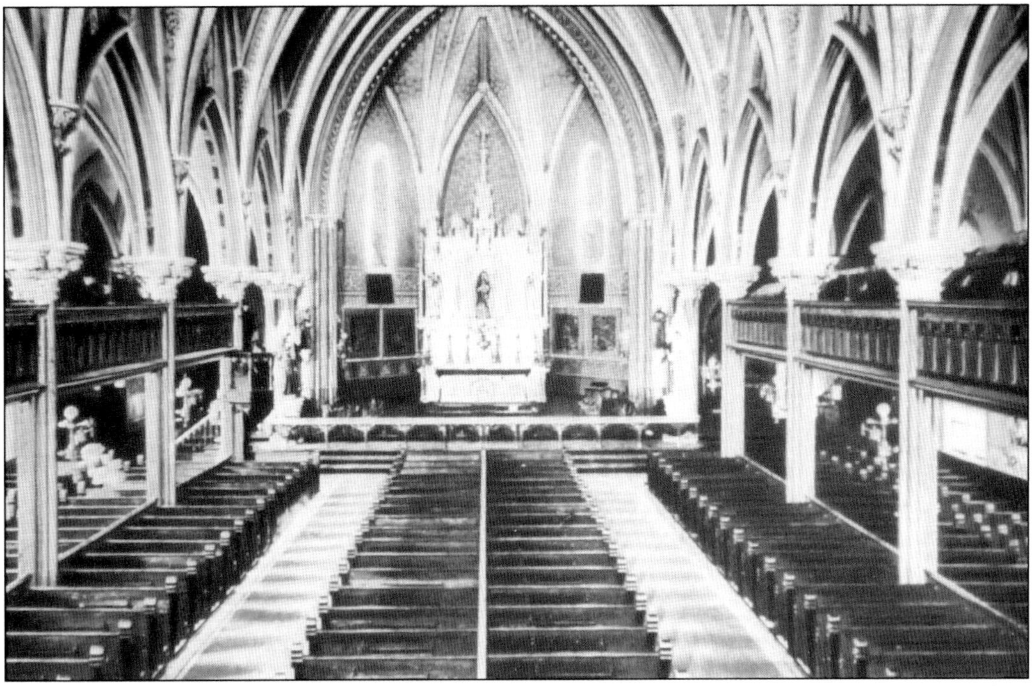

The interior of the Church of the Precious Blood, *c.* 1915. Fine polychrome stenciling ornamented the interior during this time. This is the oldest French-Canadian parish in Woonsocket. (Woonsocket Harris Public Library.)

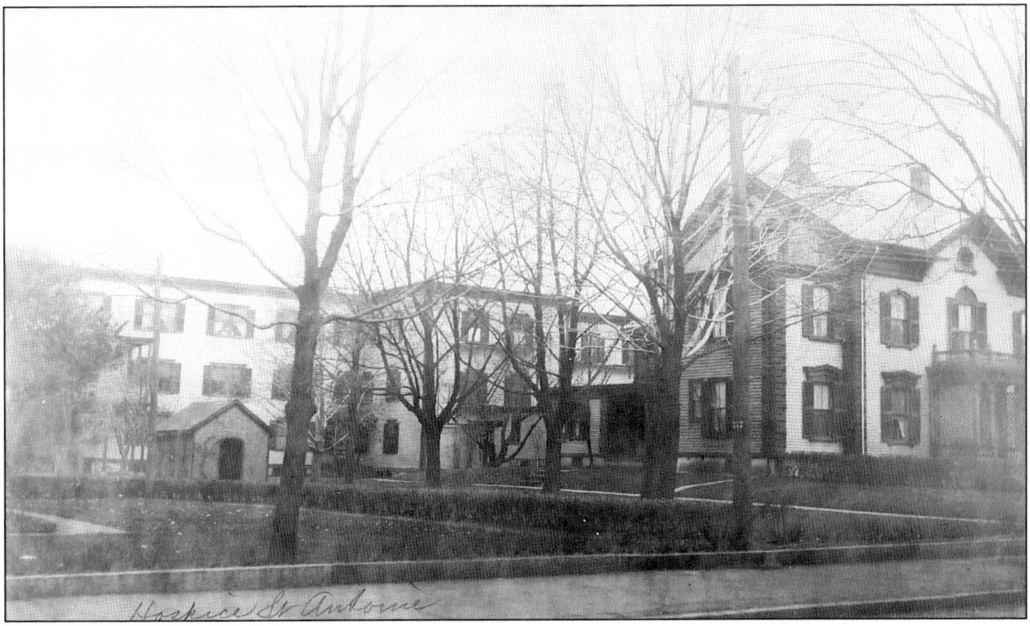

The original L'Hospice Saint Antoine home for the aged on Hamlet Avenue, *c.* 1920. It opened on January 9, 1914, in a remodeled house, as Saint Joseph's Home for the Aged. The Grey Nuns of Saint Hyacinthe, Quebec, staffed the home. The institution eventually became known as L'Hospice Saint-Antoine. In 1941, "L'Hospice" moved to larger and more modern facilities in North Smithfield. (Saint Antoine Residence.)

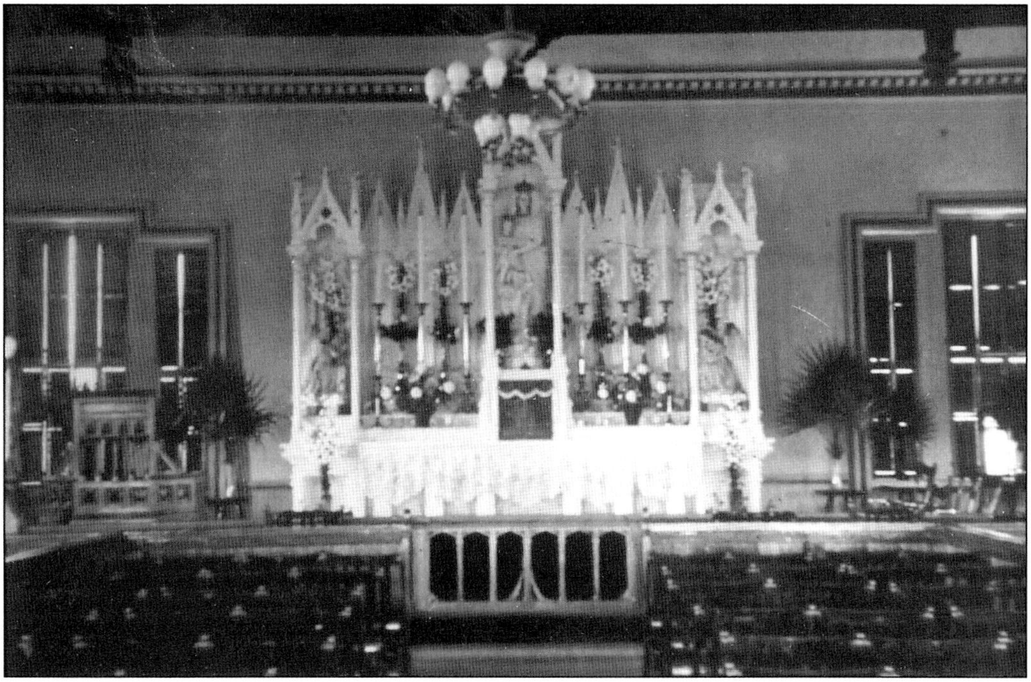

The interior of Our Lady of Victories Church, on Social Street, *c.* 1915. The parish, created in 1909 with the Reverend J.M. Leon Giroux as pastor, rented Social Hall from the Manville Company and later purchased the building in 1910. The former hall, used for religious services, also quartered the clergy and served as a school. Governor Aram J. Pothier donated the main altar pictured. (Woonsocket Harris Public Library.)

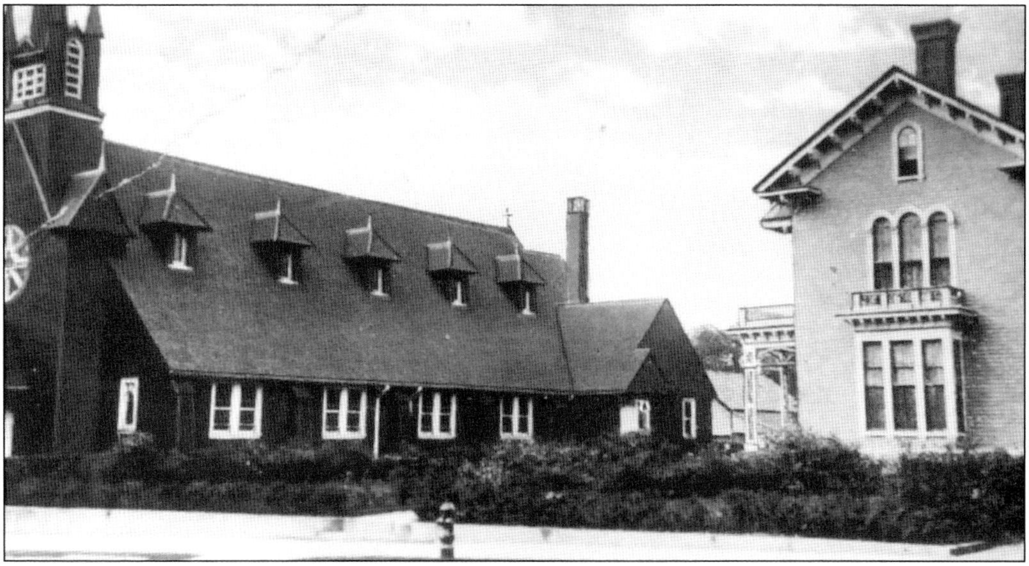

The Saint Stanlislaus Kostka Church and former rectory on Harris Avenue, *c.* 1915. Constructed in 1905 on the former estate of Mayor George Greene, the parish served the Polish population of Woonsocket. There are excellent stenciled decorations that grace the interior. Above the pillars of the nave are portraits of the saints. The rectory pictured is the former home of Mayor Greene. (Woonsocket Harris Public Library.)

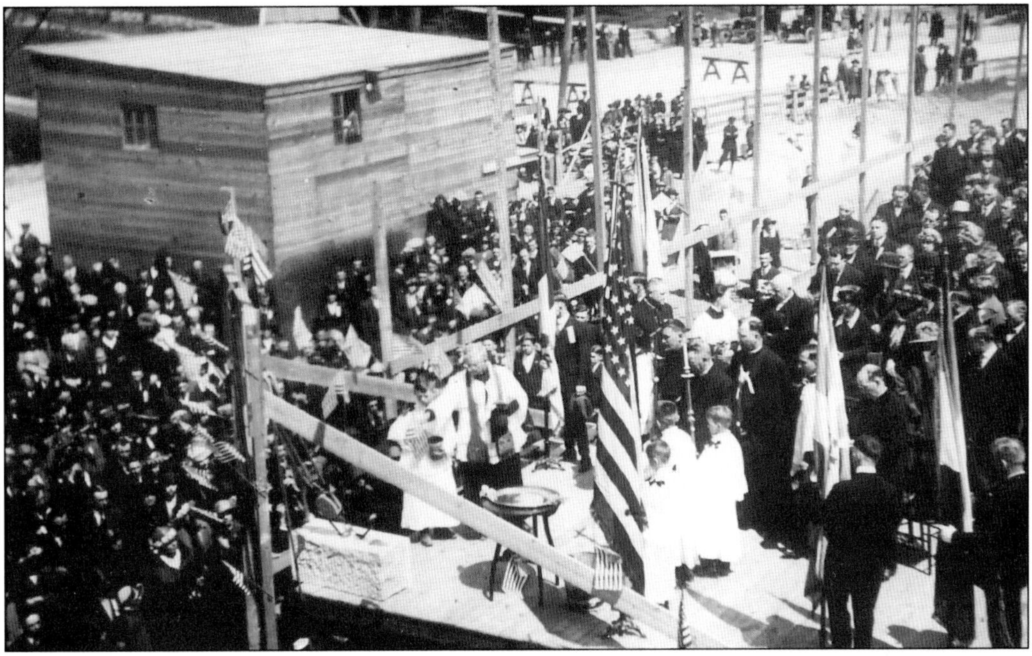

The dedication ceremonies for Saint Louis Church, at the corner of Rathbun and Privilege Streets, in 1957. Established in 1902, the parish took the name of Saint Aloysius De Gonzaga. It was a basement church for fifty-five years until a stone upper church building was dedicated on December 15, 1957. The structure cost $600,000. The parish was the site for Sentinellist meetings during the 1920s. (Woonsocket Harris Public Library.)

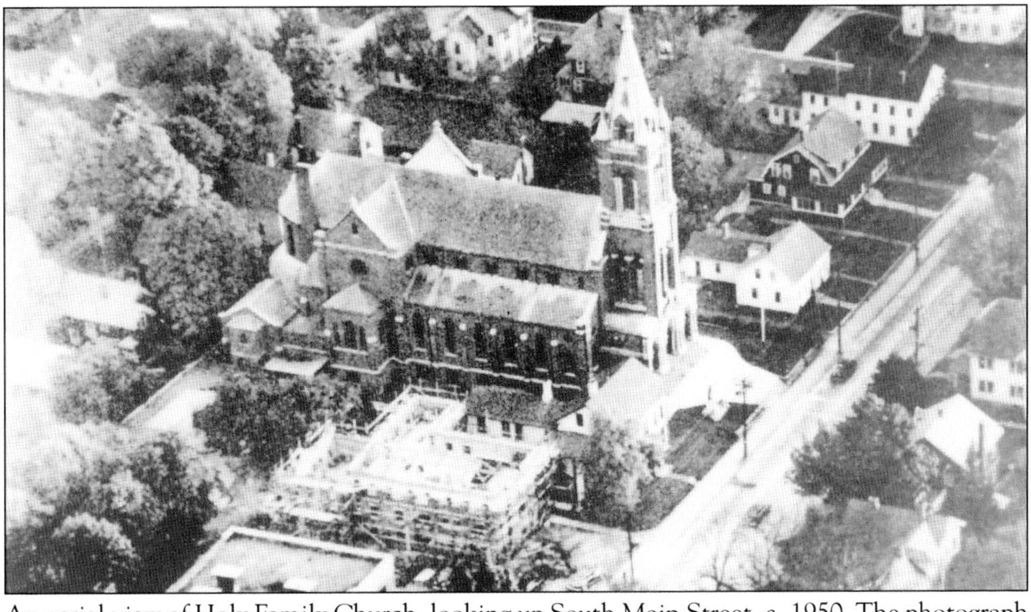

An aerial view of Holy Family Church, looking up South Main Street, c. 1950. The photograph shows the parish complex, including the church, school, and rectory. Designed by Walter Fontaine, construction on the church began in 1909, with formal dedication ceremonies taking place on January 22, 1911. The church has a magnificent polychrome interior. (Woonsocket Harris Public Library.)

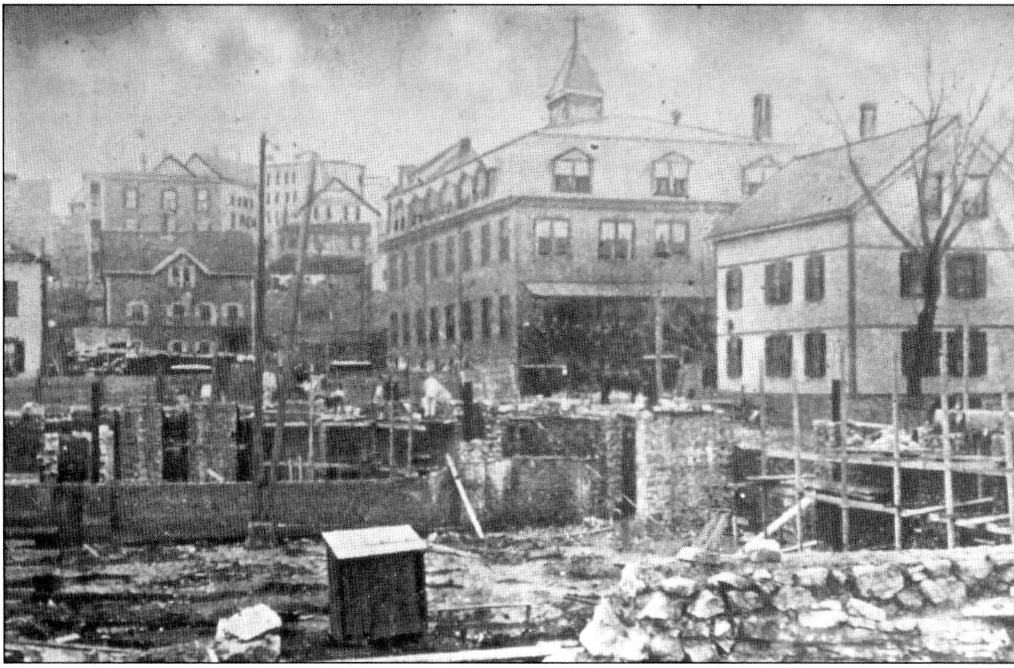

The construction of Saint Ann's Church on Cumberland Street, *c.* 1914. Established in 1890, the parish would have the Reverend Napoleon Leclerc as its first pastor. The architect for Woonsocket's most impressive church was Walter Fontaine. It is a grand, monumental structure, built of yellow brick with twin towers. The original Saint Ann's church-school building on Gaulin Avenue is in the background. (Woonsocket Harris Public Library.)

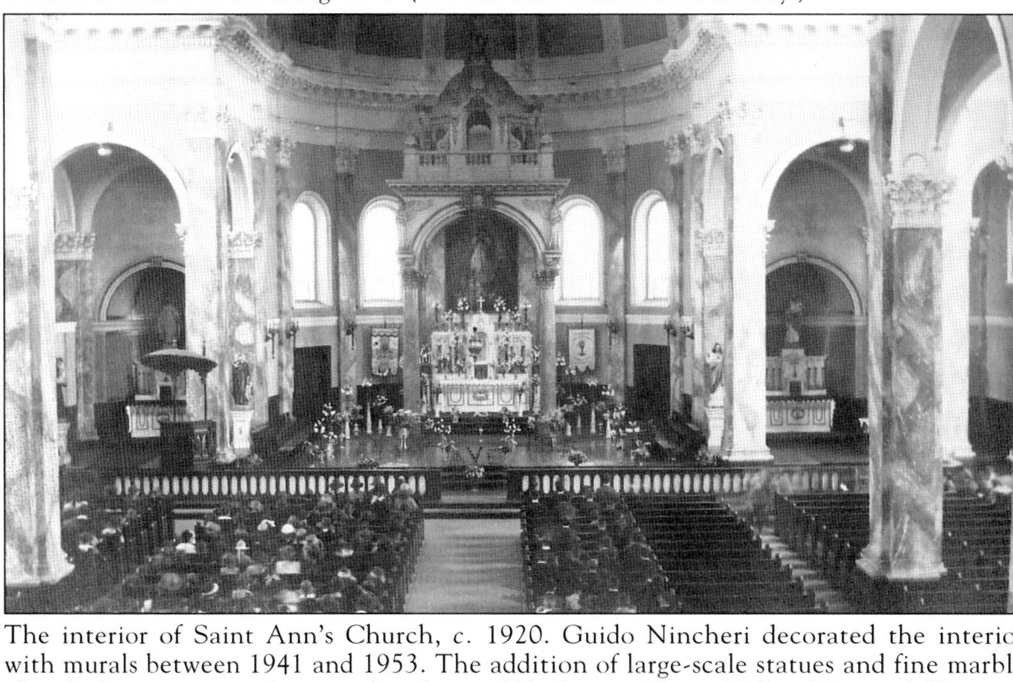

The interior of Saint Ann's Church, *c.* 1920. Guido Nincheri decorated the interior with murals between 1941 and 1953. The addition of large-scale statues and fine marble church furniture complement this decor. (Blackstone River Valley National Heritage Corridor Commission.)

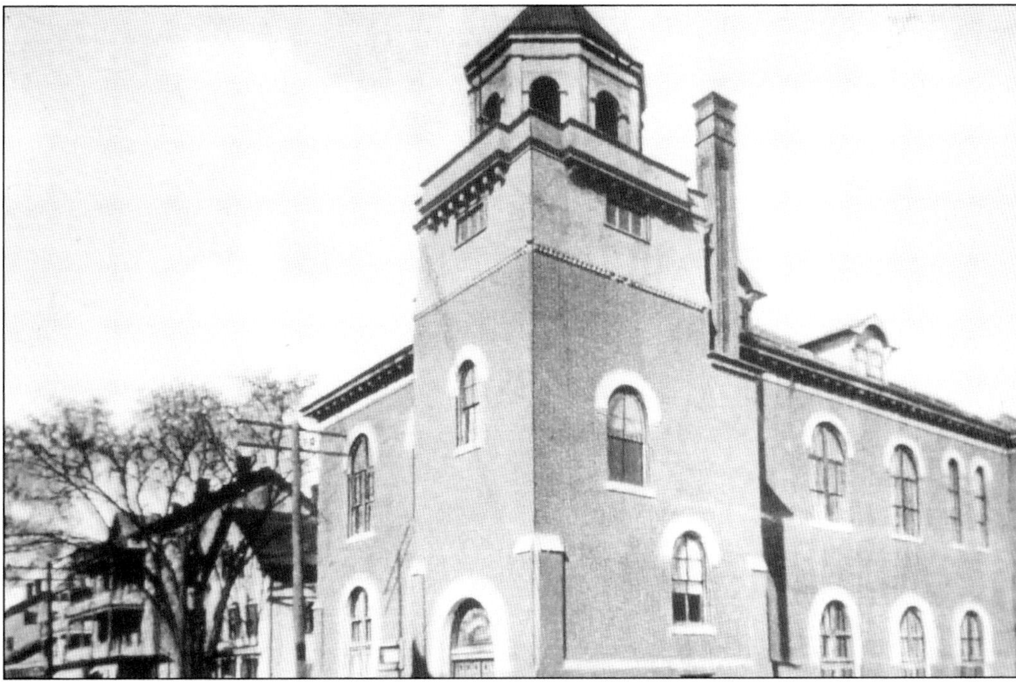

Saint Ann's Gymnasium on Cumberland Street, *c.* 1915. This was the first major commission for architect Walter Fontaine and was built in 1894 in the "Moorish" style. It originally housed a 700-seat theater and a gymnasium. French-Canadians from the Social District flocked here to attend concerts and French language plays, many written by local author Victor Vekeman. Adherents of the Sentinellist movement used the building during the 1920s for speeches and rallies. In 1942 it became the home for the French-Canadian organization, the Club Marquette. The Marquette Credit Union also began here. (Woonsocket Harris Public Library.)

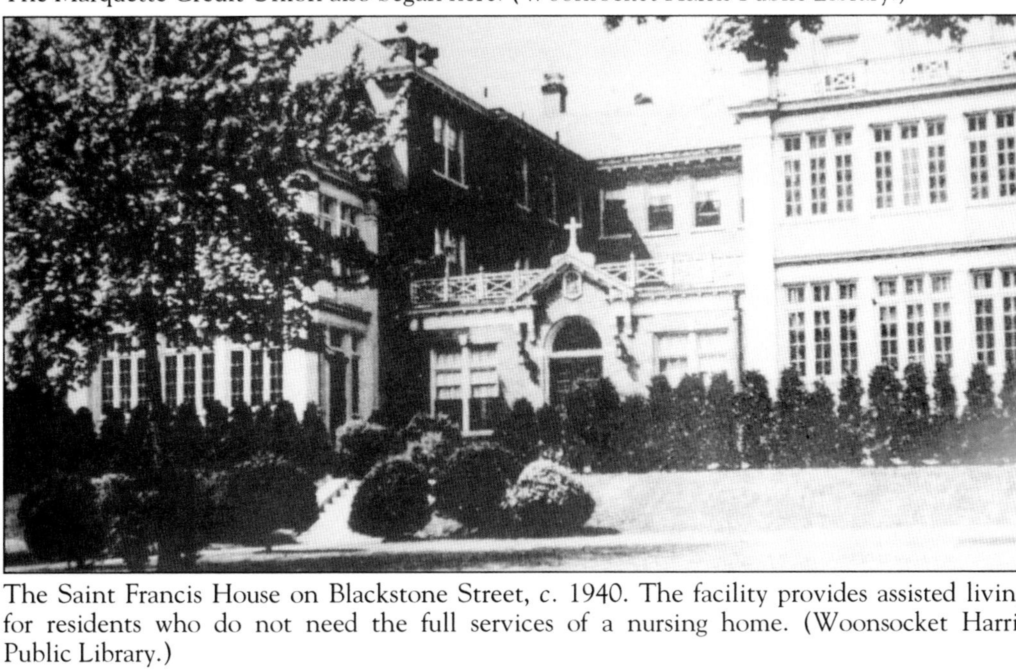

The Saint Francis House on Blackstone Street, *c.* 1940. The facility provides assisted living for residents who do not need the full services of a nursing home. (Woonsocket Harris Public Library.)

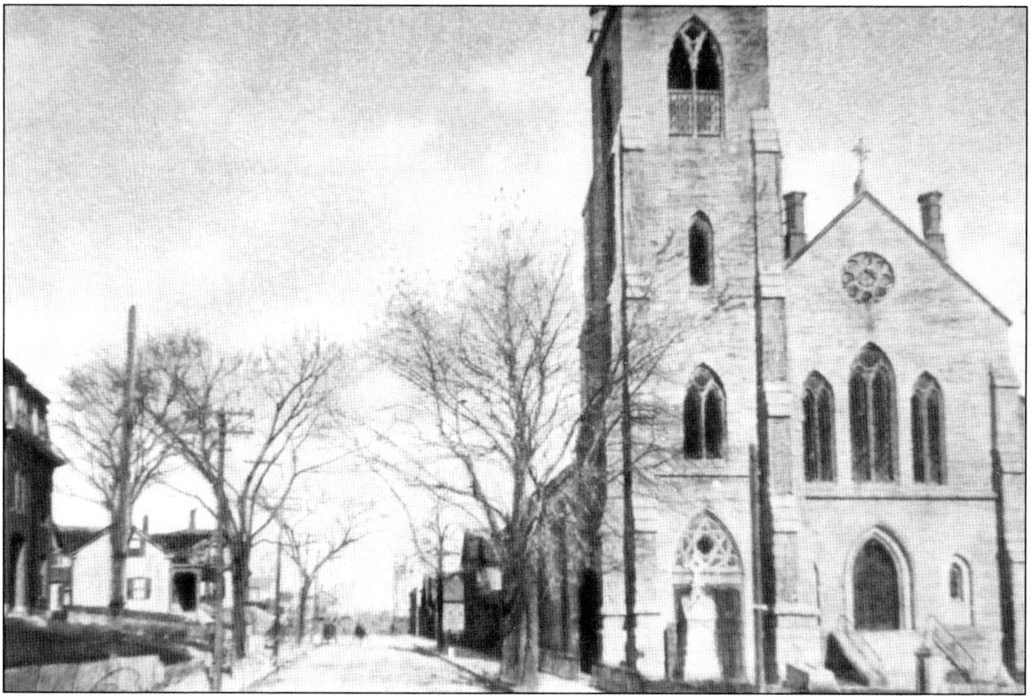

Saint Charles Borromeo Church, looking up North Main Street, *c.* 1915. Designed by P.C. Keeley, a New York architect, and built 1862–71, it is a fine stone Victorian Gothic edifice, which reminds the viewer of "an Irish cathedral." This parish, established in 1846, was Woonsocket's first Roman Catholic church. The rectory (above left) was built *c.* 1865, and is a two-and-one-half-story brick mansard-roofed structure. (Woonsocket Harris Public Library.)

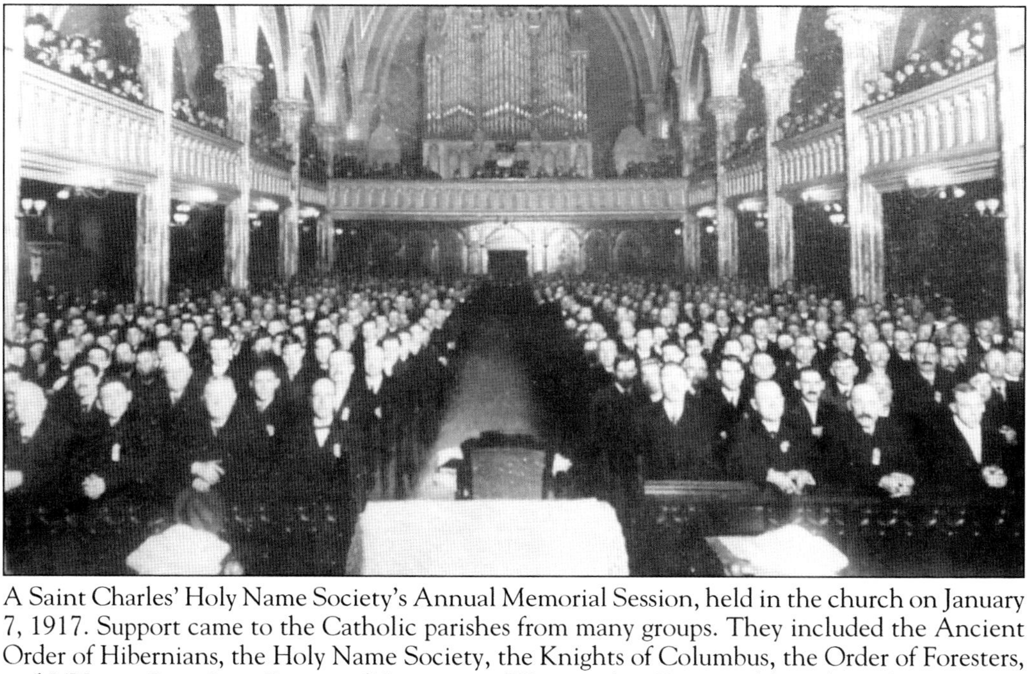

A Saint Charles' Holy Name Society's Annual Memorial Session, held in the church on January 7, 1917. Support came to the Catholic parishes from many groups. They included the Ancient Order of Hibernians, the Holy Name Society, the Knights of Columbus, the Order of Foresters, and L'Union Saint Jean Baptiste d'Amerique. (Woonsocket Harris Public Library.)

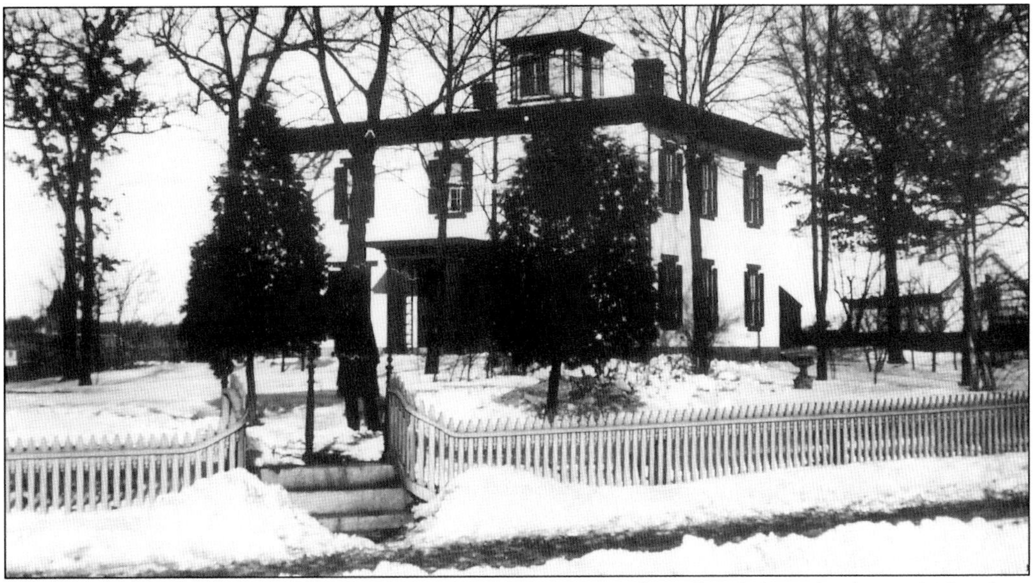

The Hebrew Free School on Hamlet Avenue, *c.* 1920s. The school dates back to 1919, when Rabbi Phineas Israeli established the school. Rabbi Israeli was New England's first Orthodox English-speaking rabbi. Solomon Trietel, considered Woonsocket's first Jewish immigrant, arrived in 1866 and established himself at Market Square as a clothier. The 1880s saw an increase in the number of Jewish immigrants into the city. By 1893, steps to form a congregation were underway. (Woonsocket Harris Public Library.)

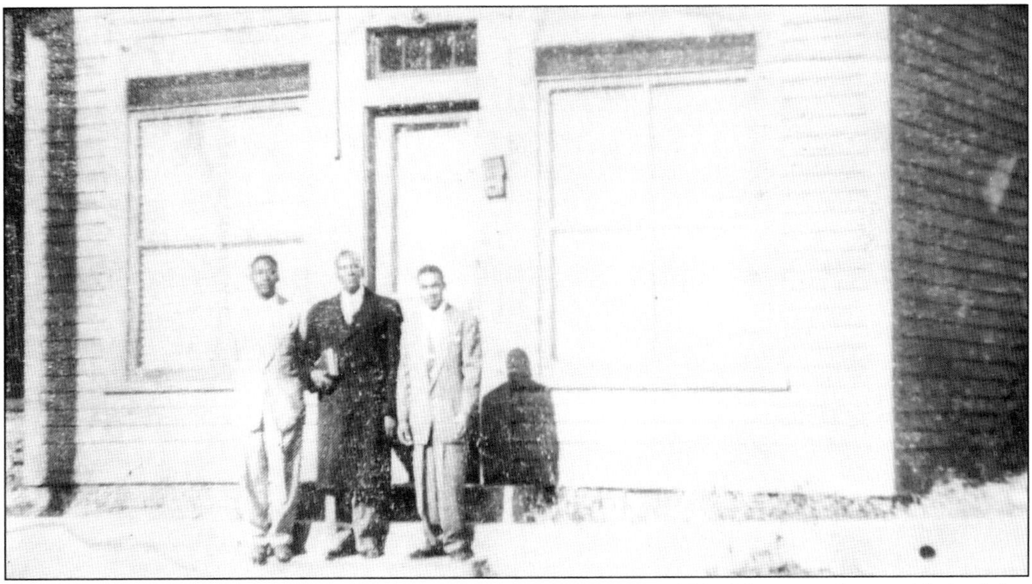

The Saint James Baptist Church, at 217 River Street, *c.* 1953. This parish, established for Woonsocket's African-American community, had as its founding pastor the Reverend James Wesley Hinson. Their first worship service took place on November 28, 1953, in this building. The parish soon outgrew its first church, and they moved to the Baker Estate, at the corner of Prospect and Winter Streets. In 1956 they purchased the former Presbyterian church at the corner of Blackstone and Spring Streets. Today the congregation worships at the former Globe Congregation Church that they now own. (Woonsocket Harris Public Library.)

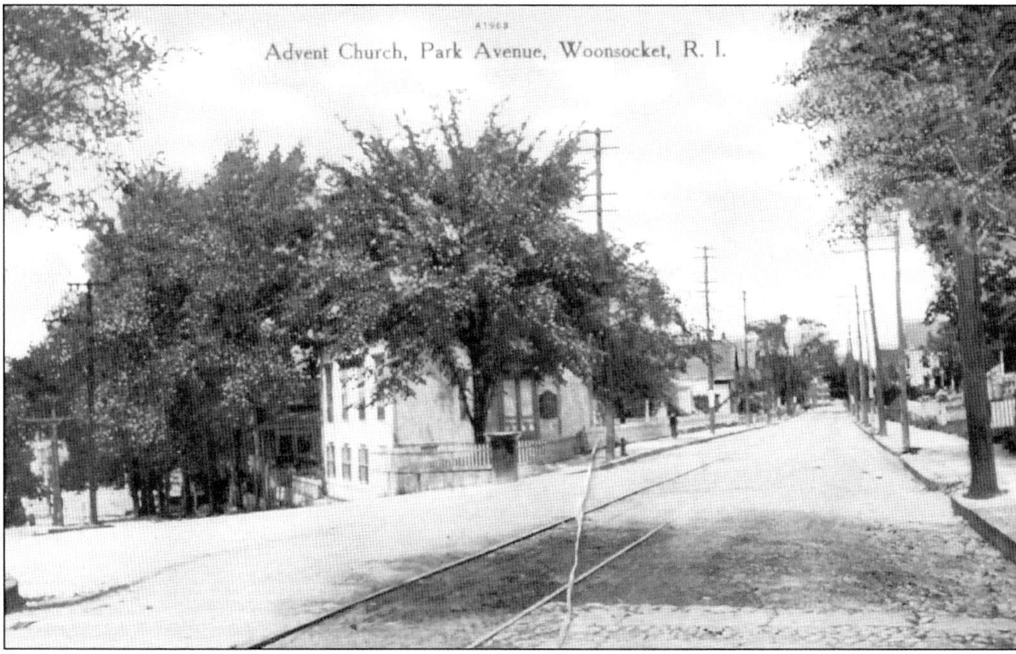

The former Advent Church, at the corner of Park Avenue and Greene Street, *c.* 1900. This chapel experienced a devastating fire on February 24, 1901. (Mr. and Mrs. Robert C. Brin.)

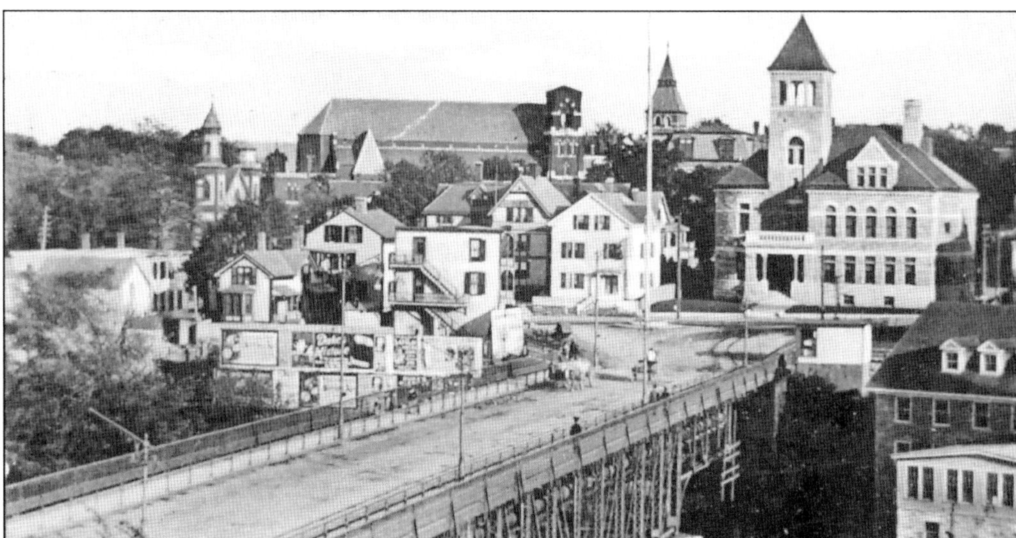

The Court Street Bridge and area around Hamlet Avenue, *c.* 1905. At left is the Saint James Episcopal Church, founded in 1832. At center left is the Church of the Precious Blood, constructed in 1881, which is the oldest French-Canadian church in Woonsocket. To the right are the former Saint Clare High School and Convent of Jesus Marie. This complex, built in 1889 with later additions, was a major Woonsocket educational institution. The Woonsocket Court House, seen at right, was constructed in 1896 and served the State Superior, Family, and District courts. (Mr. and Mrs. Robert C. Brin.)

Seven

Workers on the Move

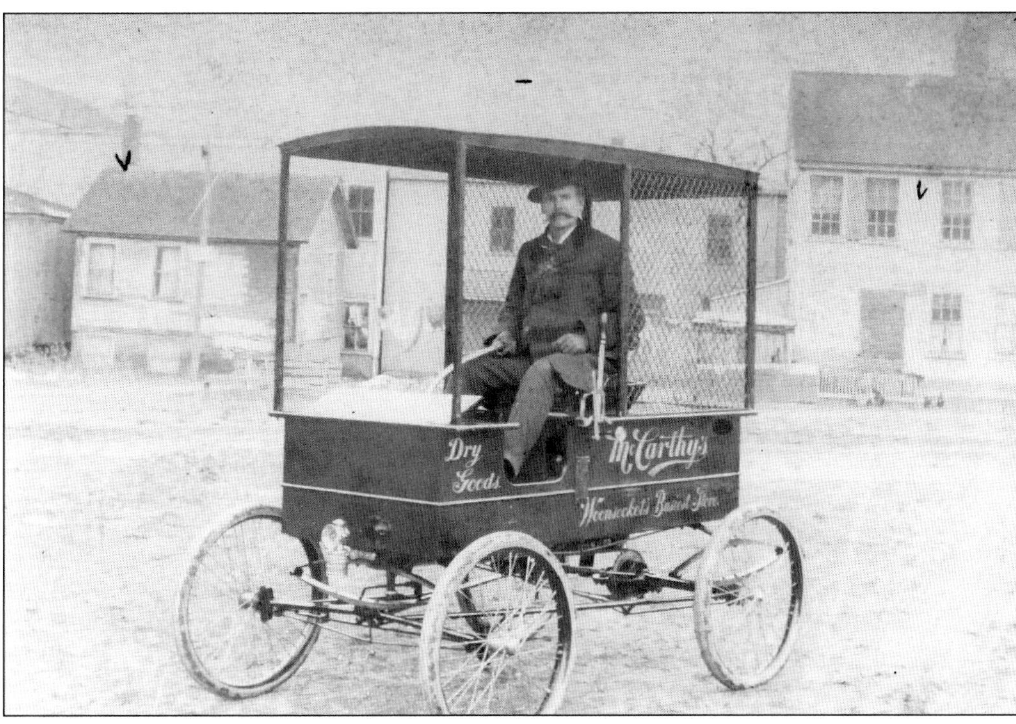

McCarthy's first delivery wagon, which operated by electric power, c. 1900. The McCarthy Dry Goods Company was founded in 1889 by James M. McCarthy. In 1914 he opened a new six-floor department store at Depot Square. (Woonsocket Harris Public Library.)

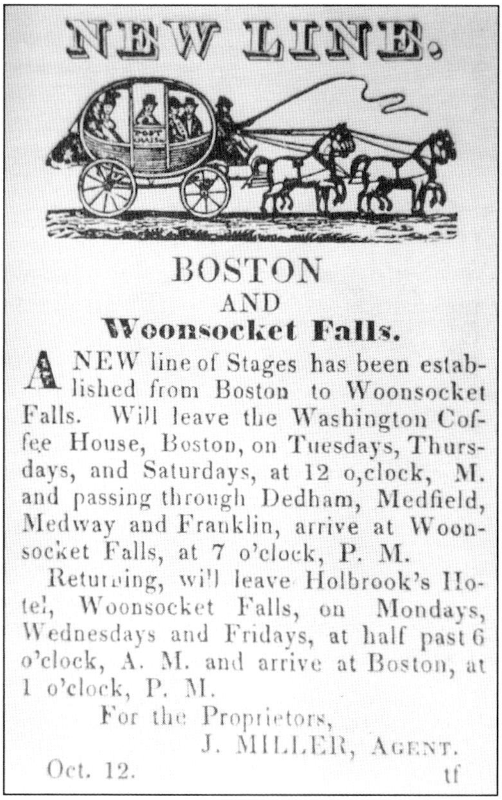

NEW LINE.

BOSTON
AND
Woonsocket Falls.

A NEW line of Stages has been established from Boston to Woonsocket Falls. Will leave the Washington Coffee House, Boston, on Tuesdays, Thursdays, and Saturdays, at 12 o,clock, M. and passing through Dedham, Medfield, Medway and Franklin, arrive at Woonsocket Falls, at 7 o'clock, P. M.

Returning, will leave Holbrook's Hotel, Woonsocket Falls, on Mondays, Wednesdays and Fridays, at half past 6 o'clock, A. M. and arrive at Boston, at 1 o'clock, P. M.

For the Proprietors,
J. MILLER, AGENT.

Oct. 12. tf

An 1833 advertisement for the new Boston and Woonsocket Falls Stagecoach line from *The Woonsocket Patriot*. Woonsocket Falls, in the early eighteenth century, was on a crossroad along the Colonial highway system, which included the Great Road and Mendon Road. By the mid-eighteenth century, the Blackstone River was being crossed at Woonsocket Falls by a highway that connected northeastern Connecticut to Boston. (Woonsocket Harris Public Library.)

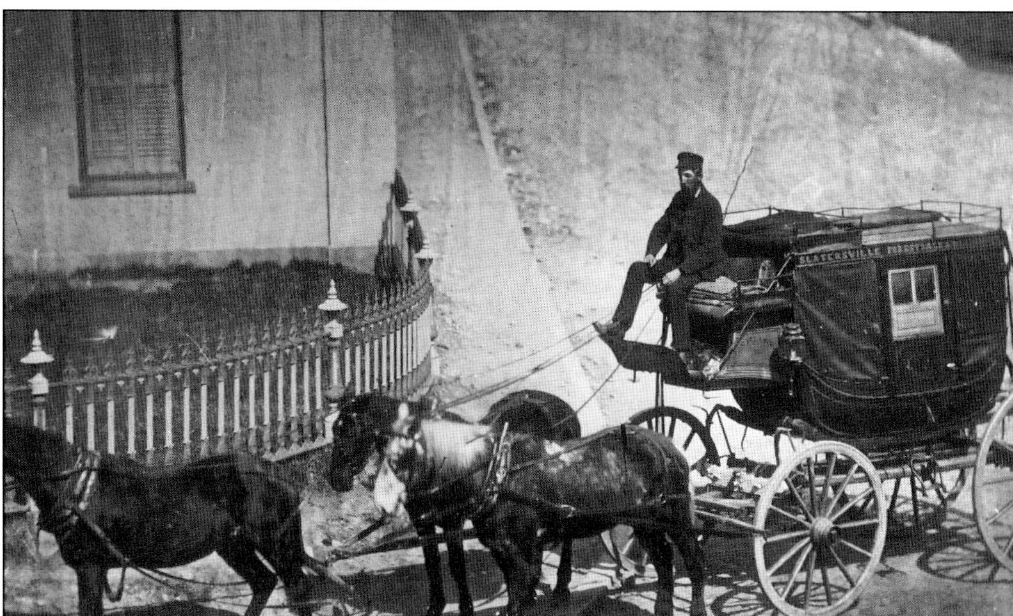

A stagecoach at Depot Square, *c.* 1860. This old coach of the Slatersville, Forestdale, and Woonsocket line is at the corner of Main and High Streets. Part of the original First Baptist Church is at upper left. (Woonsocket Harris Public Library.)

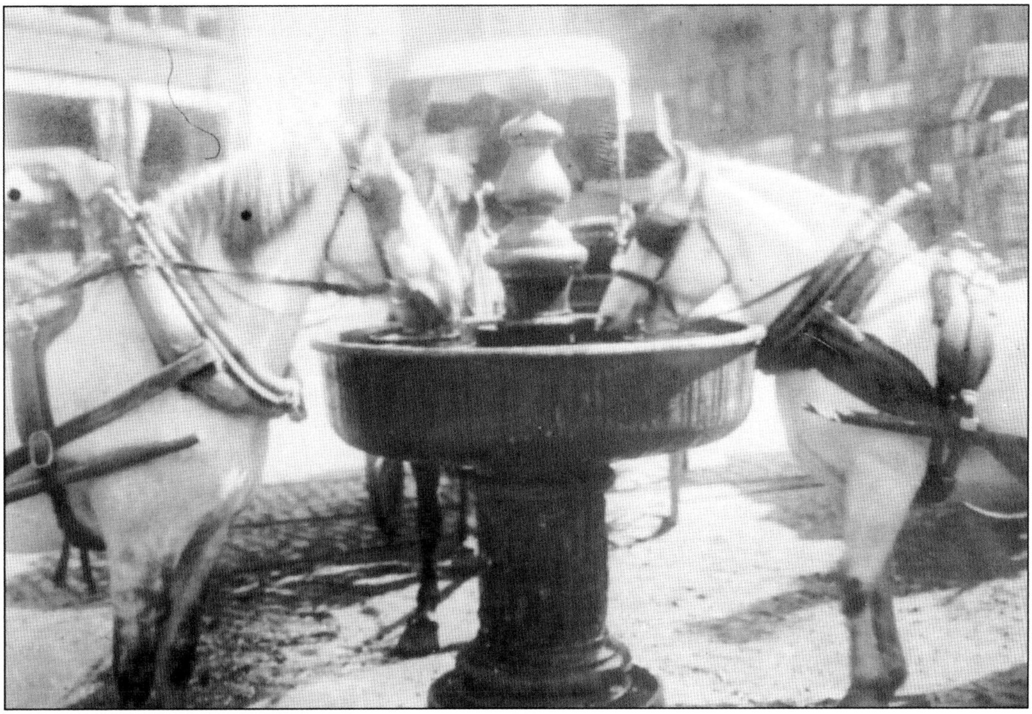

A water trough for horses, photographed *c.* 1900. In the age of the "horse and buggy," it was a common sight to see "beasts of burden" refreshing themselves at troughs similar to this one. (Woonsocket Harris Public Library.)

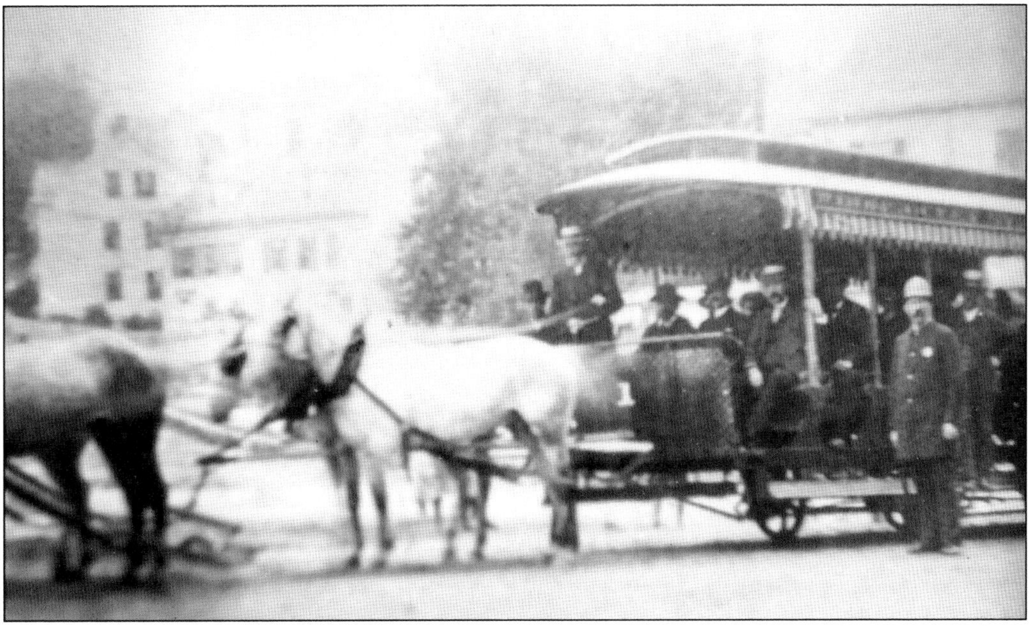

The first run of a horsecar in Woonsocket, August 14, 1887. The initial route was from Monument Square to South Main Street. In trial runs it took a team of four horses nineteen minutes to complete. The first day of operation saw 638 passengers pay 5¢ to ride this new form of "mass transit." (Woonsocket Harris Public Library.)

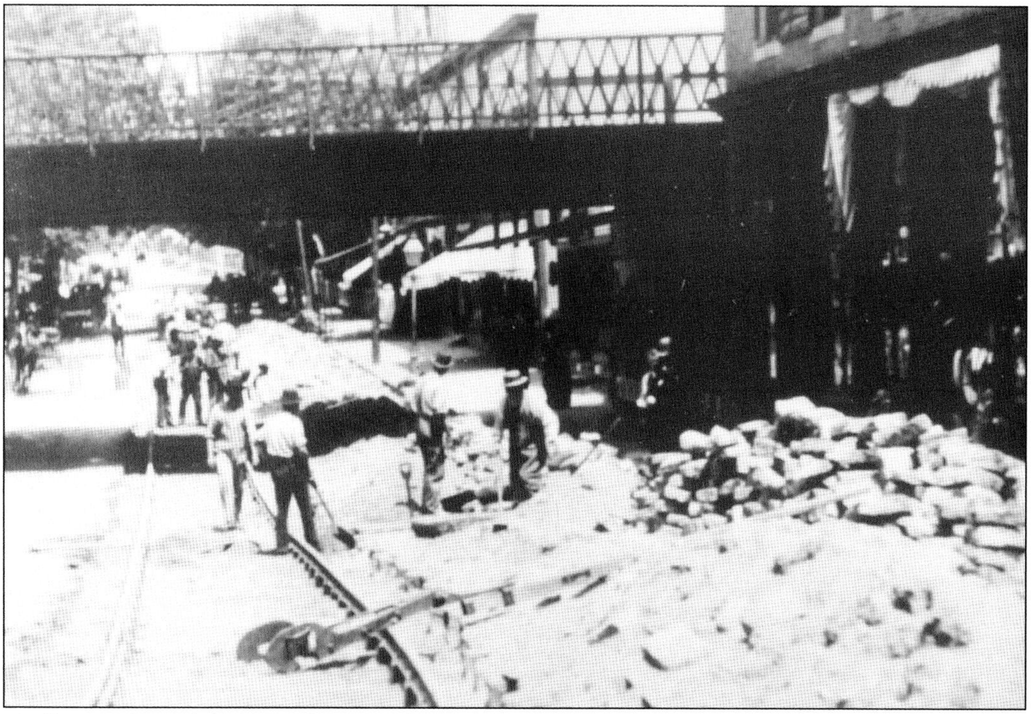

Trolley tracks and the Providence and Worcester Railroad Bridge on Main Street in 1887. The Woonsocket Street Railway Company's original route from Monument Square to South Main Street would eventually extend 6 miles by 1889. (Woonsocket Harris Public Library.)

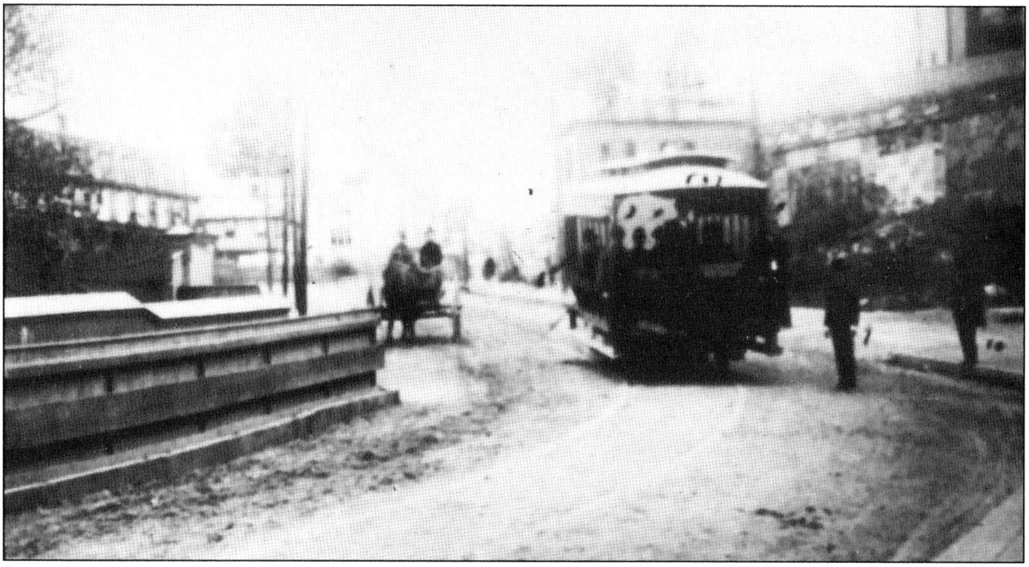

Rhode Island's first electric trolley on Globe Bridge, South Main Street, photographed in 1887. The Woonsocket Street Railway Company equipped a small horsecar with an electric motor that drew its power from overhanging wires. The experiment would run a distance of five-sixths of a mile from Market Square, up South Main Street, to Shove Street. After trial runs, and concerns from company engineers, the city's fire department, and the telephone company, the street railway continued with horse-drawn cars. (Woonsocket Harris Public Library.)

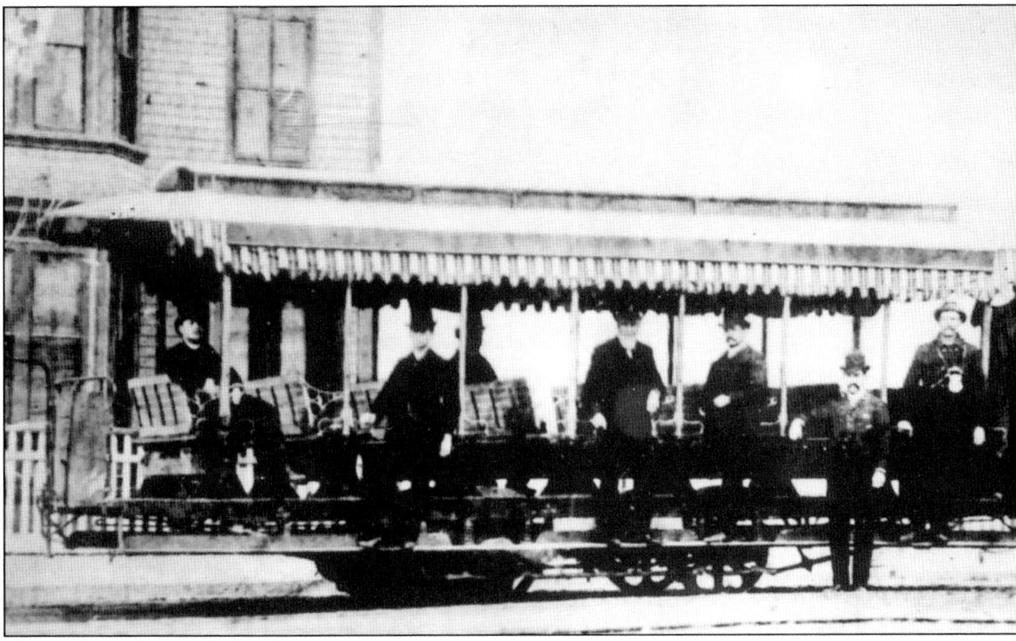

A view of Woonsocket's first electric street railway car, *c.* 1887. Residents of Woonsocket viewed these initial experiments in electrification as a novelty and a "wonder." Few people considered this a serious means of transportation and many thought it would be "an absurd failure." (Woonsocket Harris Public Library.)

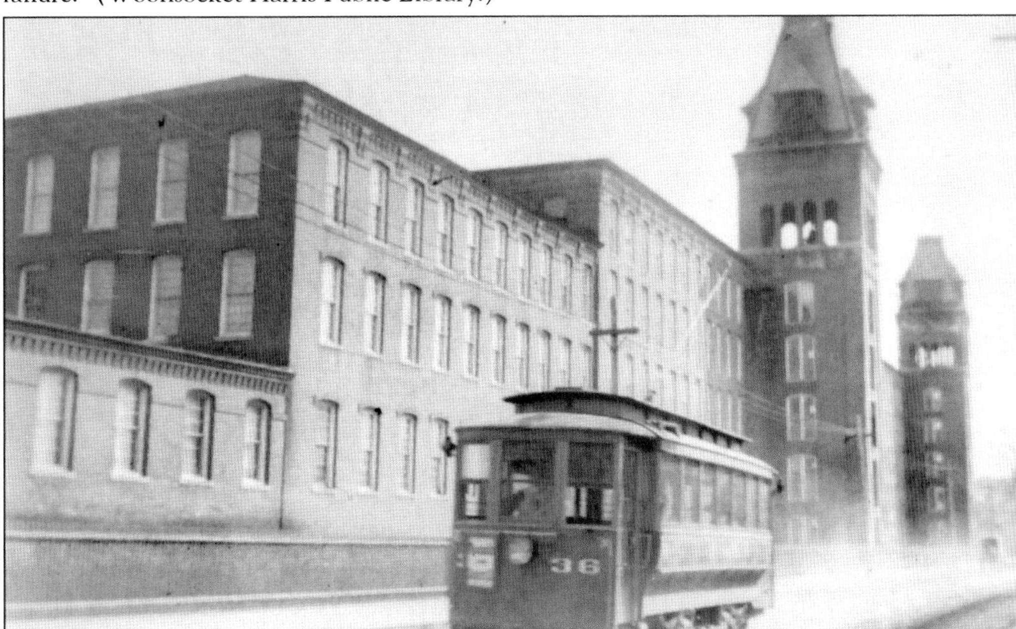

A trolley on Social Street heading toward Monument Square *c.* 1900. By 1906, the Woonsocket Street Railway Company had 22.8 miles of track in Woonsocket and in nearby towns. Trolleys allowed workers to work in one neighborhood or village and live in another. In the background is the huge Social Mill, incorporated in 1810, which grew and expanded until it closed in 1927. (Woonsocket Harris Public Library.)

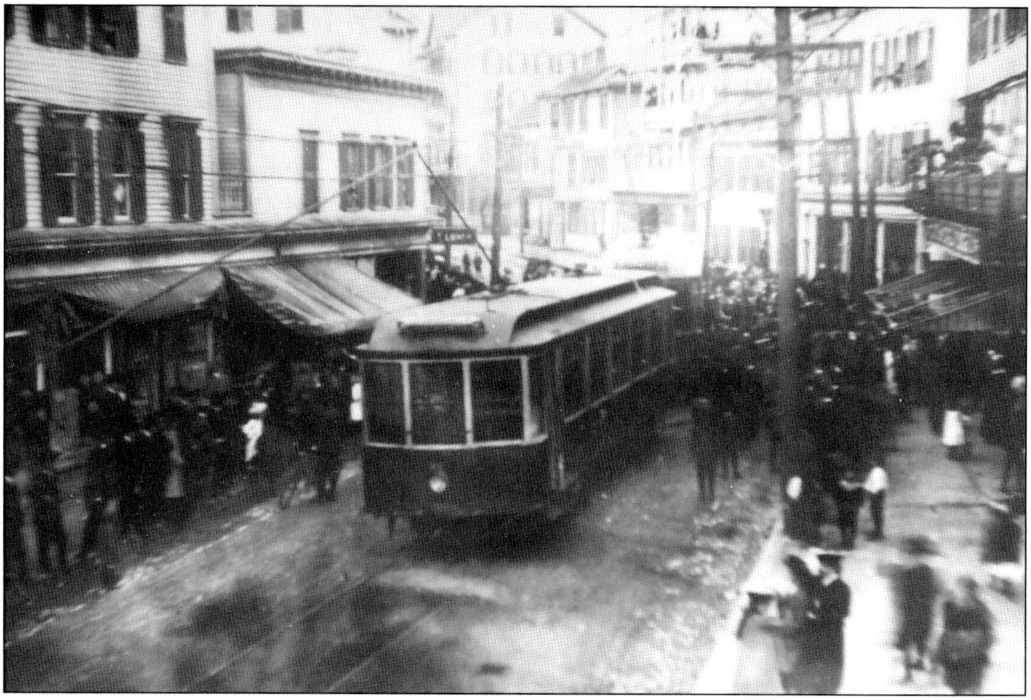

A trolley car collision on Social Street, *c.* 1908. All the major streets of Woonsocket had trolley lines by 1906. There were also more than 70 miles of tracks that emanated from the city. Workers could work in one section of the city and live in another because the trolley service was convenient and inexpensive. (Woonsocket Harris Public Library.)

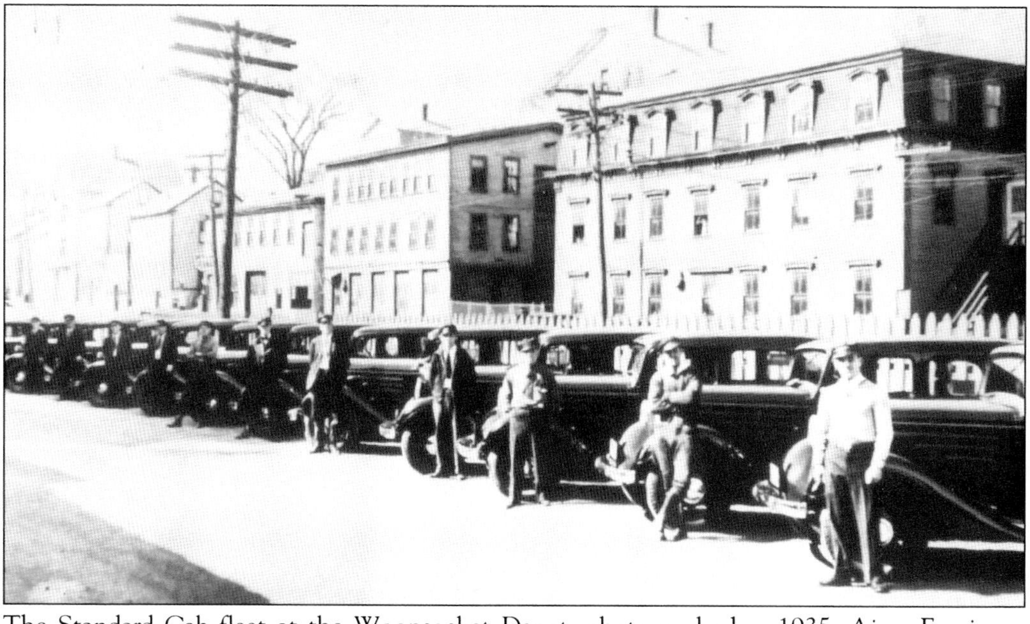

The Standard Cab fleet at the Woonsocket Depot, photographed *c.* 1935. Aime Forcier, a local resident, operated Woonsocket's first motorized taxicab in 1909. His cab was a Chalmers Detroit model with parking lamps that burned carbide gas. Fifty cents was the maximum fare. (Woonsocket Harris Public Library.)

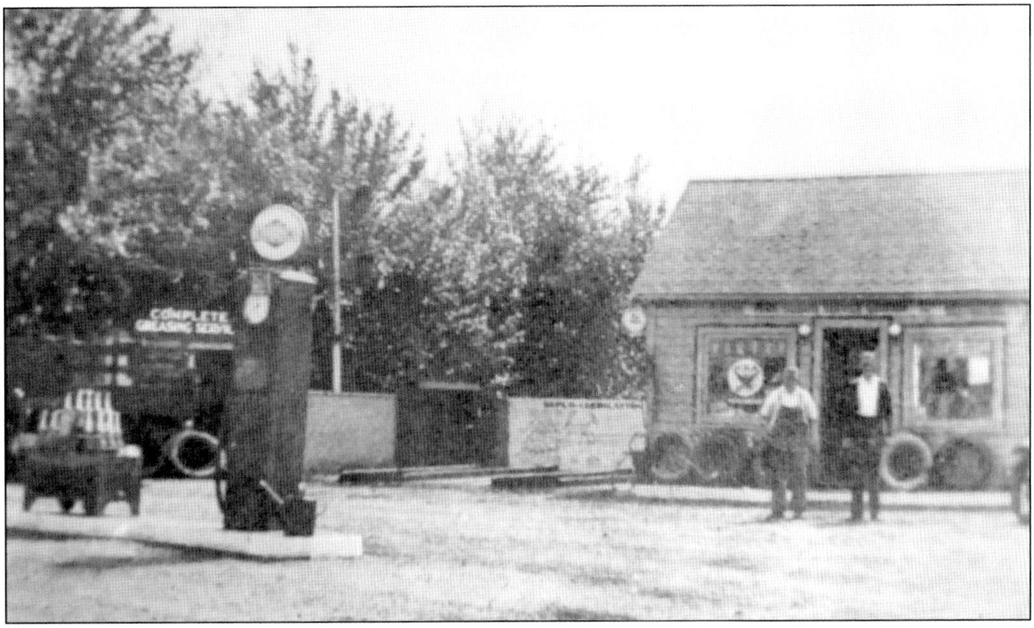

The Park Square Service Station, *c.* 1930s. Automobiles were commonplace on Woonsocket's streets beginning in the 1920s. It was also during this decade that service stations, similar to the one in this scene, could be found throughout the city's neighborhoods. (Woonsocket Harris Public Library.)

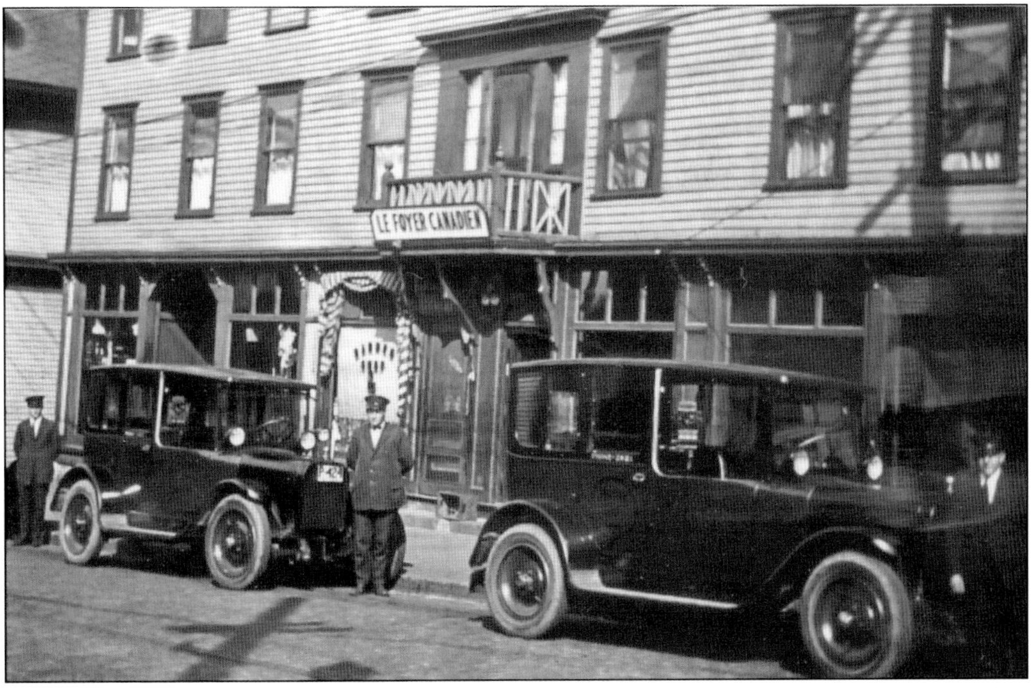

A Charles S. Lawton photograph of the fleet of the Yellow Cab Company, *c.* 1920. Arthur Legare operated this fleet from his headquarters at Nine Social Street. Le Foyer Canadien, at Five Social Street, is in the background. Eugenie Lizotte also operated a boarding and rooming house at this location. (Woonsocket Harris Public Library.)

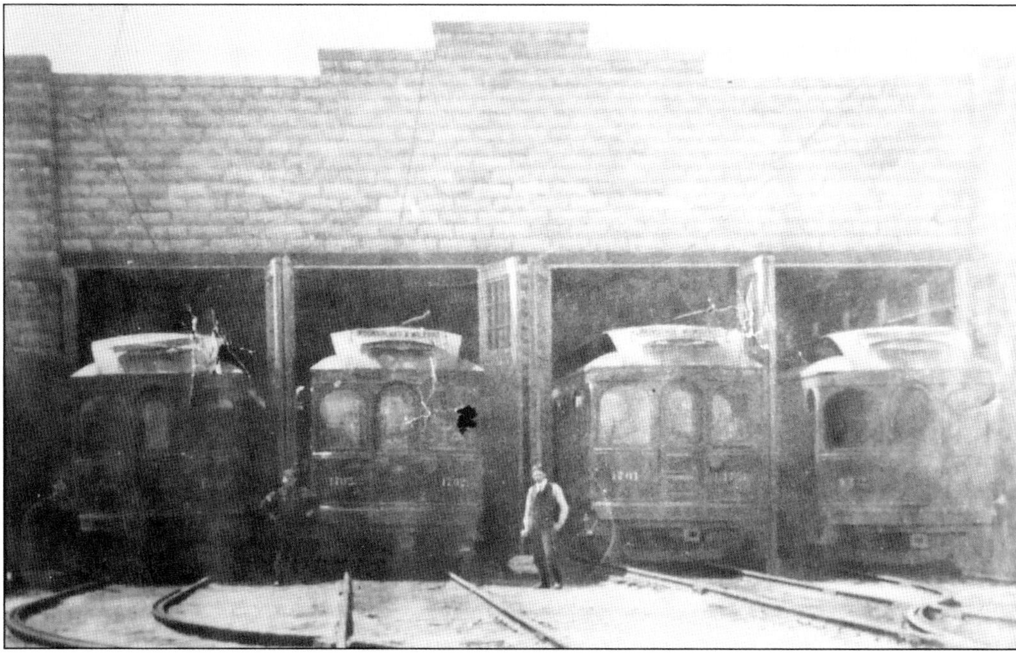

The car house of the Providence and Burrillville Street Railway at Park Square, constructed in 1905. At the time of this photograph, *c.* 1910, the company was part of the Woonsocket Division of the Rhode Island Company. Inside the car house are a few of the Rhode Island Company's 1700 series trolley cars. (Woonsocket Harris Public Library.)

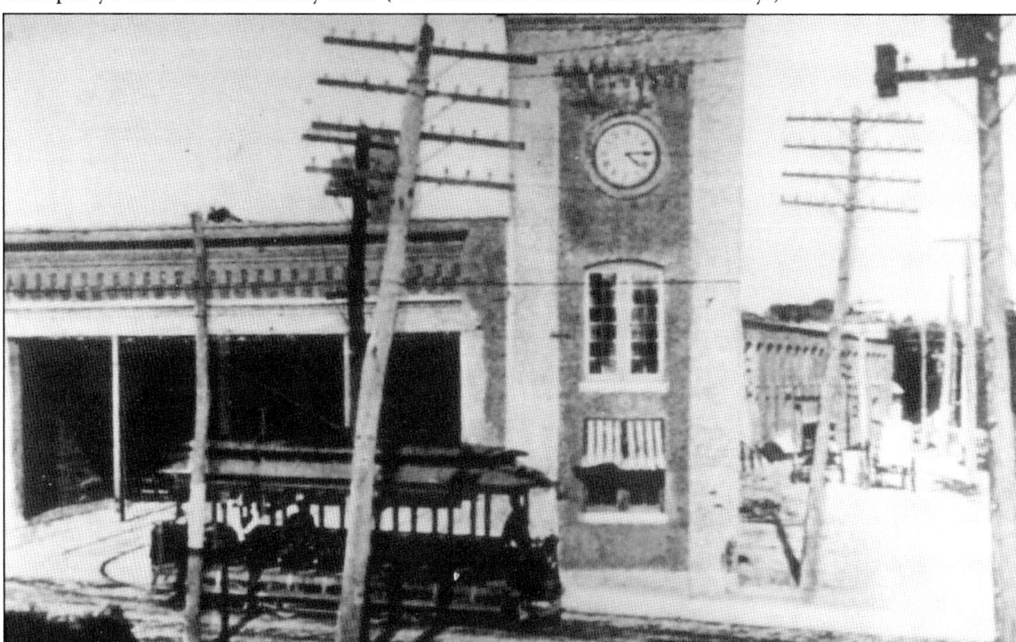

The carbarn at the corner of Social Street and Diamond Hill Road, *c.* 1900. The street railways allowed the average worker the opportunity to travel some distance from home. Resorts and amusement parks were some favorite destinations for workers during their precious leisure hours. (Woonsocket Harris Public Library.)

Eight

When Working Waters Rage

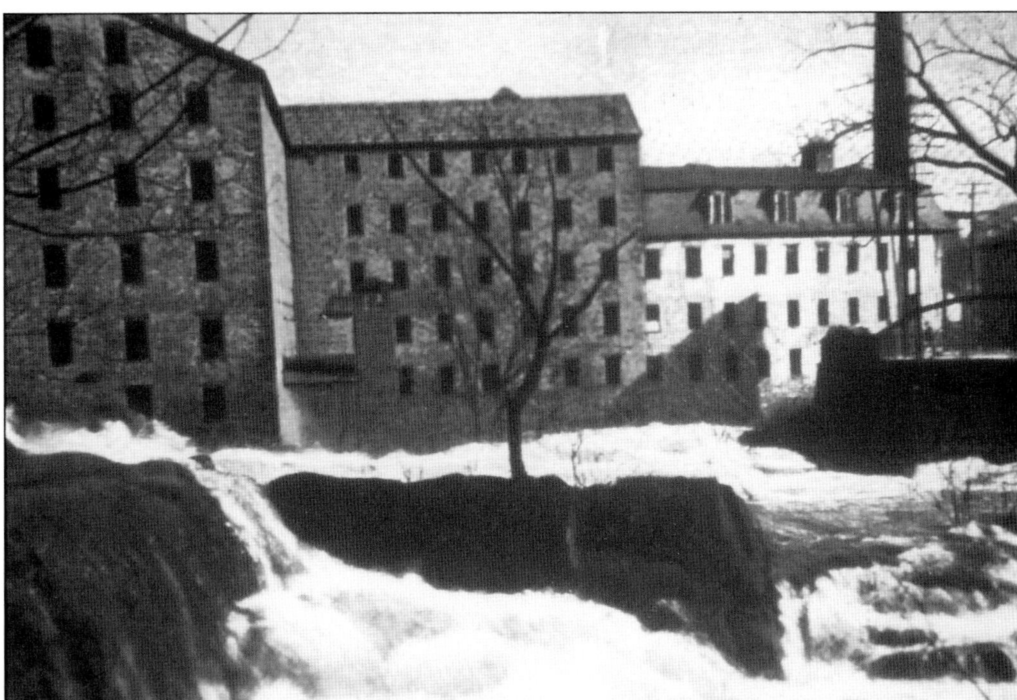

Woonsocket Falls and the mills at Market Square during a raging Blackstone River, *c*. 1900. Woonsocket has seen the wrath of "mother nature" often. A "freshet" struck in 1807, flood waters caused extensive damage to mills in 1886, and four major floods caused property losses between 1927 and 1939. The greatest natural disaster was the flood of 1955.

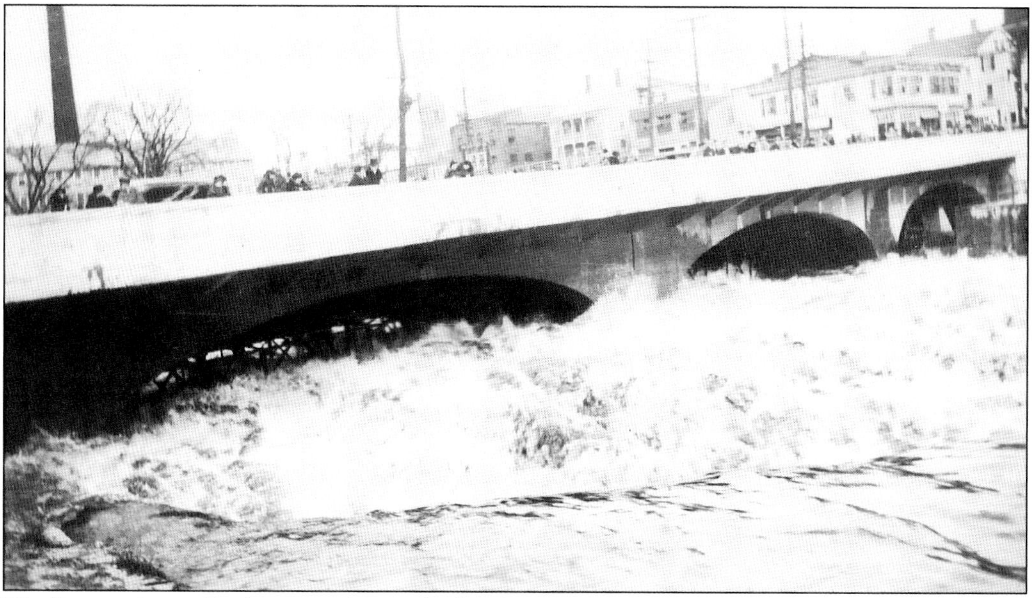

The Bernon Street Bridge, seen during the flood of 1938. Constructed in 1912, the Bernon Street Bridge was a graceful reinforced concrete span that withstood the pounding of the Blackstone River. The hurricane struck Rhode Island on September 21, 1938. Woonsocket's damage occurred due to hurricane force winds and flood waters. (Mr. and Mrs. George E. Brin.)

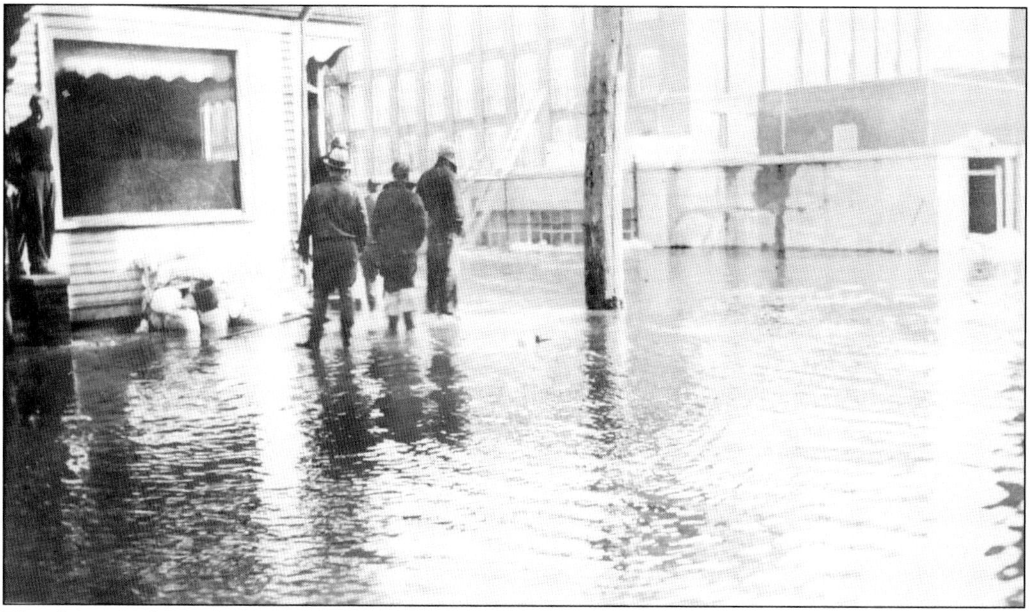

Flood waters from the Hurricane of 1938, seen at the corner of Fairmount and Water Streets. The mill in the background is the former Desurmont Worsted Yarn Mills, built in 1907. This overwhelming four-story brick mill received flood damage on its lower floors. (Mr. and Mrs. George E. Brin.)

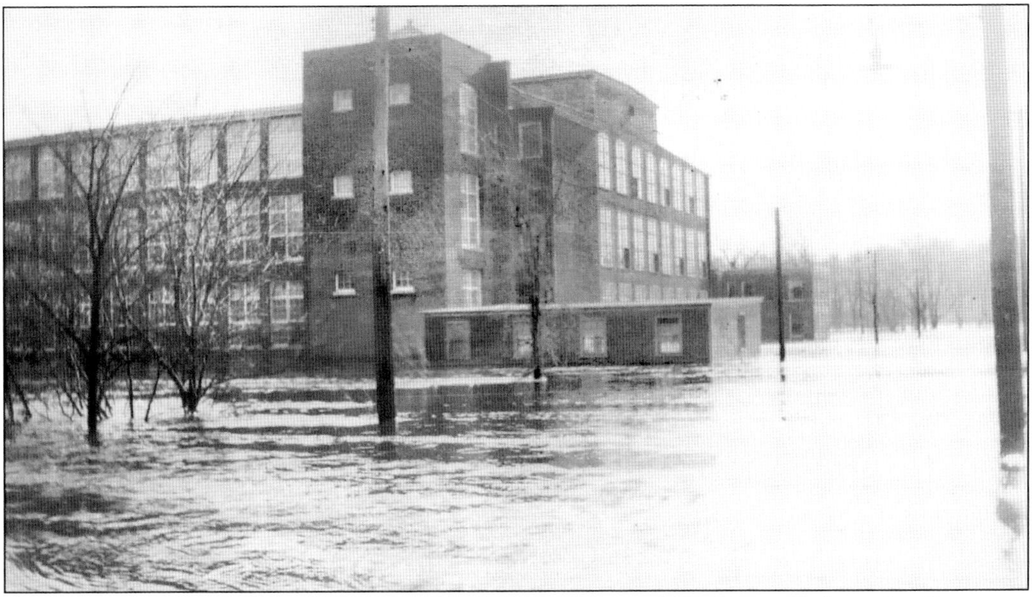

The former Samoset Worsted Mills on Singleton Street, with flood waters from the Hurricane of 1938. This three-story factory, built *c.* 1911, is an example of the last flowering of textile mill construction in Woonsocket. The mill employed more than three hundred persons. (Mr. and Mrs. George E. Brin.)

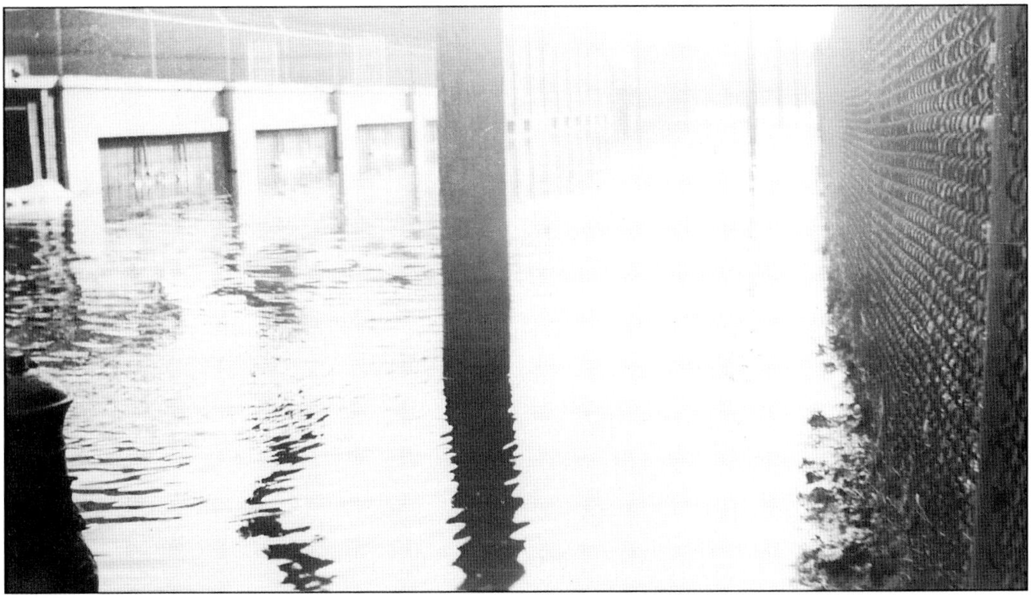

Fairmount Street during the Hurricane of 1938. Woonsocket experienced extensive wind damage including the loss of old and stately trees, snapped power and telephone lines, and many broken window panes and business display windows. Mills suffered roof damage, especially the Lafayette Worsted Company and the Alice Mill of the United States Rubber Company on Fairmount Street. (Mr. and Mrs. George E. Brin.)

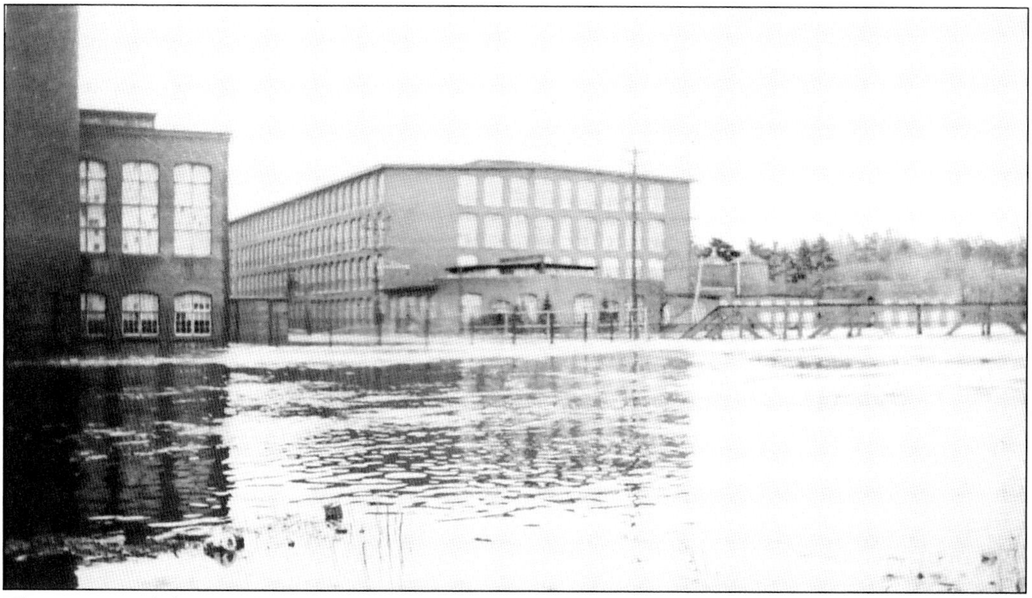

The waters of the Blackstone River and the Nyanza Mill during the Hurricane of 1938. The former Nyanza Mills, built *c.* 1910, is in the background. This four-story brick mill employed hundreds of area residents. It was part of the last great expansion of textile mills built in Woonsocket. (Mr. and Mrs. George E. Brin.)

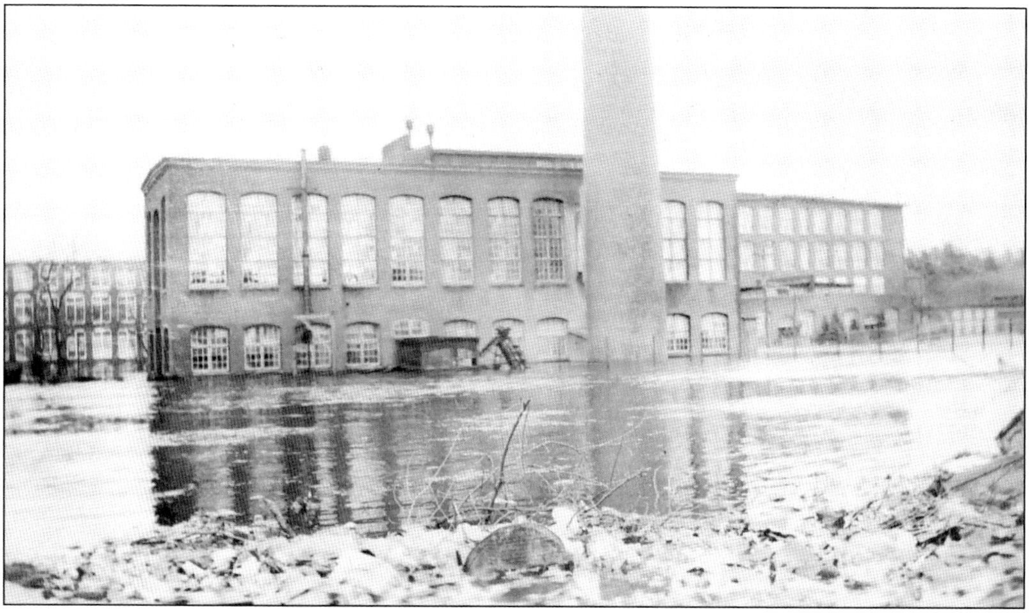

Another view of the flooding that occurred from the Hurricane of 1938. This view is of the steam power plant that supplied power to the mills along Singleton Street. By the 1860s coal burning plants, such as this one, produced steam and power that at first supplemented the water power the mills were using. Later they provided all necessary power to the mills. (Mr. and Mrs. George E. Brin.)

Damage sustained by the Lafayette Worsted Company from the wind that Woonsocket experienced during the Hurricane of 1938. The mill, located on Hamlet Avenue, lost part of its roof. When constructed, *c*. 1900, it was part of the French corporate textile migration into Woonsocket. The company produced worsted wool by the French method. (Mr. and Mrs. Aram Archambault.)

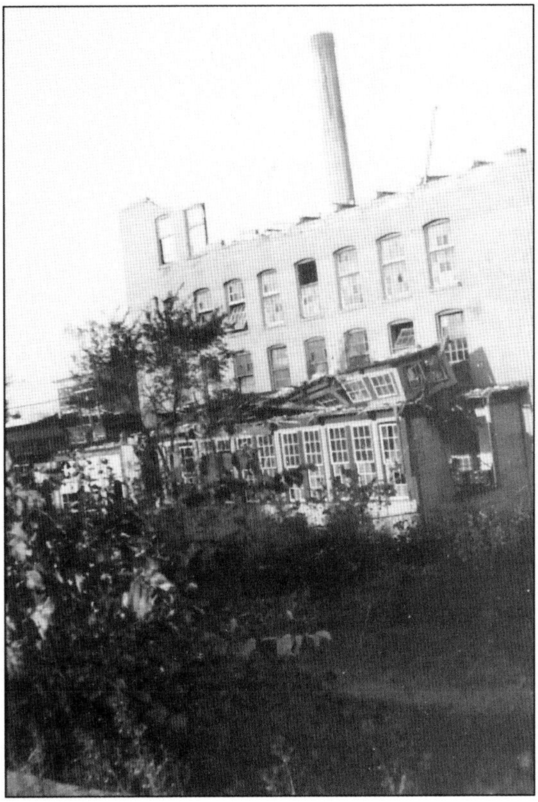

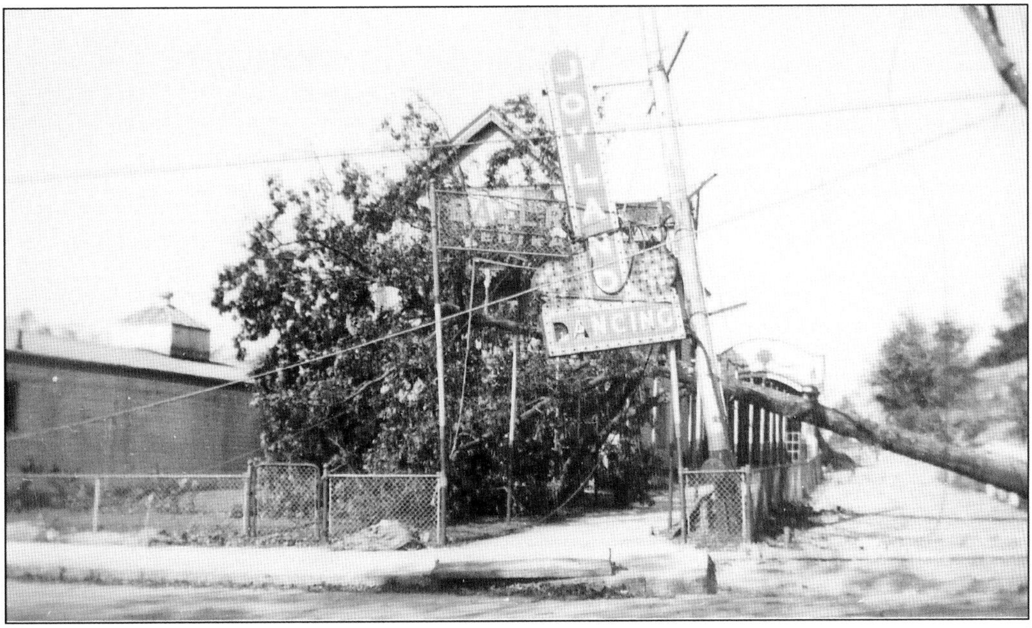

The Joyland Ballroom sign, damaged during the Hurricane of 1938. Located on Cumberland Hill Road, and built by Ovilard S. Fournier, the ballroom formally opened on May 4, 1927. The Joyland Ballroom became a roller-skating rink after its purchase, in 1958, by Samuel Phillips of Somerset, Massachusetts. (Mr. and Mrs. Aram Archambault.)

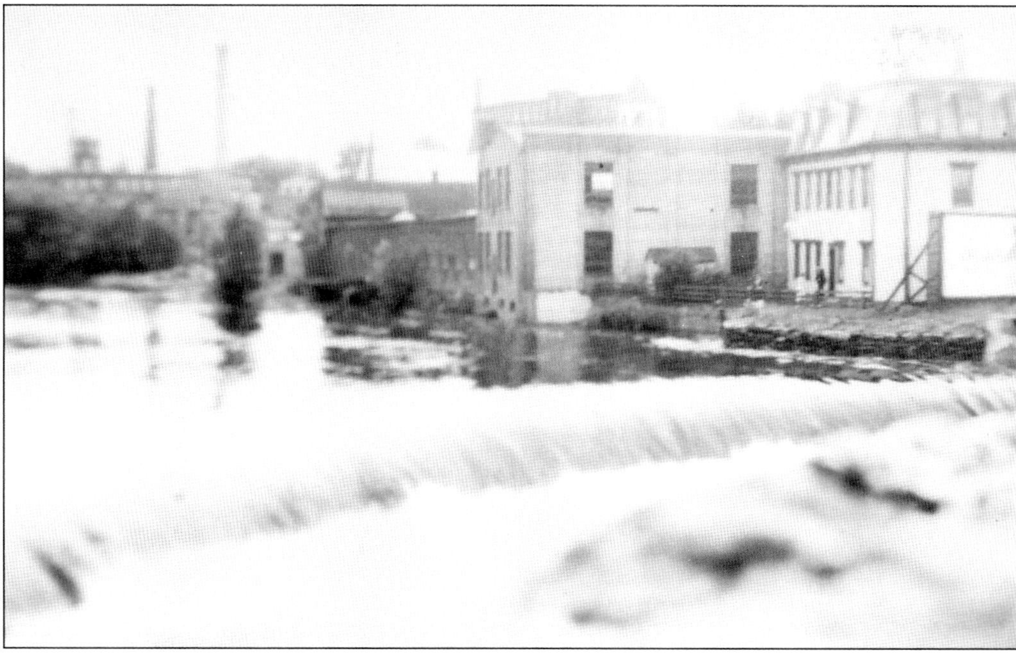

A raging Blackstone River over the Bernon Dam during the Hurricane of 1938. Woonsocket experienced mainly wind damage, with wind speeds reaching a top speed of 121 miles per hour, and also water damage, as the Blackstone River overflowed its banks. (Woonsocket Harris Public Library.)

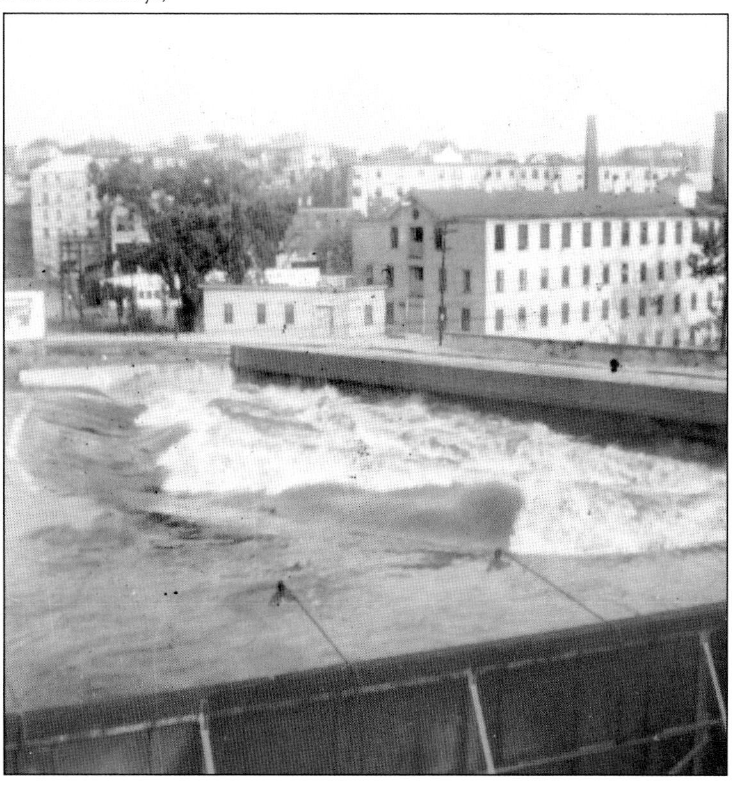

Bernon Dam and Bridge during the flood following the Hurricane of 1955. This hurricane was Woonsocket's greatest natural disaster and caused widespread damage throughout the city. "Diane" (the name for the hurricane of 1955) caused $31 million in damage to the city. In the background is the former Narragansett Knitting Mill on Bernon Street. (Mr. and Mrs. George E. Brin.)

Nine

Working on the Railroad

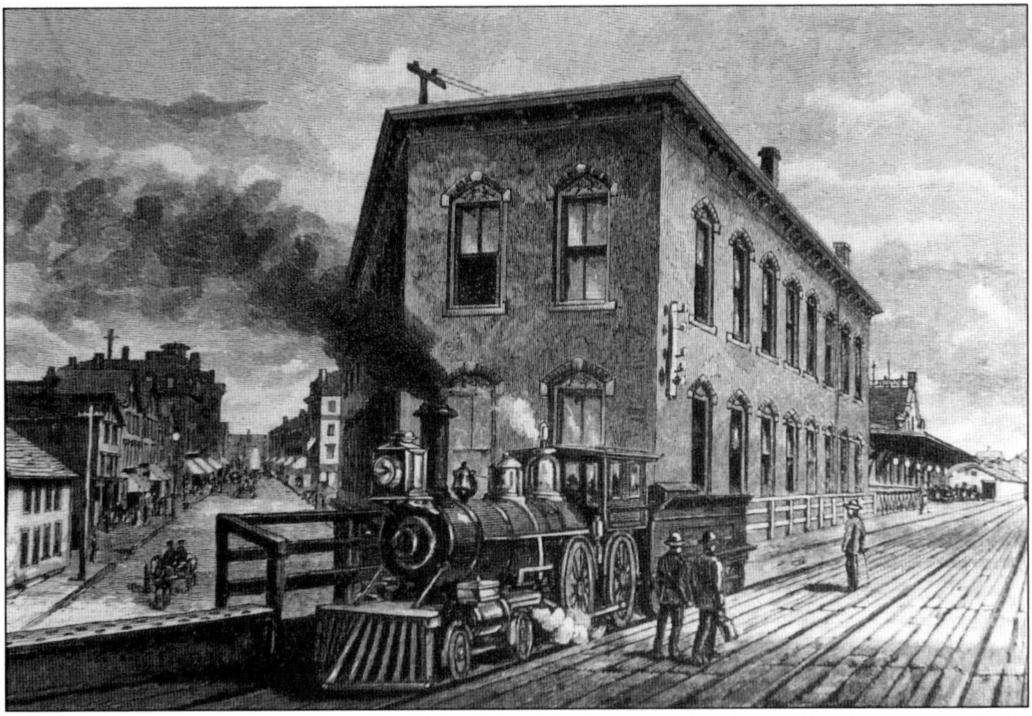

A Providence and Worcester Railroad locomotive alongside the Hope Building, at trackside level, in 1886. The Providence and Worcester Railroad arrived in Woonsocket in 1847 and became a key transportation element for industrial growth. The Hope Building, constructed c. 1876, is in the background. It is a three-story brick block building. (Woonsocket Harris Public Library.)

rovidence & Worcester Railro

PASSENGER NOTICE.

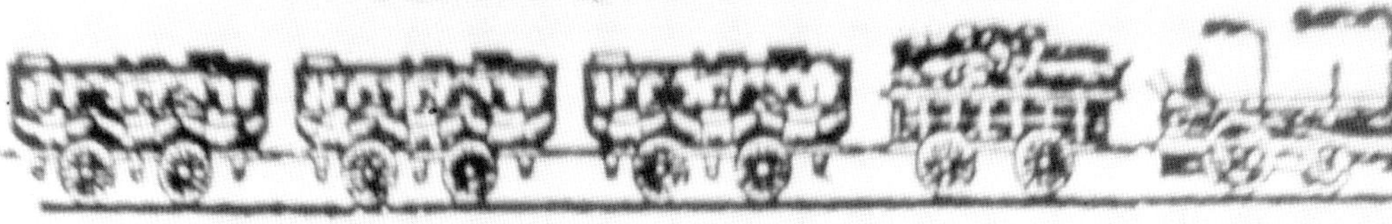

ON and after Wednesday, March 15th, 1848, trains run as follows:

THROUGH TRAINS

Leave Worcester at 7.30 A.M. and 3 45 P.M.

Leave Providence at 7 A.M. 3.15 P.M.

Morning and evening trains connect each way with ewport boats..

Morning and evening trains from Providence connec Vorcester with trains for Albany and Norwich.

Tickets sold at Providence for Albany and stations orwich and Worcester Railroad.

FREIGHT TRAIN, with Passenger Car attached, lea Ierchandise Depot, Green St., Worcester, at 11.30 A.M

SPECIAL TRAINS

Leave Uxbridge for Providence at 6.20 A.M. & 1.05 P.

Leave Providence for Uxbridge at 11.15 A.M. & 5.40 P

The 6.20 A.M. train from Uxbridge will connect at P acket with train for Boston.

The 5.40 P.M. train for Uxbridge will connect at P acket with train from Boston.

No 2d class tickets sold for freight train or special tr

Trains stop at Millbury, Wilkinsonville, Grafton, F omsville, Northbridge, Whitin's, Uxbridge, Millv lackstone, Waterford, Woonsocket, Hamlet, Manv lbion, Ashton, Lonsdale, Valley Falls, Central Falls id Pawtucket. ISAAC HINCKLEY, Sup't

FREIGHT NOTICE—Goods remaining at depot

A train schedule advertisement for the Providence and Worcester Railroad's passenger service in 1848. The original depot, constructed in 1847, was the busiest stop on the railroad's line throughout the nineteenth century. Automobiles and buses eventually decimated rail passenger service in the mid-twentieth century. (Woonsocket Harris Public Library.)

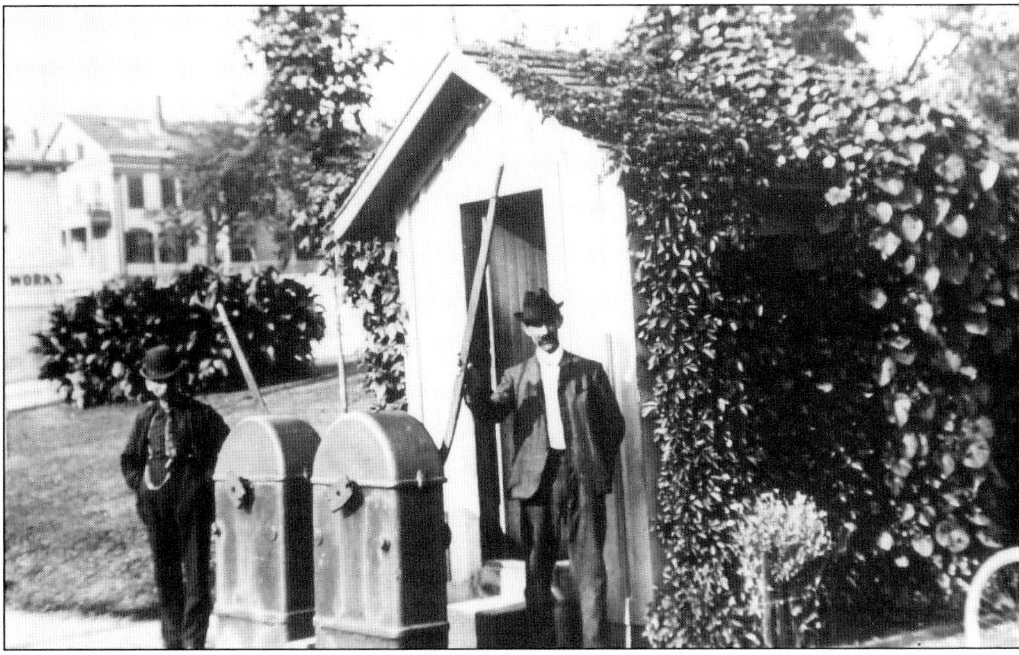

The railroad crossing tender shanty at the corner of North Main and Prospect Streets, *c.* 1890. These tracks, installed in 1863, were part of a rail line that linked Woonsocket with Boston. (Woonsocket Harris Public Library.)

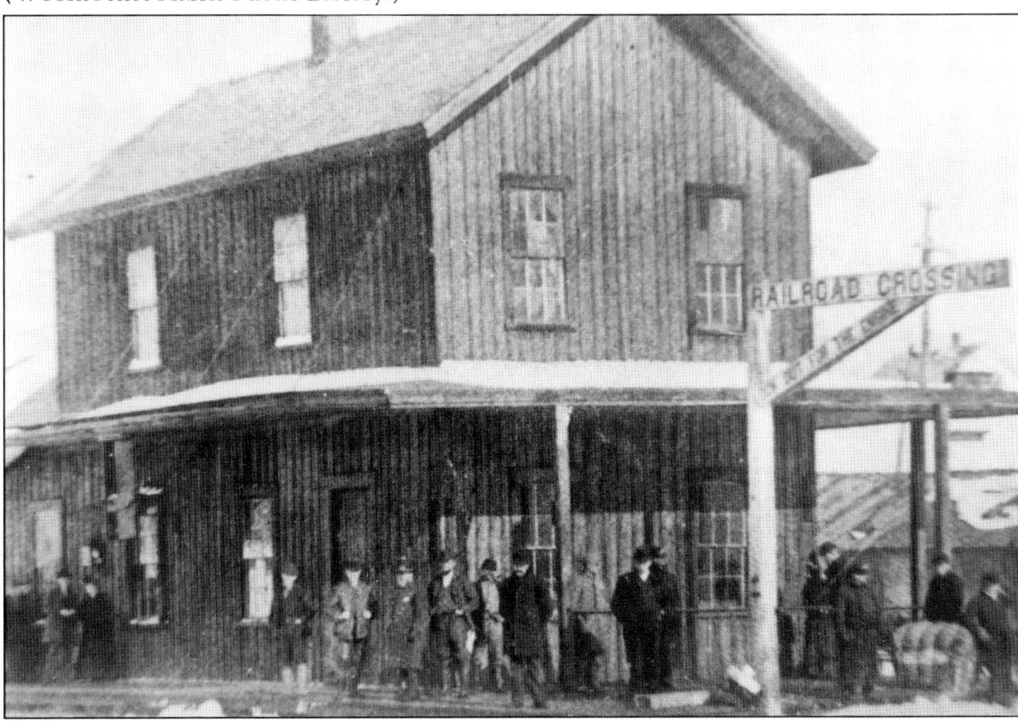

The Woonsocket Station, on Railroad Street, of the New York and New England Railroad, photographed in 1890. This major rail line, built in 1863, linked Woonsocket with Boston. (Woonsocket Harris Public Library.)

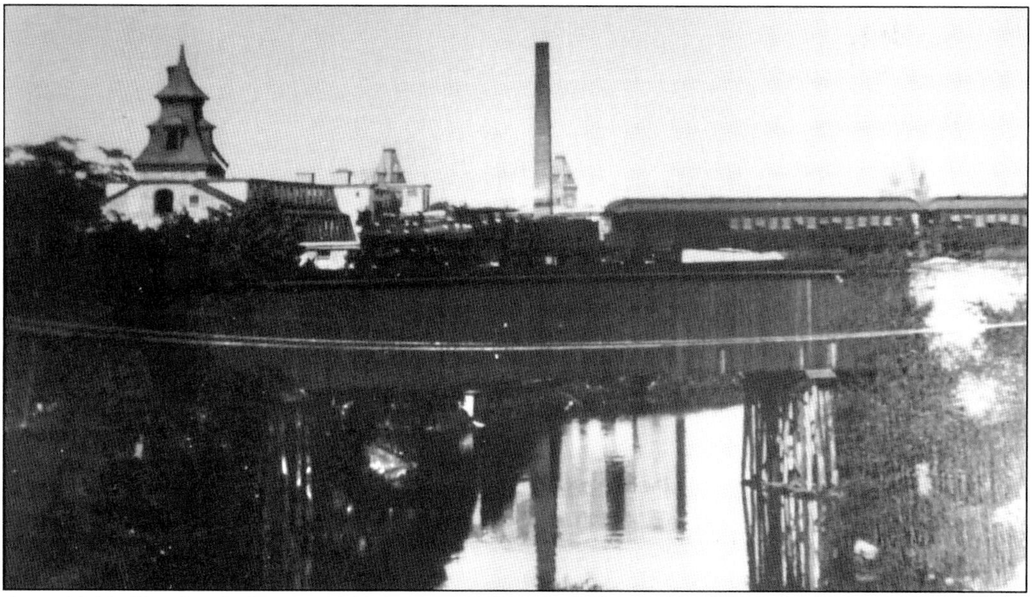

A *c.* 1900 Charles S. Lawton photograph of a northbound train carrying passengers on the Providence and Worcester Railroad, on the bridge over the Blackstone River, just south of the depot. In 1893, the New York, New Haven, and Hartford Railroad leased the Providence and Worcester line for ninety-nine years. Local services and operations did not change immediately under their control. (Woonsocket Harris Public Library.)

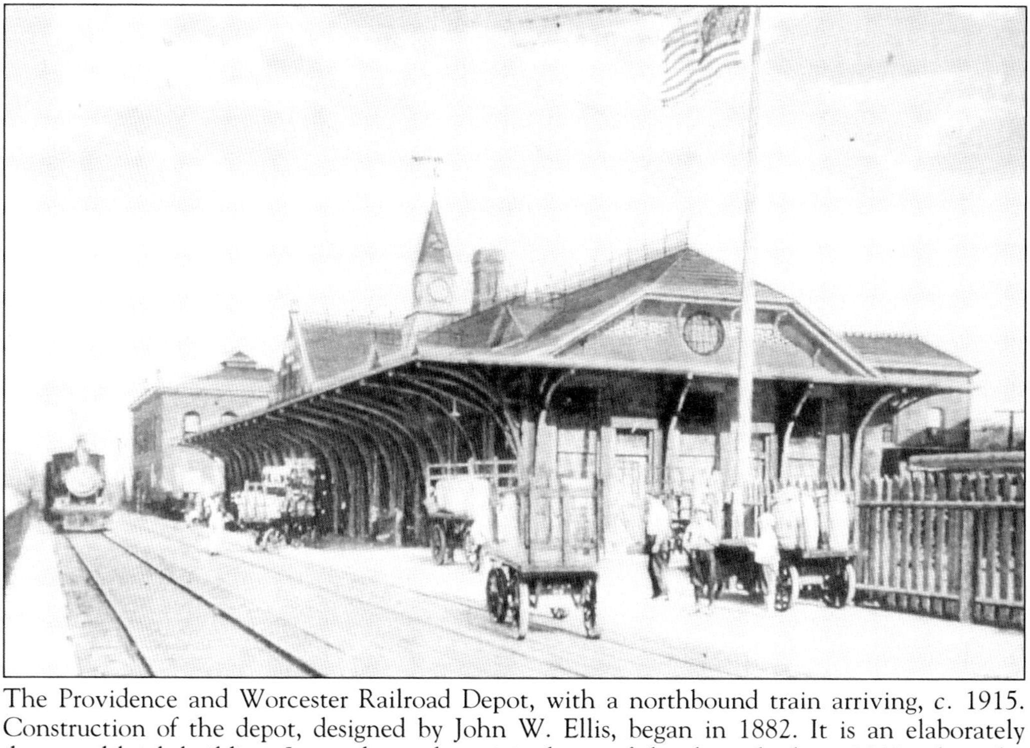

The Providence and Worcester Railroad Depot, with a northbound train arriving, *c.* 1915. Construction of the depot, designed by John W. Ellis, began in 1882. It is an elaborately decorated brick building. It stands on the original site of the depot built in 1847, when the Providence and Worcester first arrived in Woonsocket. (Woonsocket Harris Public Library.)

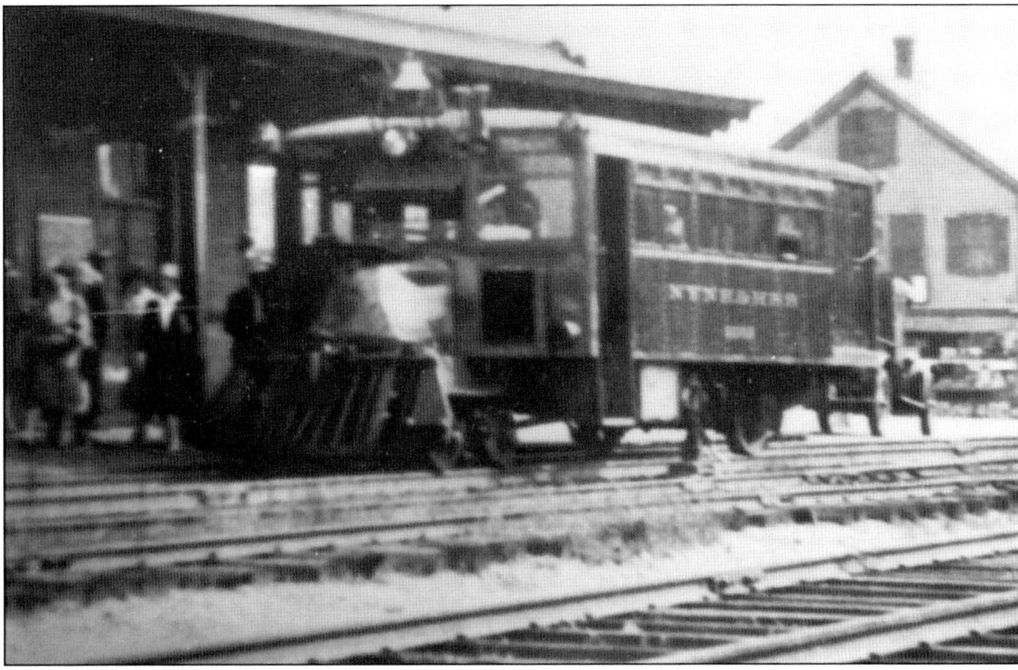

A New York, New Haven, and Hartford Railroad Mack gas railbus, #9002, at the River Street Station. This Boston-bound bus is on the New Haven's Boston-Pascoag branch and was photographed on August 13, 1929. (Woonsocket Harris Public Library.)

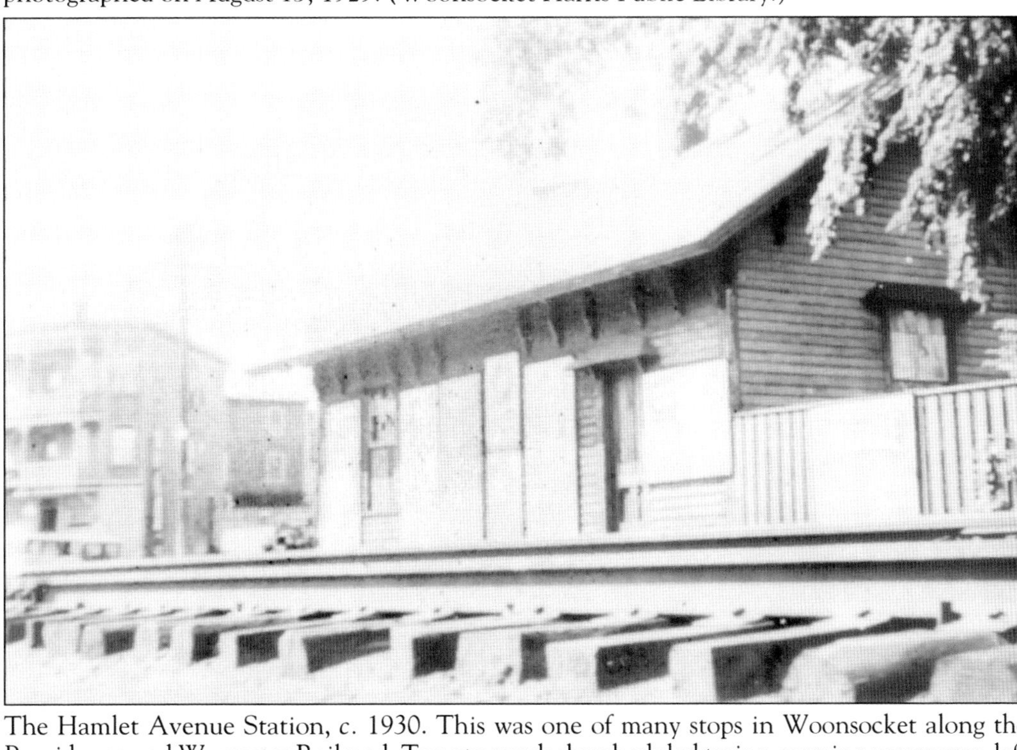

The Hamlet Avenue Station, *c.* 1930. This was one of many stops in Woonsocket along the Providence and Worcester Railroad. Twenty regularly scheduled trains, carrying passengers, left Woonsocket every weekday in 1929. (Woonsocket Harris Public Library.)

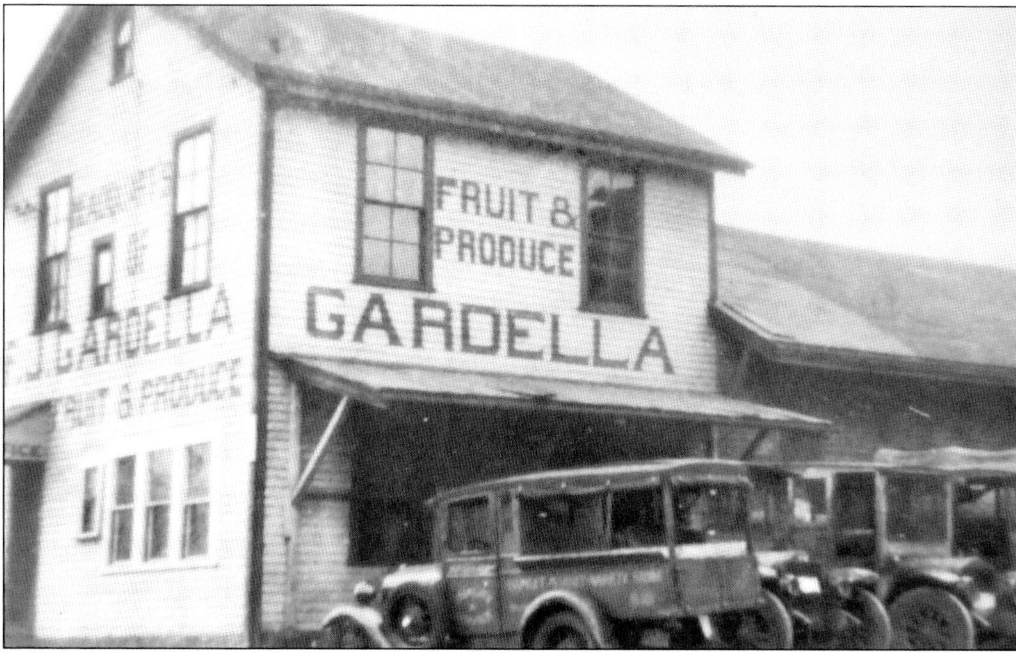

Gardella's Fruit and Produce Warehouse, April 1931. This was the old Woonsocket Station-Freight House on the New York, New Haven, and Hartford Railroad's Boston-Pascoag line. Francis J. Gardella established F.J. Gardella's and Sons in 1928. (Woonsocket Harris Public Library.)

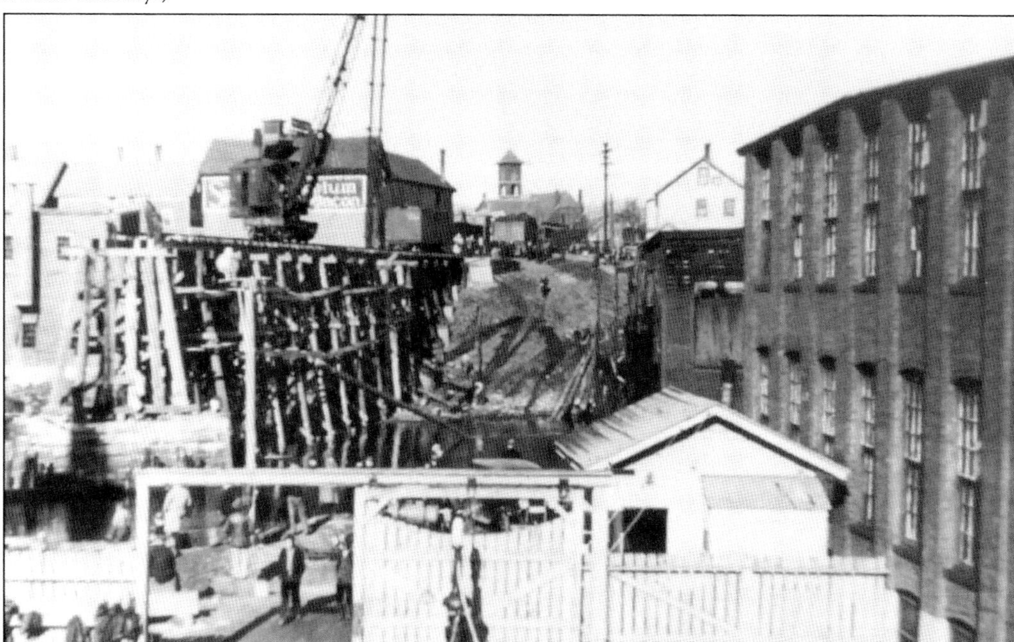

The construction of the Bandwagon Bridge, bridge 29-18, on the New York, New Haven, and Hartford Railroad's Boston-Pascoag line, April 19, 1935. The Boston-Pascoag line was part of the old New York and New England Railroad. In the background is the tower of the First Baptist Church on Blackstone Street. (Woonsocket Harris Public Library.)

Ten

Workers Escape

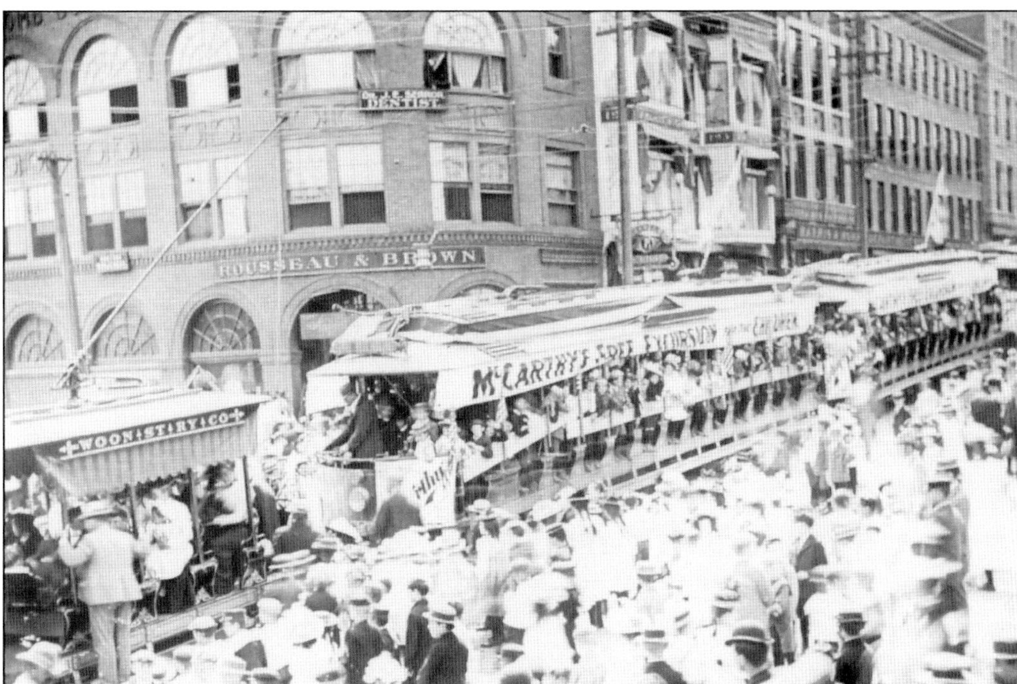

An outing for children, sponsored by the McCarthy Dry Goods Company, at Depot Square, c. 1910. To the left of the center, in the background, is the old Slocomb Building. McCarthy's, founded in 1889, would grow to become "Woonsocket's Largest Store," and would eventually expand into this building. (Woonsocket Harris Public Library.)

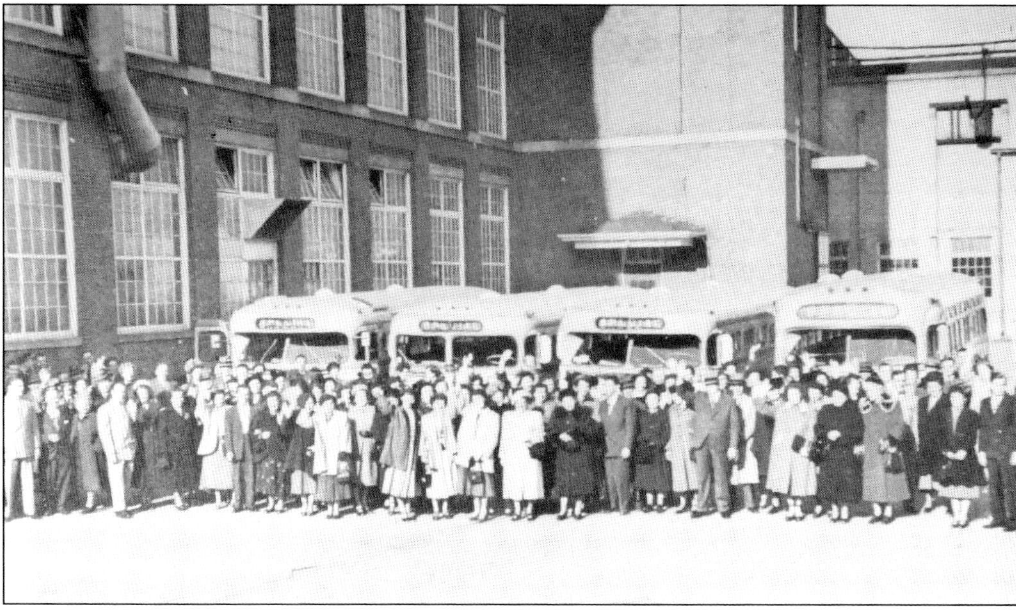

Argonne Worsted workers leaving for their 50th anniversary banquet on October 29, 1949. Hamlet Avenue was the location for The Argonne Worsted Company's mill yard. (Woonsocket Harris Public Library.)

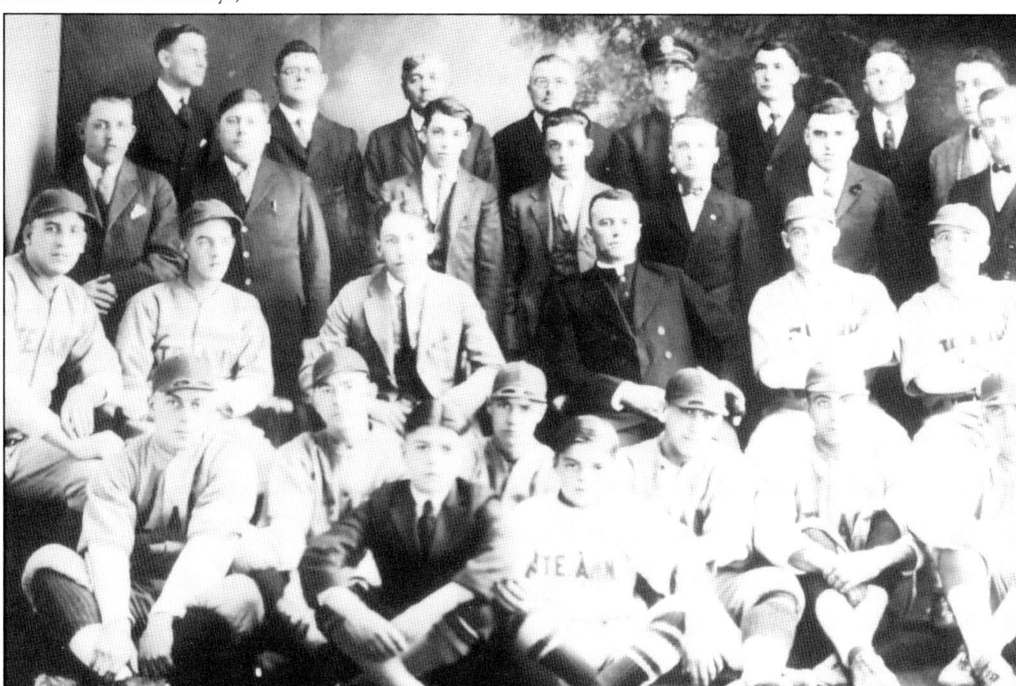

The Saint Ann's baseball team, *c.* 1920s. Baseball was a popular sport with the residents of Woonsocket. Whether they played for teams in the "Blackstone Valley League" or for schools and churches, city residents and their excited fans enjoyed this popular diversion. Saint Ann's Park, at the corner of Cass and Dulude Avenues, was the site of many games. (Woonsocket Harris Public Library.)

Napoleon Lajoie (1875–1959), *c.* 1905. Born in Woonsocket, Lajoie began playing baseball for local teams in the 1890s, later playing his first professional games for a minor league team in Fall River in 1896. He was picked up by the Philadelphia Phillies, later joining the American League Philadelphia Athletics, and ended his career with the Cleveland Indians. The Baseball Hall of Fame inducted him in 1937. (Woonsocket Harris Public Library.)

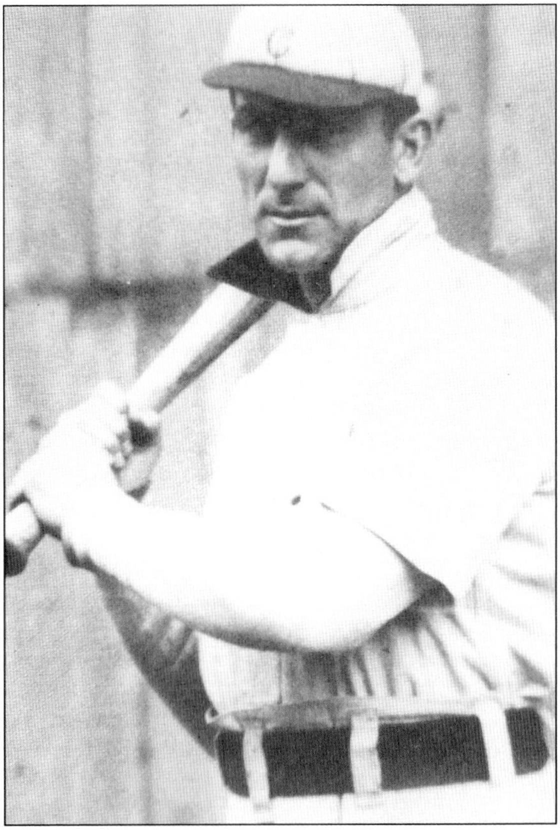

The Woonsocket Plant baseball team of the United States Rubber Company, *c.* 1930. Many mills sponsored baseball teams that challenged each other and had countless loyal fans. Attendance at Sunday afternoon games was always in the hundreds. (Woonsocket Harris Public Library.)

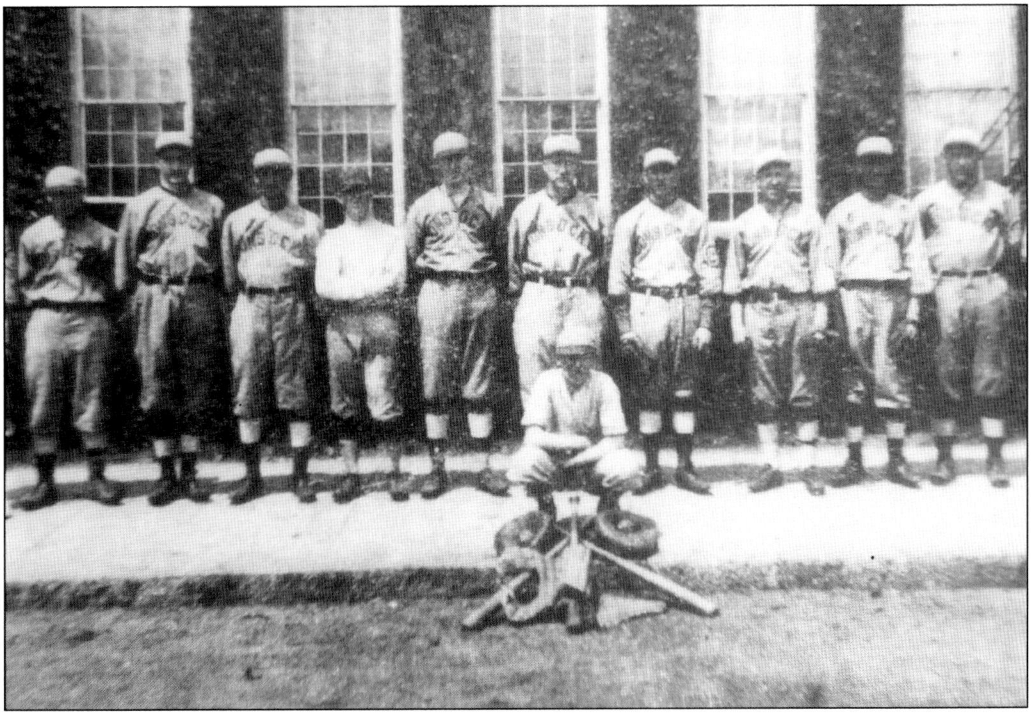

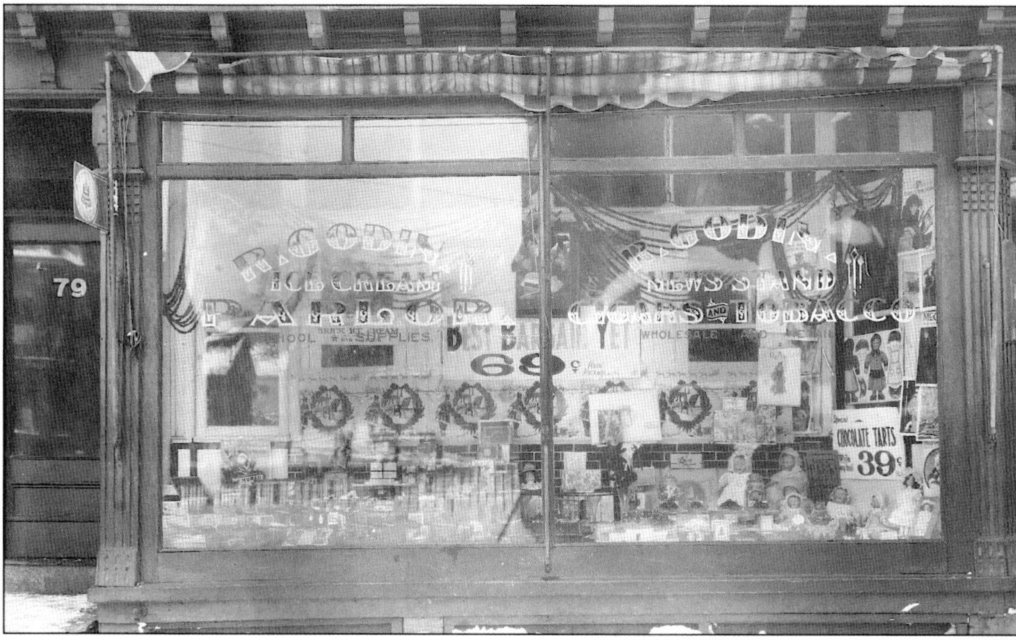

R. Godin's Ice Cream Parlor and News Stand, *c.* 1910. Small "Mom and Pop" operations like this one were popular places for young and old alike. Besides serving ice cream, you could also purchase school supplies, magazines, newspapers, tobacco products, and other items. (Blackstone River Valley National Heritage Corridor Commission.)

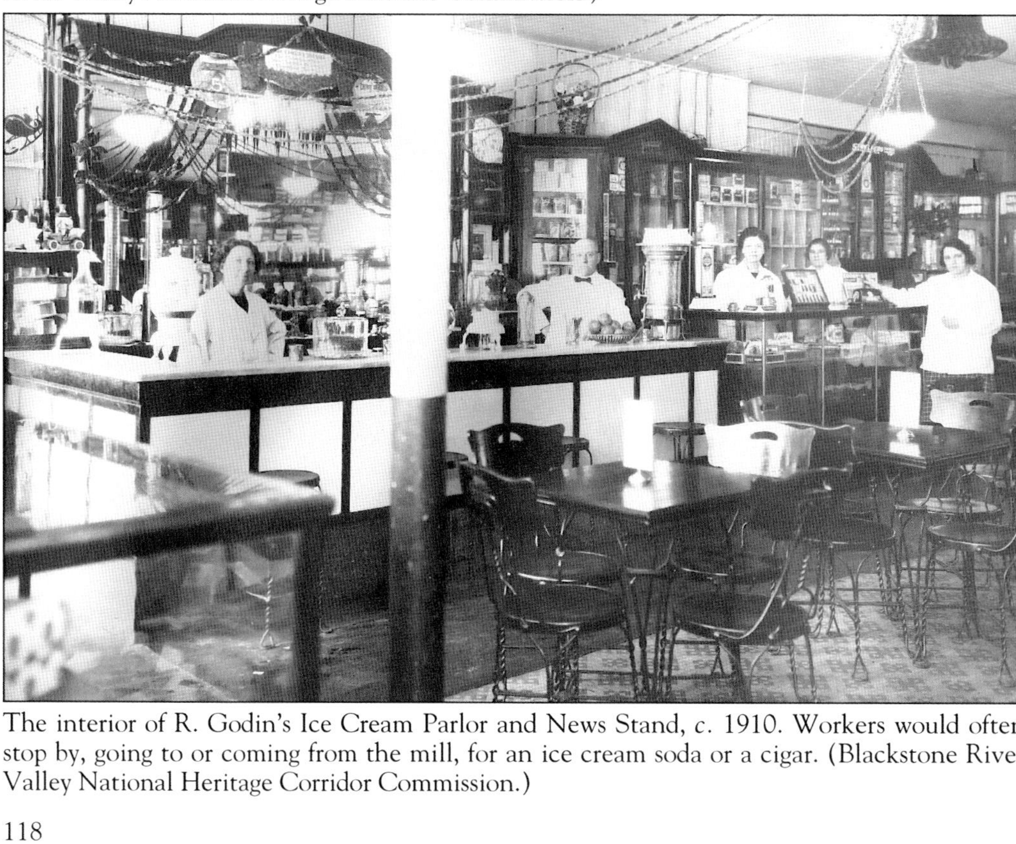

The interior of R. Godin's Ice Cream Parlor and News Stand, *c.* 1910. Workers would often stop by, going to or coming from the mill, for an ice cream soda or a cigar. (Blackstone River Valley National Heritage Corridor Commission.)

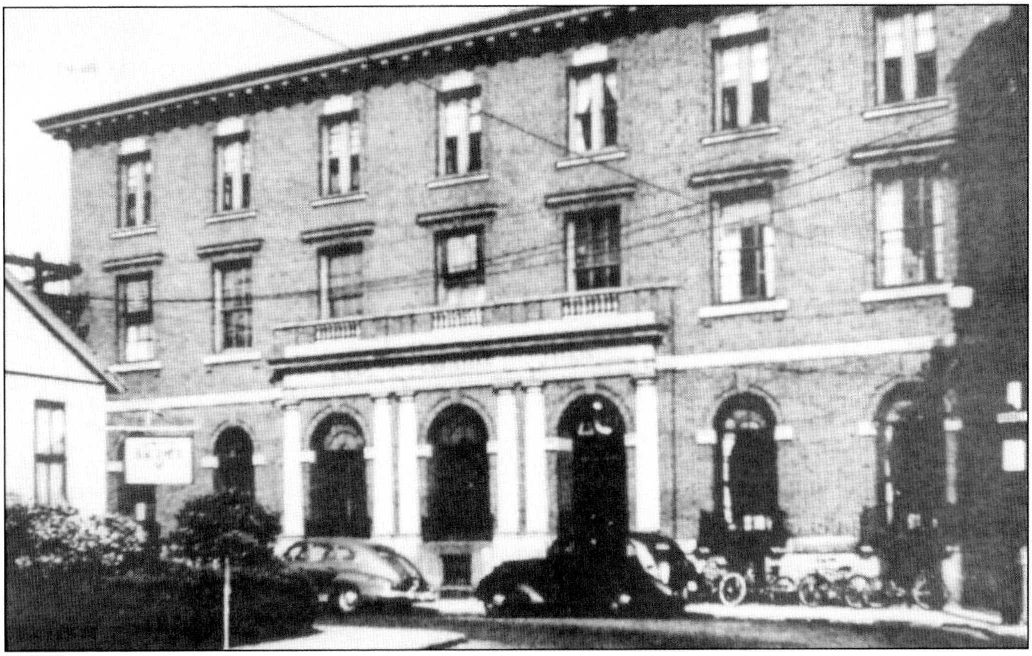

The Woonsocket Young Men's Christian Association building, *c.* 1940s. Designed by Walter Fontaine and constructed in 1920, it is a functional three-story brick building. This simple yet dignified structure has been an important civic center over the years. The building on the left is the former Young Women's Christian Association. (Woonsocket Harris Public Library.)

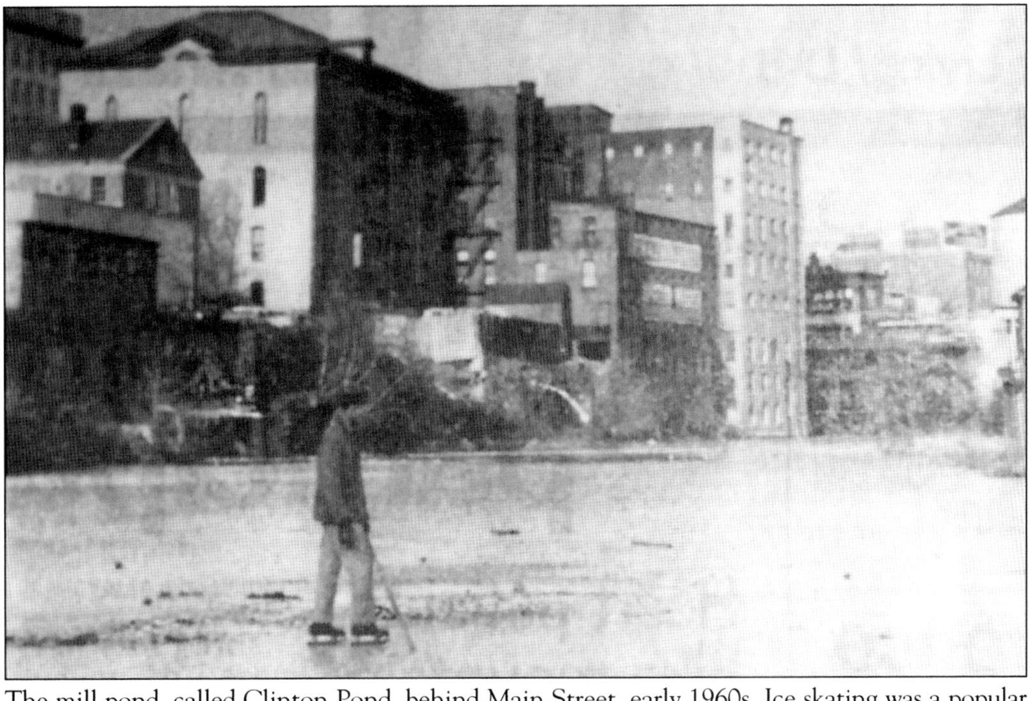

The mill pond, called Clinton Pond, behind Main Street, early 1960s. Ice skating was a popular recreation on the city's many mill ponds and trenches during the winter. Today automobiles on the Truman Bypass travel where Clinton Pond used to be. (Woonsocket Harris Public Library.)

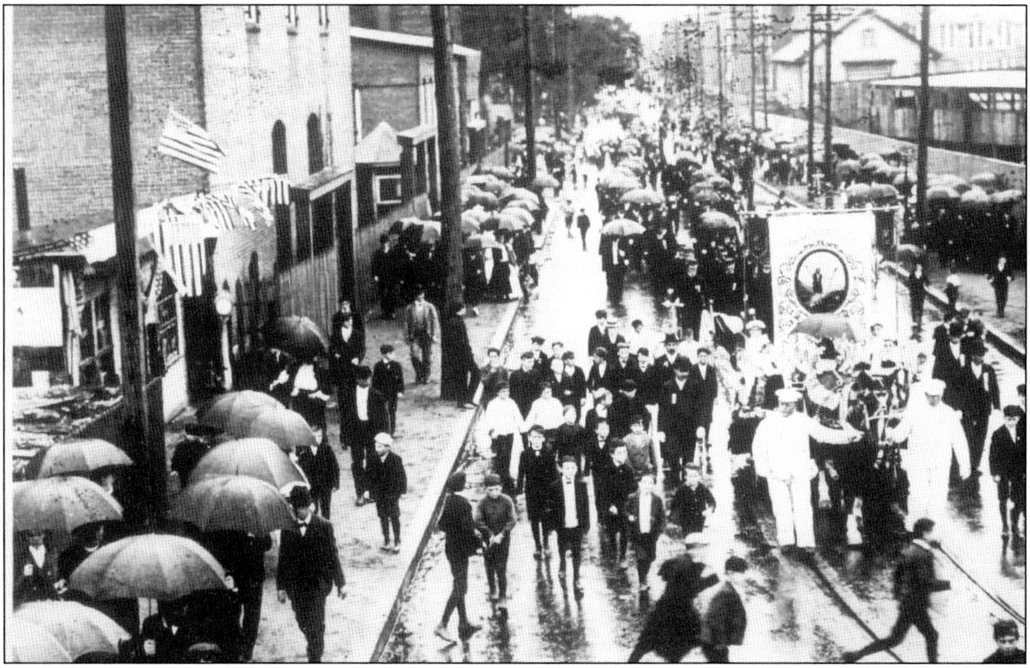

A 1906 Saint Jean Baptiste Day parade on Clinton Street. June 24 is the feast day of Saint Jean Baptiste, the patron saint of the French-Canadians. These festivities would usually include a mammoth parade, picnic, and concert.

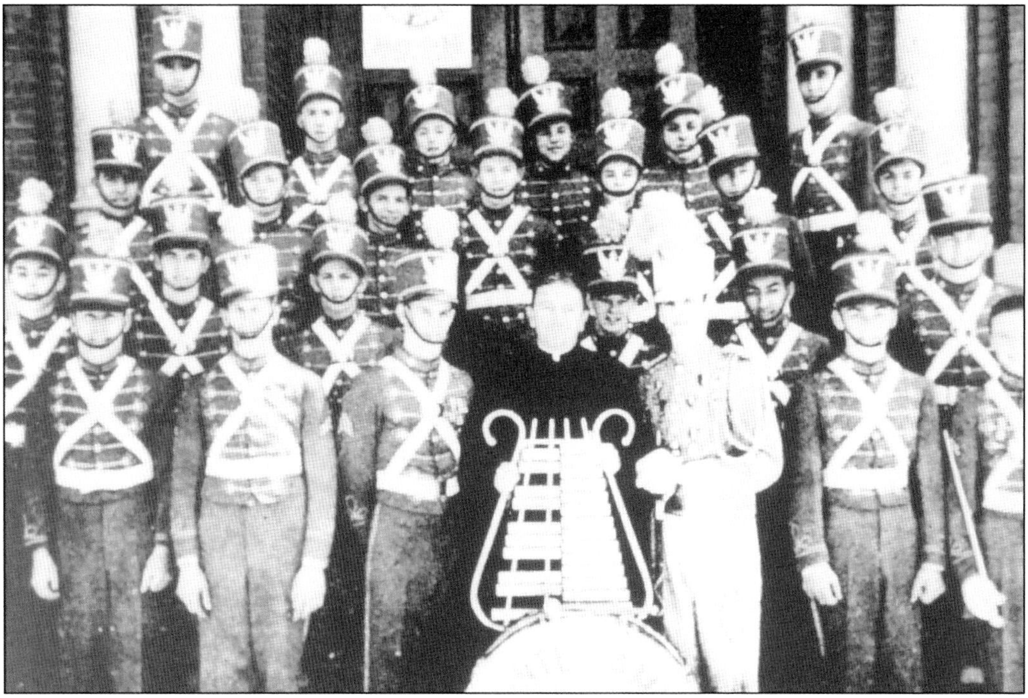

The Holy Family Church Drum and Bugle Corps in April 1952. Musical groups provided many hours of recreational opportunities to city residents. Some of these groups were as good as professional musicians in larger cities. (Woonsocket Harris Public Library.)

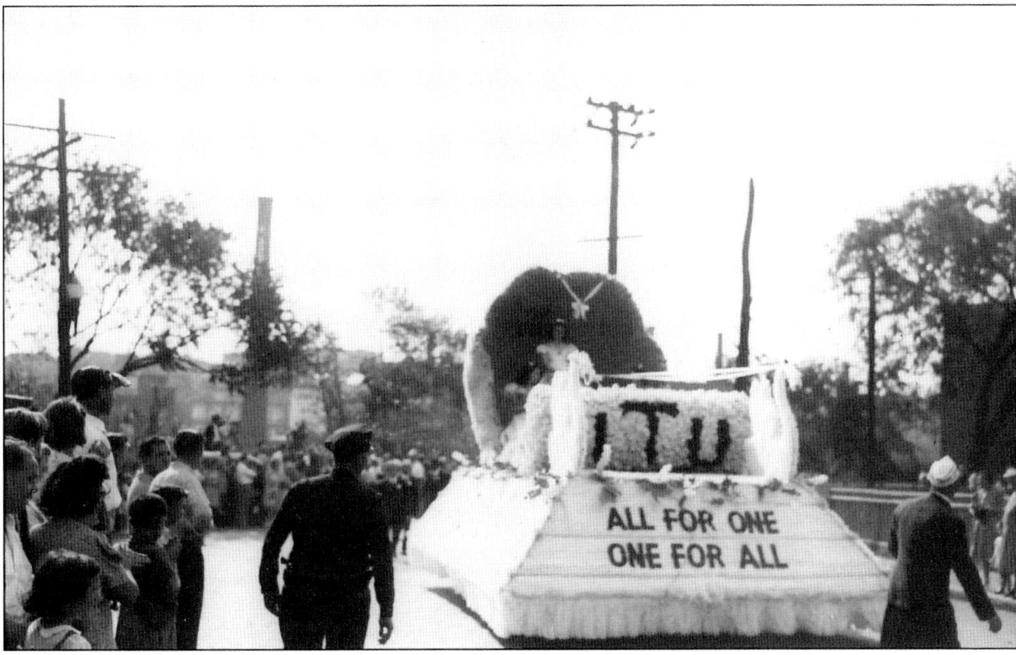

The Labor Day Parade in Woonsocket in September 1941. Depicted is a parade float sponsored by the Industrial Trades Union. This union, formed in Woonsocket, began as the Independent Textile Union in 1931 and by 1936 had over 6,000 members.

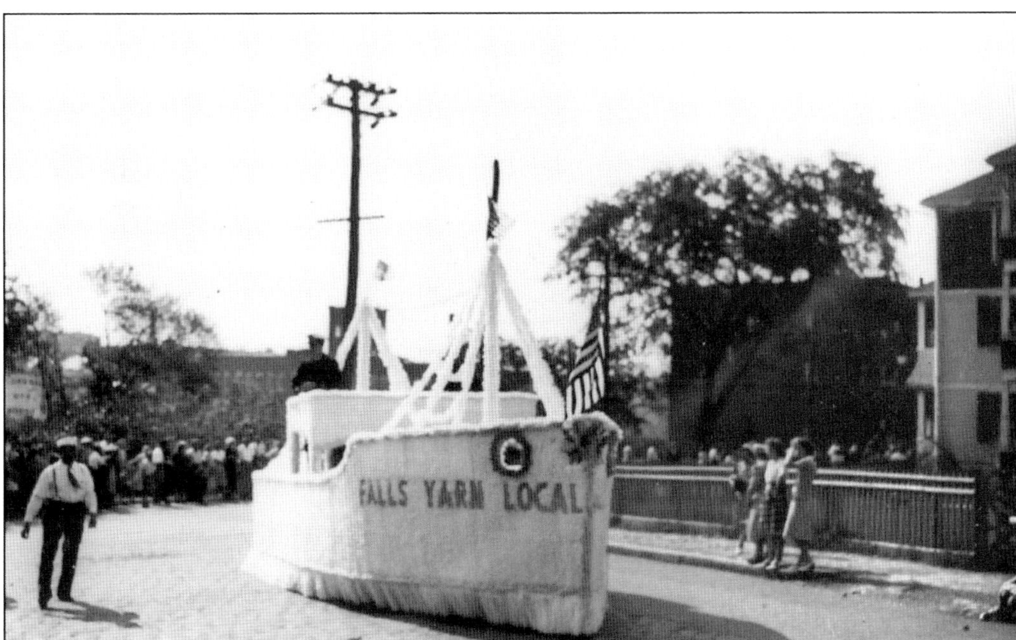

Another view of the Labor Day Parade in Woonsocket in September 1941. The union local representing workers at the Falls Yarn Mills sponsored this parade float. The Industrial Trades Union's social concerns extended to their subsidy of a medical clinic, life insurance plan, cooperative financing for single-family homes, and educational interests.

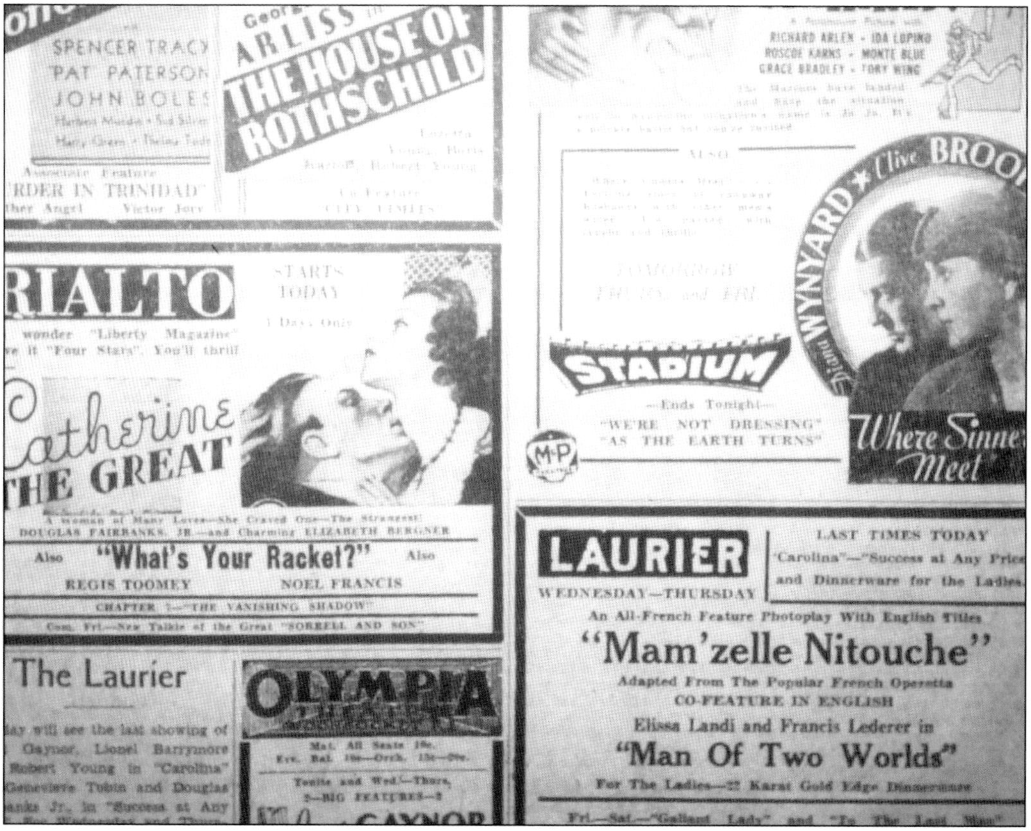

An advertisement for movie theater shows from *The Woonsocket Call* in 1934. By the 1950s Woonsocket residents would have a choice of six movie theaters. On Main Street, one could find the Bijou, Rialto, Olympia, and Stadium Theaters. The Laurier Theater was on Cumberland Street, and the New Park Theater was on North Main Street. (Woonsocket Harris Public Library.)

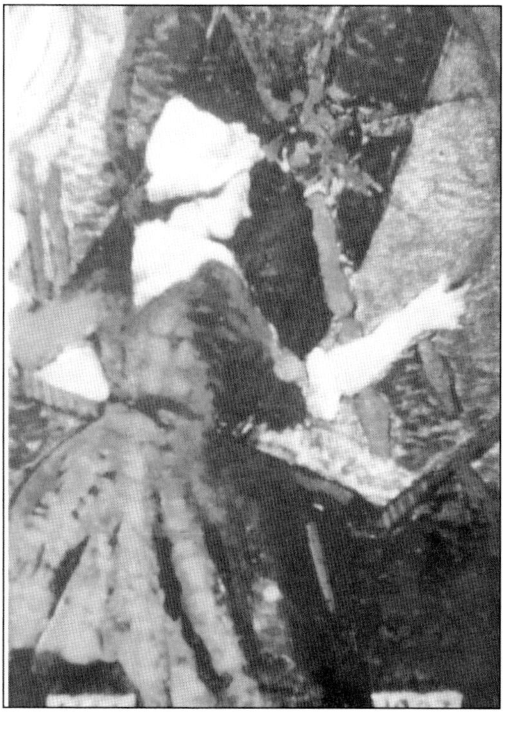

Part of the mural in the Stadium Building depicting a spinning wheel, photographed in 1928. The mural, located beneath the main staircase, is in the four-story Stadium Building on Main Street. (Woonsocket Harris Public Library.)

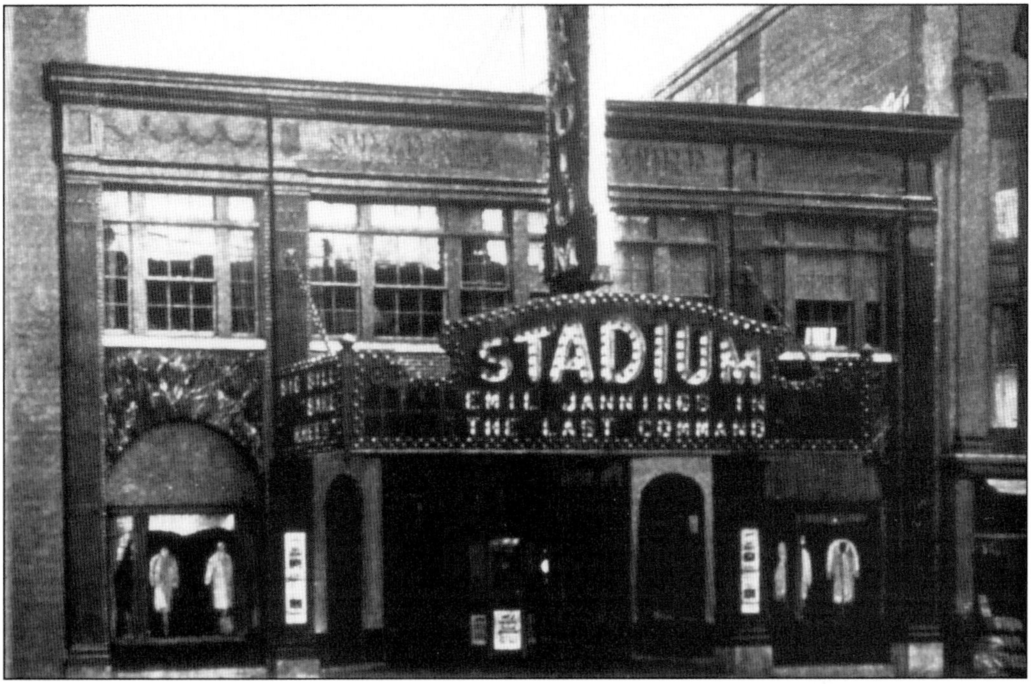

The entrance and marquee to the Stadium Theater, photographed in 1928. Designed by Perry and Whipple of Providence, the Stadium Theater, constructed in 1926, forms a lovely backdrop to Monument Square. Arthur I. Darman, a local industrialist who had a love for vaudeville theater, had it built. An elegantly designed shopping arcade provides an entrance to the theater. (Woonsocket Harris Public Library.)

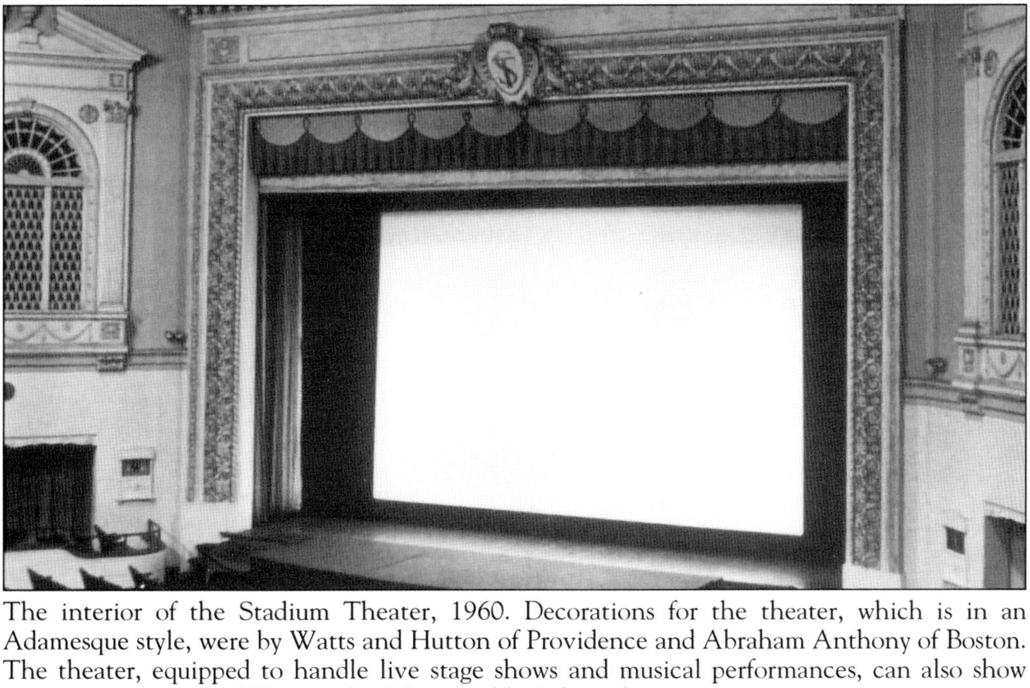

The interior of the Stadium Theater, 1960. Decorations for the theater, which is in an Adamesque style, were by Watts and Hutton of Providence and Abraham Anthony of Boston. The theater, equipped to handle live stage shows and musical performances, can also show movie presentations. (Woonsocket Harris Public Library.)

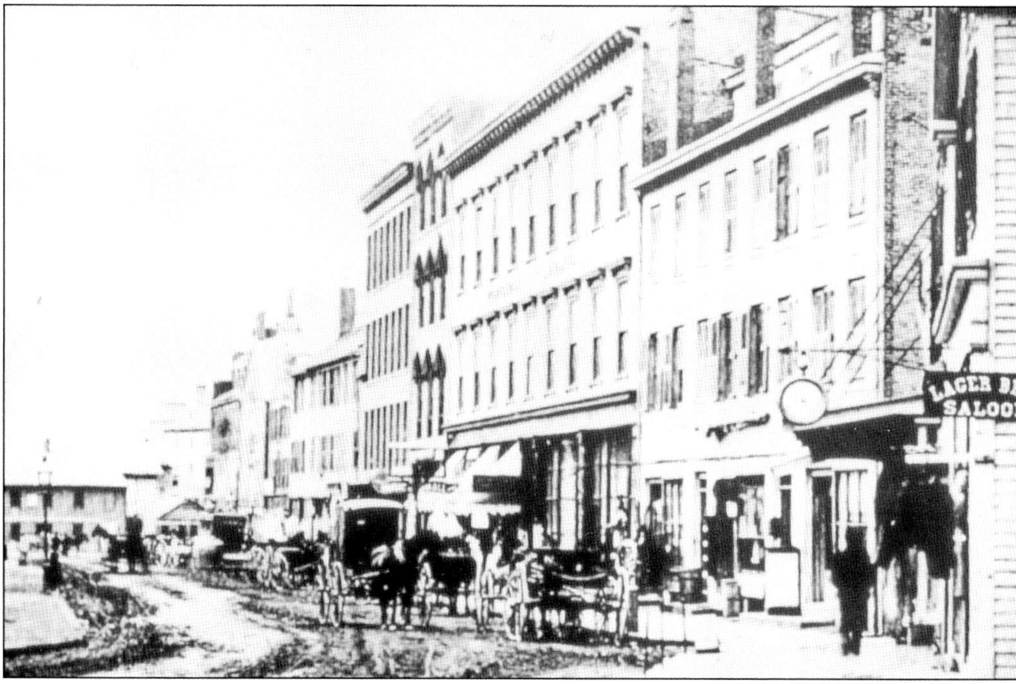

The site of the Olympia Theater, near Market Square, on Main Street *c.* 1870. As with most theaters during the heyday of movie houses, the Olympia Theater had matinees and evening performances, and usually featured two movies. During the 1950s, as an enticement to boost attendance, viewers could play "Honey" for cash prizes. (Woonsocket Harris Public Library.)

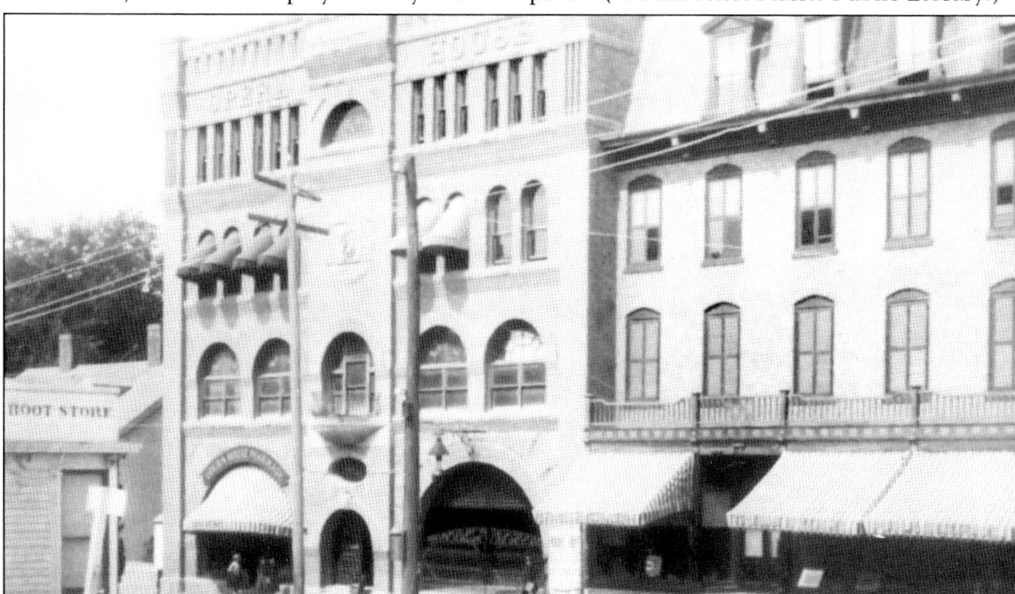

The Woonsocket Opera House, as seen through the lens of Charles S. Lawton in 1900. Completed in 1888 on North Main Street, the opera house cost $80,000 to build. Designed in the Romanesque style by architect Willard Kent, the theater also contains offices, a store, hotel annex, and lobbies located in the front of the building. (Woonsocket Harris Public Library.)

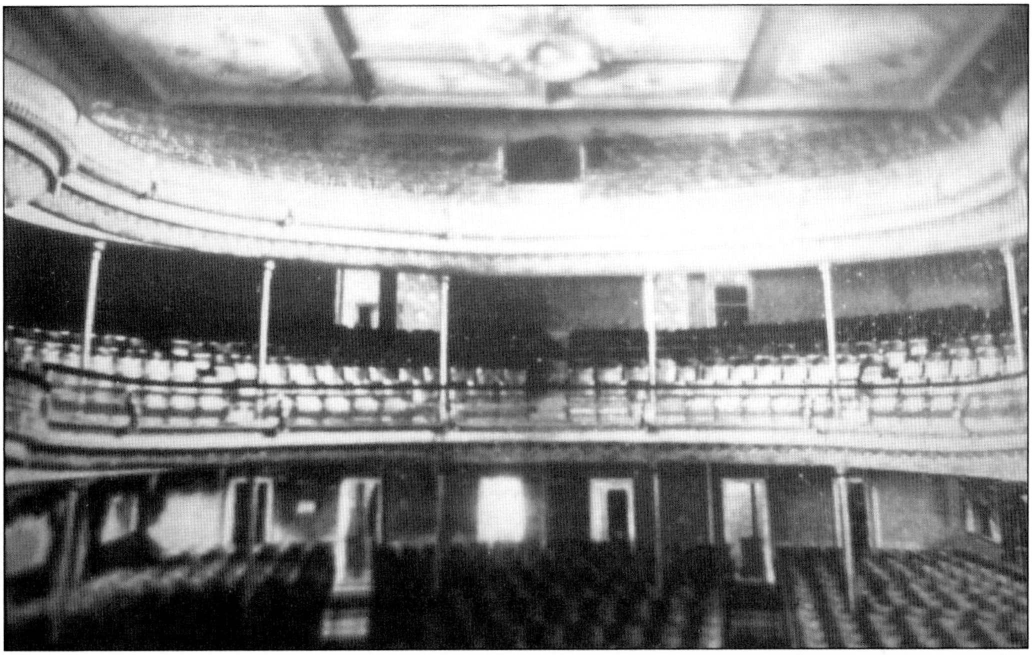

The interior of the Woonsocket Opera House from the stage, *c.* 1900. The opera house had a seating capacity of 1,500 and a stage that was 54 feet deep and 65 feet wide. Later converted to a movie theater named the Park Theater, it showed its last movie in 1963. Fire destroyed this impressive and imposing structure on September 22, 1975. (Woonsocket Harris Public Library.)

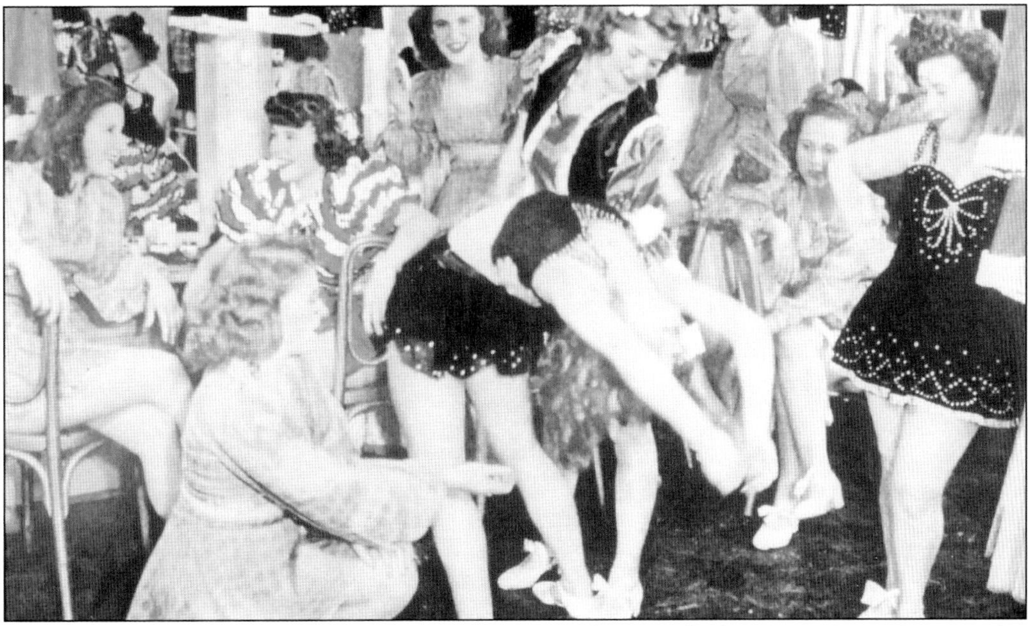

Entertainers in the dressing room of the Park Theater, photographed on June 23, 1945. Located at Monument Square on North Main Street, the former Woonsocket Opera House, later renamed the Park Theater, provided war-weary citizens with much-needed vaudeville entertainment. Arthur I. Darman, its owner, brought the stage back to life with live shows during World War II. (Woonsocket Harris Public Library.)

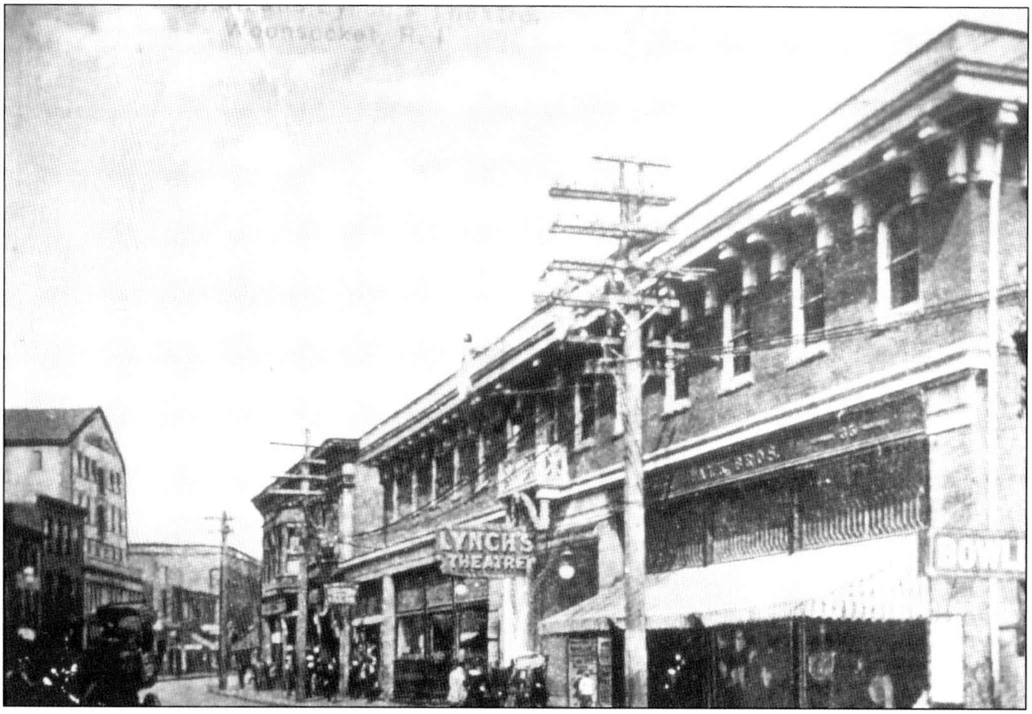

Lynch's Theater, later the Rialto Theater, *c.* 1915. Lynch's Theater, on Main Street, was near Market Square. (Woonsocket Harris Public Library.)

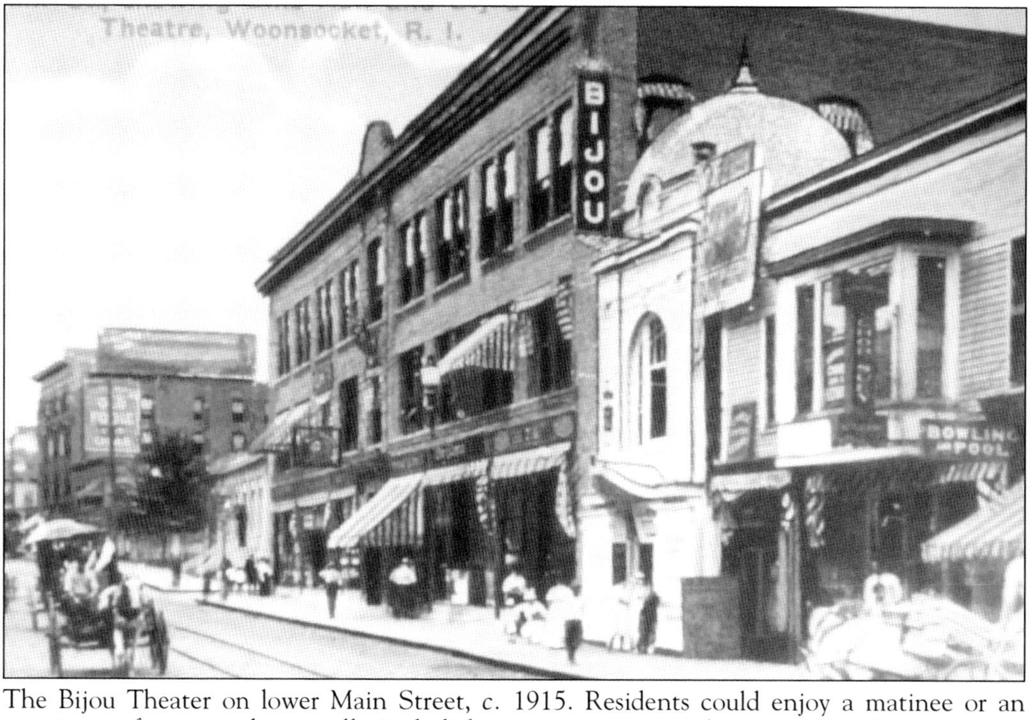

The Bijou Theater on lower Main Street, *c.* 1915. Residents could enjoy a matinee or an evening performance that usually included a cartoon or a serial, newsreel, and two movies. (Woonsocket Harris Public Library.)

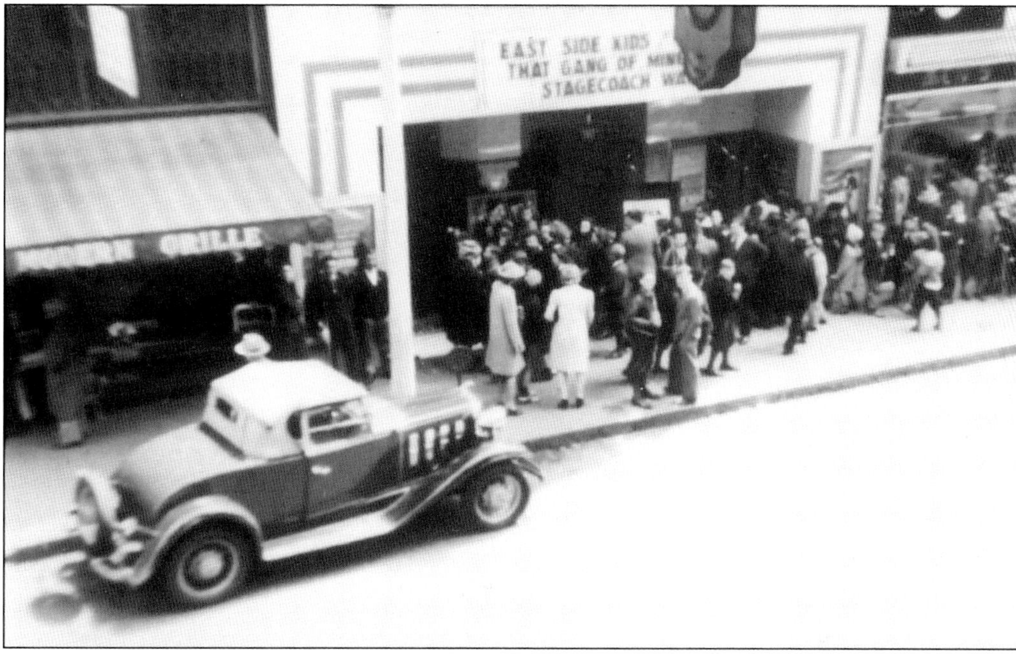

The Rialto Theater, in the Market Square area on Main Street, photographed in 1941. (Woonsocket Harris Public Library.)

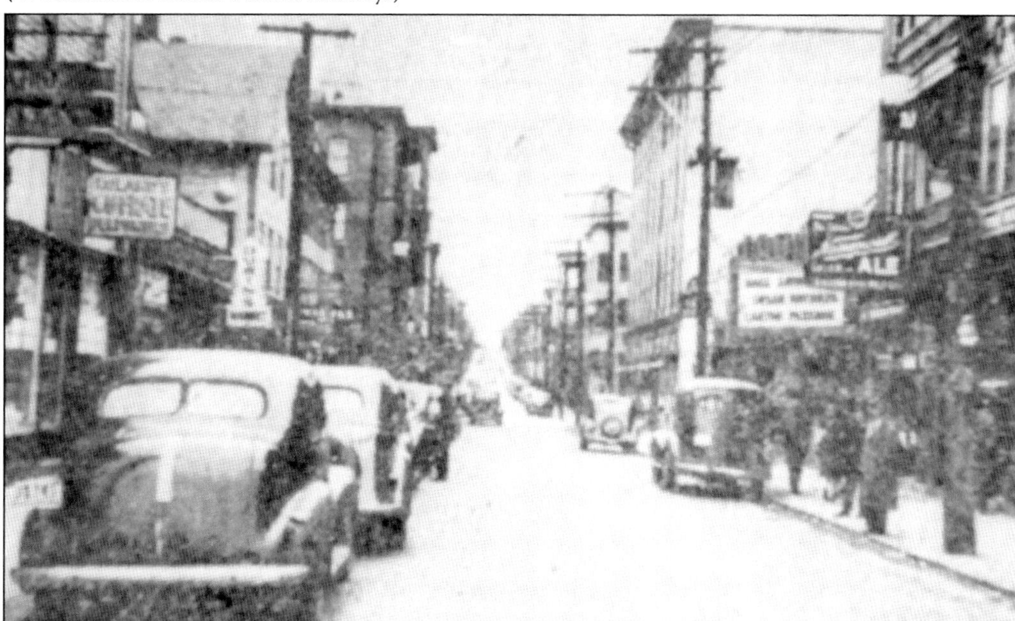

Cumberland Street, near Social Corner, with the Laurier Theater at right, photographed in November 1947. The theater opened in 1920, and was named in honor of Sir Wilfrid Laurier, the first French-Canadian to be elected premier of Canada. The Laurier strove to promote French culture in Woonsocket. It eventually became a second-run movie house that operated until severely damaged in the flood of 1955. It was demolished three years later. (Woonsocket Harris Public Library.)

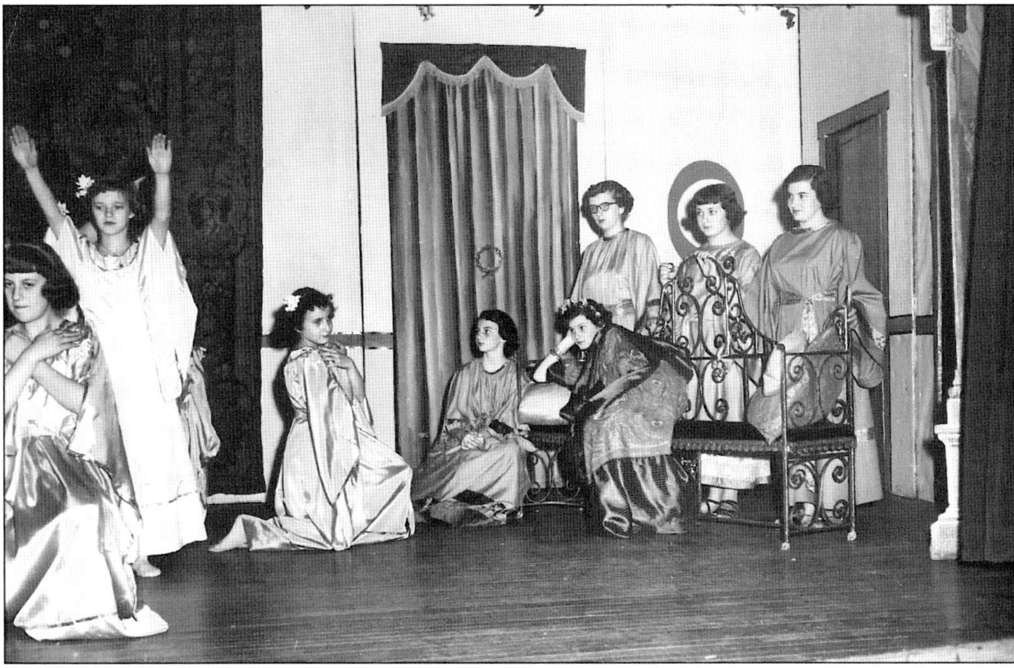

A play by students of Saint Clare High School, *c.* 1954. The Saint Clare High School was a major Woonsocket educational institution founded by Monsignor Dauray, of the Church of the Precious Blood, in 1911. Students participating in this production include, from left to right: unknown, Jackie Levreault, Therese Cyr, unknown, Irene Carriere, Lucille Brousseau, Louise Milot, and Muriel Houle. (Mr. and Mrs. George E. Brin.)

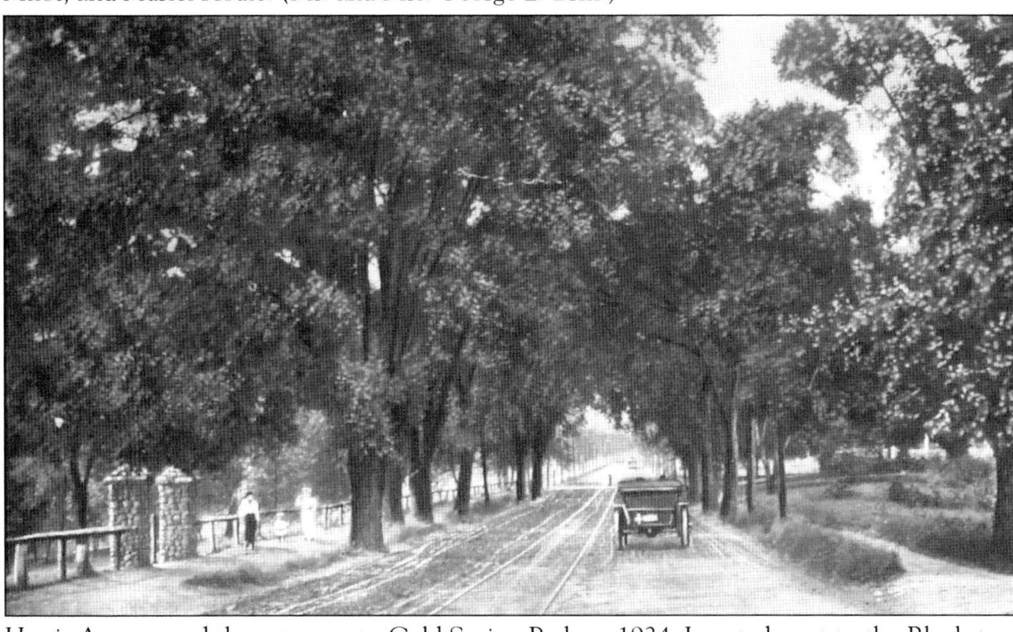

Harris Avenue and the entrance to Cold Spring Park, *c.* 1924. Located next to the Blackstone River, this pleasant park has been a place of recreation since the early 1840s. Advocates of a liberalized state constitution, called the "Dorrites," held enormous clambakes and rallies here. (Mr. and Mrs. Robert C. Brin.)